PARTICIPATION

AND POWER

Civic Discourse in
Environmental Policy Decisions

W. MICHELE SIMMONS

STATE UNIVERSITY OF NEW YORK PRESS

Published by
STATE UNIVERSITY OF NEW YORK PRESS,
Albany

© 2007 State University of New York

For information, address State University of New York Press
194 Washington Avenue, Suite 305, Albany, NY 12210-2384

Production by Laurie D. Searl
Marketing by Anne M. Valentine

Library of Congress Cataloging-in-Publication Data

Simmons, W. Michele, 1969–
    Participation and power : civic discourse in environmental policy decisions /
W. Michele Simmons.
       p. cm. — (SUNY series, Studies in scientific and technical communication)
    Includes bibliographical references and index.
    ISBN-13: 978-0-7914-6995-8 (alk. paper)
    ISBN-13: 978-0-7914-6996-5 (pbk. : alk. paper)
    1. Environmental policy—Decision making.   2. Environmental policy—Citizen
participation.   3. Communication in science.   I. Title.   II. Series.

GE170.S56 2007
363.7'0525—dc22   2006007840

10 9 8 7 6 5 4 3 2 1

CONTENTS

ILLUSTRATIONS

FIGURES

TABLES

ACKNOWLEDGMENTS

This book has evolved from a research project because of the generous contributions of many. I thank my professors at Purdue who helped me focus my research interests. Johndan Johnson-Eilola and Irwin Weiser asked questions that broadened my thinking and offered sage advice that kept me on track. I am especially grateful to Pat Sullivan and Jim Porter for teaching me to think about whom research serves and the social change it should seek. I have learned much from them, and I continue to learn. My colleagues from graduate school, Jeff Grabill, Stuart Blythe, Libby Miles, and Meredith Weisberg Zoetewey, have provided invaluable feedback on this project through their conversations, collaborations, and readings of earlier drafts. I am grateful for their continued friendship. Thanks also to the spokespeople of the citizen groups and the depot whose generosity with their time and information was immeasurable.

I thank my colleagues at Miami University who have been supportive of my work, especially Jennie Dautermann, Jean Lutz, Laura Mandell, Kate Ronald, Paul Anderson, and Morris Young, who provided feedback on different components of the project. My students in the spring 2004 graduate information design course challenged my thinking about participatory design in the classroom in productive ways. I also thank Miami University for an assigned research appointment that enabled me to complete portions of the book.

Finally, I thank my parents for their support, and most of all I thank Josh, who encourages and inspires me every day.

Selected passages of this book have appeared previously in different forms. Permissions have been granted for the use of the following materials. Chapters 1 and 2 include revised selections from "Toward a Critical Rhetoric of Risk Communication: Producing Citizens and the Role of Technical Communicators," Jeffery T. Grabill and W. Michele Simmons (1998). *Technical Communication Quarterly*, 7(4), 415–441 with permission from the Association of Teachers of Technical Writing.

Figures 6.1 and 6.2 are reprinted from the Clermont County StormWater Pollution Prevention Website with permission.

CHAPTER ONE

CITIZENS, INSTITUTIONS,
AND THE CONSTRUCTION OF
ENVIRONMENTAL POLICY

When Congress began passing environmental regulations that mandated public involvement in approving environmental policies, citizens legally became an important component in the decisions of environmental management.[1] The National Environmental Policy Act (NEPA) passed in 1969, and the Comprehensive Environmental Response, Compensation, and Liability Act (CERCLA) passed in 1980, for example, mandate that the public be notified and allowed to respond to any remediation plan before it is adopted. Risk communication evolved out of the legislated need of risk assessors to gain public acceptance for policies grounded in risk assessment methodologies and generally came to be defined as "any purposeful exchange of scientific information between interested parties regarding health or environmental risks" (Covello, Sandman, & Slovic, 1988). Conflicts began to arise between the quantitative approach to risk assessment and the public's perceptions of risk. Risk assessment, according to Plough and Krimsky (1988), is the characterization of potential adverse health effects based on an evaluation of results of epidemiologic, toxicologic, and environmental research. As a result of the conflicts, experts in risk assessment and management worked to design models for explaining risk to the public. A problem with these models is that too many have been arhetorical—typically decontextualizing risks, failing to consider the knowledge local citizens can contribute, and striving to influence/educate citizens in order to bring their perceptions into conformity with scientific rationale. (For examples of these models see Russell, 1986; Sandman, 1990; Slovic, 1986.) This failure to see risk (and environmental policy) as socially constructed leads to unethical and oppressive risk communication

1

practices because the public[2] is denied democratic participation in the decision-making process.

For example, in August 1999, the United States Army held a public meeting to inform local residents of Newport, Indiana, about the technology chosen to destroy 1, 269 tons of VX nerve agent—the deadliest substance known—onsite at the Newport Chemical Depot. Using a technology called "supercritical water oxidation," the VX nerve agent would be neutralized, and the remaining effluent from the neutralized agent would be dumped into the nearby Wabash River. Representatives from the Army and the subcontractor hired to dispose of the VX agent stood by posters describing the disposal process. A number of local residents and other concerned citizens walked around tables littered with information maintaining the safety of the disposal process. At this meeting I met a representative from the Army who asked if I had any questions about the disposal process. When I asked if this process had been implemented elsewhere, she replied, "You aren't from here are you? None of the other citizens around here have asked that question." When I commented that I was not from Newport but was interested in the ways in which the public participated in policy decisions, she told me that public participation in technical decisions such as this "goes against [her] way of thinking." Acknowledging that such response was required, she wanted to tell me of an idea the Army was implementing in which local residents were invited to a roundtable with two Army representatives familiar with the events at the Newport Chemical Depot. At this roundtable discussion, the residents were given free pizza and allowed to vent their concerns. "So that the residents don't feel intimidated," she reported, "their responses aren't written down; they are completely off the record." Her intention for public participation may have been sincere, but to her it made little difference whether public comments were factored into a decision as long as the public was allowed to comment. When I asked how the decision makers learned of the citizens' concerns and feedback, she told me that was not the purpose of the meeting.

Such an approach to public participation is not uncommon in environmental policy debates. This book examines both historical and firsthand accounts of risk communication and public participation practices as a way to examine how public participation is currently defined and practiced by institutions and subsequently, how citizens are positioned in the decision-making process. These accounts show that the citizens' status is most often marked by low interaction with the technical experts as well as little power in influencing the final policy. These examples illustrate that public participation practices focused on either (1) bombarding the public with a one-way flow of information in an effort to bring their perceptions about an issue into conformity with the technical experts or (2) holding public meetings and allowing public comments that attempt to placate publics, but that do not influence the final policy. According to the cases examined, publics often react, not to the technology chosen but to not being involved in the decision-making process. These cases suggest that current models of risk communication and public participation are ineffective for involving the public in the decision-making process in ethical and significant ways.

THE COMPLEXITIES OF CIVIC DISCOURSE IN POLICY DECISIONS

Most risk researchers acknowledge the need to involve the public more significantly in the decisions of risk policies; however, the complex issues involved in risk assessment, governmental law, and governmental agencies present challenging obstacles to negotiating a policy that all involved parties consider just. By *just*, I mean that all affected by the decision had the ability to actively participate in the decision-making process. I draw this notion from Iris Marion Young (1990) who argues that justice is

> The institutional conditions that make it possible for all to learn and use satisfying skills in socially recognized settings, to participate in decision-making, and to express their feelings, experience, and perspective on social life in contexts where others can listen . . . Justice . . . requires, however, participation in public discussion and processes of democratic decision-making. (p. 91)

Yet little work has been done to examine the institutional conditions that promote or prevent citizen participation in the decision-making process of environmental policy as a way to develop a more just approach to risk communication practices.[3]

This book examines the ways in which citizens are allowed to participate in decisions of environmental policy and constructs a theory of democratic and ethical public involvement for environmental policy and, subsequently, an alternative model of public participation that grants citizens more power in the decision-making process. Despite requirements that mandate public participation, citizens have very little say and almost no power to influence environmental decisions, even when it affects their own neighborhoods. Citizens have valuable knowledge to contribute to policy decisions and are capable of participating in significant ways, yet this study illustrates how institutional practices and current models of public participation exclude citizens from actively participating. This denied participation not only is unethical, but it can result in inappropriate policies—policies that do not sufficiently address community needs. When citizens believe that policies are not reflective of their local situation, environmental debates often become hostile, resulting in long-term and costly issues for the government and other involved organizations. Yet, if policies are to become more just and public participation is to become more significant in policy decisions, the process for decision making must change.

All policies are made through discourse (Rude, 2000, p. 5). Yet all policies involve technical information. Technically complex public issues complicate the traditional notion of discourse because technical experts claim ownership of the technical issues and close off public debate even though these issues affect the public in very concrete ways. As a result, a rhetoric for civic discourse in policy debates is needed.

In order to develop such a rhetoric of civic discourse for policy debates, this book uses historical accounts and a firsthand case of public participation in environmental policy to examine institutional assumptions and views of public participation in order to show the public's marginalized status in policy debates. It then investigates the level of power and degree of interaction citizens have in the decision-making process to argue that a more critical rhetoric of debates is needed to dissolve the separation of risk assessment from risk communication (or technical decisions from public discourse) and locate epistemology within the process that involves the public. Drawing in part from a range of critical theorists, I use critical in this context as a perspective that aims toward both identifying oppressive power relations and seeking to redesign or change the practices that cause the oppression (Feenberg, 1991; Foucault, 1984; Porter & Sullivan, 1997). This critical rhetoric for just policy debates must address ways to (1) identify and bring to the forefront the unequal power relations that currently work to marginalize public involvement, (2) see the public as capable of contributing useful knowledge to the decision-making process, and (3) offer ways to include the public earlier and more significantly in the decision-making process. Such a framework can offer policy makers, community groups, and rhetoricians strategies for evaluating policy debates and encouraging more active public participation. Such a participatory framework can also inform classroom pedagogy, service learning, and community-based projects.

Good policy decisions require both scientific knowledge and social justice, and an ethical framework, or approach, for decision making is needed to ensure that both are reflected in a policy (Rowan, "What Risk," p. 304). However, most current approaches to studying risk communication have not pursued such a framework. Indeed, most risk communication research concerning public participation has focused on either providing theoretical models to *predict* citizen perception/participation or describing public participation in a particular risk situation via qualitative studies. Neither of these two approaches fully addresses (1) how institutions warrant certain notions of risk communication or (2) what institutional conditions make possible certain subject positions within the social space of the risk communication process. And neither works toward developing a framework for encouraging significant participation by all involved parties.[4]

Researchers in rhetoric and composition, as well as professional writing, know little about the range of writing and communication practices in community contexts such as those required for participating in public policy decisions. While rhetoric and professional communication courses have often included public policy writing as part of their curricula (indeed, a historical purpose of rhetoric included helping citizens participate in public discussions necessary for democratic government), there has been little inquiry into how citizens use their professional knowledge in arguing positions in the public sphere. By crossing traditional boundaries in rhetoric and composition and professional writing to include studies of civic discourse, both fields can glean a richer understanding of the everyday literacy practices necessary for collaborative decision making in the community (Sullivan, 1990). Such research could further work toward designing a curriculum that encourages our students to see the strategies they learn in composition and professional writing courses as useful for affecting social change in the workplace *and* the community.

This book is a first step both in addressing these gaps and in answering the call of governmental agencies for ways to better involve the public in the risk communication process. While most agencies acknowledge the need to involve citizens, they claim that they do not know how to do so. Further, working toward a more ethical approach that encourages significant public participation could ease the hostility currently present in risk communication situations and bring about more just policies.

A DIFFERENT WAY OF LOOKING AT PUBLIC PARTICIPATION IN ENVIRONMENTAL POLICY

A number of scholars have drawn on Jürgen Habermas' theory of communicative action/rationality to consider whether policy debates constitute democratic discourse (See Blyler; Dayton; Karis; Killingsworth & Palmer; Hynds and Martin; and Wells). Certainly, Habermas has contributed much to our understanding of deliberation in the public sphere. Habermas' notion of discourse ethics and his distinctions among types of communications are valuable for identifying common approaches to public involvement in policy decisions. For example, his concept of strategic action as a manipulative attempt to coerce others (*Moral Consciousness*, p. 58) and his concept of instrumental rationality as an attempt by those in power to maintain the current system (*Theory of Communicative Action, vol.2*) can serve as markers for oppressive discourse—markers to which I will return later. And while I agree wholeheartedly with his belief that participation must occur early in the decision-making process in order to avoid coercion, I see his system of rational discourse for enabling citizens to affect policy decisions as limited in two ways. First, his belief that rules for discourse are universal seem to me to discount the influence of the social context of a particular situation that often result in unequal power relations and opportunities for participation. (See also Hauser, 1999; Porter, 1998; Grabill and Simmons, 1998 for critiques of Habermas' universal norms.) The idea that everyone capable of speech has an equal opportunity to participate in deliberations seems optimistic. In environmental public debates, the local citizen is rarely discussing her concerns on an equal playing field with the "technical expert." Habermas himself acknowledges that a "technocratic consciousness" (*Toward*, 105–115) may preclude public and democratic deliberation on scientific issues. Some scholars have questioned then whether the public can influence debates on technical and scientific issues (Blyler; Parks). Drawing from Habermas, Parks (1993) maintains: "[t]hose who command expert knowledge also dominate any debate concerning issues of public interest because the noninitiated are unable to enter the scientized universe of discourse, as they lack the technical terminology and specialized language of argumentation" (7). Yet, a framework for evaluating public debates that questions the very possibility seems limited.

Second, his criteria for communicative action—for evaluating norms of validity (e.g., truth, sincerity, comprehensibility, and appropriateness) (*Communication*, 118) seem inadequate for going beyond mutual understanding to seek places where change is possible and to understand what strategies might encourage more access to and influence in the decision-making process. It is identifying these spaces where change is possible that is likely to enable real public influence on policy issues. Perhaps, then, we need to expand the framework for evaluating public deliberation in policy debates to include a closer look at the local situation and the unequal power relations in debates of technical and scientific policy issues.

Rather than a strictly Habermasian approach that assumes the ideal speech communication ("the communication of equals who attempt to understand each other") as normative (qtd in Blyler, 1994, p. 127; see also Wells), an approach that incorporates institutional critique to focus on the unequal power relations in local settings and has as its goal finding ways to dismantle that inequality seems useful for policy debates where control and power are often points of contention among stakeholders.

All participation is not equal—encouraging citizens to contribute knowledge about how a policy will affect their community at the onset of a decision-making process is quite different from allowing citizens to respond to policies already determined. While the former represents an approach that sees policies as socially constructed by groups that value the contributions that each can make to the decision-making process, the latter represents a more common approach that sees the public as an entity to be managed and educated by the experts, not capable of contributing significantly to the development of the policy. Democratic participation—the kind of participation required for just policies—occurs only when all affected parties have both the access and the ability to *actively* participate in the decision-making process (Young, 1990, p. 91). Democratic participation cannot occur, Young maintains, if there is an unequal distribution of power or privilege granted to particular groups. This unequal distribution of power is often visible in risk communi-

cation practices when health experts or government agencies determ
risk policy and involve citizens only to the point of allowing them to respon.
to their decision as illustrated in the opening example. According to Young,
a policy or decision can only be considered just when "it has been arrived at
by a public which has truly promoted the free expression of all needs and
points of view. Tyrannized publics, publics manipulated by officials, and media
publics with little access to information and communication do not satisfy
this requirement" (1990, p. 92). Young describes these tyrannized and manipulated publics as oppressed in that they are inhibited by institutional
conditions from participating in decisions that affect their lives.

Oppression, she argues, has five faces, but one face, powerlessness, seems
especially appropriate for discussions of public participation in environmental policy decisions. According to Young, the powerless lack the "technical
expertise, authority . . . and status" needed to participate directly in decisions
that affect their lives (pp. 56–57). Further, she notes,

> direct participation in public policy is rare, and policy implementa-
> tion is for the most part hierarchical, imposing rules on bureaucrats
> and citizens. Thus most people in these societies do not regularly
> participate in making decisions that affect the conditions of their
> lives and actions, and in this sense, most people lack significant
> power. (1990, p. 56)

It is only when oppressed groups are able to "express their interests and
experience in the public on an equal basis with other groups" that decision-
making processes can be considered ethical (p. 95). It is important to begin
a discussion of ethical decision making with an explanation of power if our
goals are to identify oppressive situations within institutions and to frame less
oppressive processes as a response. I argue, then, that if we hope to change the
unequal distribution of power in risk communication practices, we must examine the ways in which power is exercised in environmental public policy decisions. But how, then, can the exercise of power be examined?

John Gaventa (1980), in his study of why Appalachian coal miners
often chose not to rebel or challenge their domination by coal companies,
asserts that participation or nonparticipation in the decision-making process
is determined almost exclusively by the exercise of power. Drawing from
theorists Freire, Bachrach, and Baratz, Gaventa asserts that "power is exercised not just upon participants within the decision-making process but also
towards the exclusion of certain participants and issues altogether" (p. 9).
Like Young, Gaventa categorizes the powerless as those who are excluded
from participating, or from discussing issues of interest to them, in the decision-making process. He argues that studies of policy must include studies of
power, specifically in terms of "who gets what, when, and how and who gets
left out, and how the two are interrelated" (p. 9). And power, he maintains,

"may be studied by examining who participates, who gains and loses, and who prevails in decision making" (p. 5). Gaventa's emphasis on who is left out is an important issue here. By examining who was "invited" to the discussions, that is, who was alerted to the meeting times and places of the policy discussions, we can see who was excluded from the beginning by the institutions arranging the decision making. Drawing on Gaventa's assertion that power is exercised by the exclusion of certain participants and issues, we can see ways in which certain publics are marginalized, if we focus on who is left out.

How and when members of the public are included in the decision-making process—essentially, their status as decision makers—are important factors in the decision-making process. I am especially interested in the ways in which the public's comments are reflected in the final policy. Even if citizens are allowed to comment on an environmental decision before it is implemented, if their comments, concerns, and interests are not considered in the final policy, they are still rendered powerless. By looking at cases of risk communication and public participation practices—from recent literature and from my observations—and examining who participates, who prevails, and how, in a number of situations, we can begin to discuss the relationship of power in the decisions of environmental public policy and work toward a more ethical approach to the decision-making process. Additionally, we can begin to understand the literacy practices necessary to gain agency to participate in technical yet civic issues.

As researchers in rhetoric and composition and professional writing, we are increasingly involved with projects that take us outside the academy to conduct studies and to affect positive change in the communities in which we live and work. Just as increasingly, however, we are finding that traditional approaches to empirical studies may not adequately accommodate the particular situations that exist in these communities. For example, rather than the traditional goal of producing new knowledge for the field, the primary goal of the project may be to bring about change in the community as well as in the lives of the research participants. Or the project may be one that has traditionally concerned those outside academia. As a result, we must employ research methodologies that can function in the spaces between the institution and the community and still yield positive and credible results. As Sullivan and Porter (1997) note, "research methodology should not be something we apply or select so much as something we construct out of particular situations and then argue for in the write up of our studies" (p. 46). As a way to consider how the public might contribute more significantly to public policy debates, I draw on Foucault (1982) to argue that we must first recognize the power structures in place that work to prevent participation. We must also understand the discourse practices that enable resistance to those power structures by analyzing the institutions that govern the policy-making processes.

This study is historical in its examination of existing cases of public participation, empirical in its firsthand observations of how the public is allowed to participate in risk decisions at particular sites including an environmental policy decision to dispose of VX nerve agent at an Army depot, and theoretical in using these examinations and observations to suggest a framework for ethical decision making that is applicable beyond individual cases. I use multiple empirical, theoretical, and analytical approaches to critique public meetings, environmental impact statements, public records, and interviews with citizen group leaders and agency officials to examine how arguments, notions of risk, and policies were constructed in the decision to dispose of VX nerve agent at the depot. Drawing from methodological approaches including cases and institutional critique (Porter et al., 2000; Sullivan and Porter, 1997; Foucault, 1982; Fine, 1992), the design of the study is an institutional case. I see an institutional case as a way to focus on a concrete, particular environment, such as a policy decision, and I use institutional critique as a way to closely examine the practices and power of institutions within that environment. In an attempt to avoid generating totalizing, decontextualized theory, the research is situated in localized sites, including the events surrounding the decision to destroy VX nerve agent at an Army depot in Newport, Indiana.

EXAMINING POWER IN POLICY DECISIONS

An institutional case focuses on a particular environment, but with a particular focus on institutional power relations. I borrow this idea from Dorothy Smith's (1987) description of institutional ethnography as well as from Jeff Grabill's (1997) description of institutional case. Smith argues that in order to avoid the "ungrounded abstraction" of theory, inquiry must focus on the "every day life" of real individuals, activities, material conditions, and the relationship between activities and material conditions. Institutional ethnographies or cases identify "institution" as a "complex of relations forming part of the ruling apparatus, organized around a distinctive function" such as education or law (Smith, p. 160). Exploring, describing, and analyzing such a complex of relations by ethnographic methods forces us to focus on specific, real, and concrete examples of the individuals or activities that make up that institution, rather than falling prey to abstract generalizations about the function of that institution (p. 160). For example, when working with citizens involved in discussions of environmental policy, institutional ethnography may allow the researcher to discuss with these citizens why participation is not currently possible at certain points of the decision-making process and suggest approaches to the citizens themselves regarding ways to participate more significantly in the process. This approach seeks to avoid ungrounded abstractions and present situated examples that might serve as heuristics for risk communication and public involvement practices.

The "institutional" focus of this study involves investigating the power relations and resulting subject positions that inhibit or encourage significant citizen participation in the decisions of environmental policy. In order to change oppressive practices, change must occur at the institutional level. Michelle Fine, for example, argues that "efforts to fix people and not to change structures" often work to "reinforce the recipient's lower power position" (p. 71). Michel Foucault (1982) likewise asserts that in order to change oppressive practices, change must occur at the institutional level. If their thinking were extended to risk communication, we would expect that changing current risk communication practices requires change at the level of the institutions involved in risk communication. Institutions regulate and constrain knowledge making, production, distribution, and consumption through a system of rules and practices (Foucault, 1982; Leitch, 1992). It is the institutions, then, with their rules and practices that determine the ways in which citizens participate in the production of environmental decisions and policy. As a result, I examine the institutional forces that regulate public participation in existing cases as well as the VX nerve agent disposal decision. I focus on practices, micropolitics, and local arrangements, using discourse to examine historically and socially situated relationships in the production of knowledge, power, and ethics. This approach illuminates how these institutions work to make certain types of participation possible and others impossible (Porter et al., 2000). Foucault (1982) further argues that by critiquing institutions, we can discover ways in which power is exercised. By understanding the ways in which power is exercised, and looking for gaps in this system, we can work toward resisting, even revising, institutions. If, then, we hope to recognize and understand the conditions that make possible significant citizen participation as well as those conditions that inhibit participation, we must examine the institutions that regulate risk communication. According to Iris Marion Young (1990), the "unquestioned norms, habits, and symbols" embedded in "assumptions underlying institutional rules and the collective consequence of following those rules" often brings about injustice through domination and oppression (p. 41). These injustices, she argues, can be "rectified only by basic institutional changes" (p. 14). Institutions are dynamic, uncontained structures and as such offer the space/possibility for such change.

CRITIQUING INSTITUTIONAL RISK COMMUNICATION PRACTICES THROUGH MULTIDISCIPLINARY DISCOURSES

Applying institutional rhetorical critique involves focusing on practices, micropolitics, and local arrangements using discourse and self-reflexivity to examine historically and socially situated relationships among discursive practices in the production of systems of knowledge, power, and ethics (Foucault, Leitch, Porter et al., Young, 1990). If we hope to understand the ways in which citizens can be granted more power in the decision-making process and insepa-rably, the ways in which the user knowledge that citizens have is valued, we must examine how institutions promote certain risk communication practices and how those practices come into play in the ways the public is allowed to participate in the decision-making process in a specific situation. I believe that examining the institutions involved with risk communication and environ-mental policy foregrounds the institutional production of knowledge about risk and reveals spaces within these systems for change. Institutions that regulate risk communication—including risk assessment, governmental law, and the Environmental Protection Agency (EPA)—all function in ways that make significant public participation difficult. The following sections illustrate ways in which each institution grants an unequal distribution of power in the de-cision-making process to experts, works to base policy on strictly technical issues, and decontextualizes the risk in individual communities.

Risk Assessment

Although risk assessment is a subject of research, I am interested in how risk assessment manifests itself in the regulatory agencies' required process for risk management. The very process involved in assessing a potential risk is difficult and time consuming. The uncertainties and probabilities that factor into the early stages of the risk assessment make knowing definite answers about the risk nearly impossible. In "The Nature of Risk Assessment," a National Academy of Science committee asserts that the first stage of risk assessment, hazard identification, rarely produces conclusive results about a risk:

> [T]he process of determining whether exposure to an agent can cause an increase in the incidence of a health condition (cancer, birth defect, etc.) . . . involves characterizing the nature and strength of the evidence of causation. Although the question of whether a substance causes cancer or other adverse health effects is theoreti-cally a yes-no question, there are few chemicals on which the hu-man data are definitive. (p. 19)

Despite this level of uncertainty, risk assessors use largely quantitative models to determine the health risk posed. Often risk assessors view this number as the "true risk," and any other nontechnical issues are considered arbitrary to determining a policy. For example, Fischhoff, Watson, & Hope (1984) note that often all risk information is not valued equally: "[T]echnial experts often distinguish between 'objective' and 'subjective' risk. The former refers to the product of scientific research, primarily public health statistics, experimental studies, epidemiological surveys, and probabilistic risk analyses. The latter refers to non-expert perceptions of that research, embellished by whatever other considerations seized the public mind" (p. 131).

Governmental Law

It is important to consider how federal laws influence risk assessment procedures and consequently citizen participation. The Comprehensive Environmental Response, Compensation, and Liability Act (CERCLA) was created in
1980 in response to citizens who wanted input into the decisions being made
about environmental hazards. Ironically, because the law was intended to ensure
public participation, it is this very document that justifies not bringing citizens
into the process until the policy is determined. CERCLA states:

> Before adoption of any plan for remedial action to be undertaken,
> the state shall take both of the following actions: (1) publish a
> notice and brief analysis of the proposed plan and make such plan
> available to the public. (2) Provide a reasonable opportunity for
> submission of written and oral comments and an opportunity for a
> public meeting at or near the facility at issue regarding the proposed
> plan. The notice and analysis published under paragraph (1) shall
> include sufficient information as may be necessary to provide a rea-
> sonable explanation of the proposed plan and alternative proposals
> considered. (42 U.S.C. section 9617 CERCLA section 117)

CERCLA mandates that after a policy has been decided, the public
must be given a set time to respond before the policy is implemented.
CERCLA also states that an explanation of why this policy was chosen must
be provided; however, CERCLA only allows that the public be made aware
of the policy *after* the decisions have been made. As a result of CERCLA,
health assessors are required to address citizens' responses but are not required to integrate them into the policy.

There has been little attempt to change this in ways that would more
significantly involve citizens in policy decisions, because government officials,
who often view citizens as both hostile and devoid of knowledge that could
inform a scientifically sound policy, argue that more significant involvement
with "lay" citizens would only delay the already long and tedious policy
process. This is evident not only in the CERCLA ruling but also in other
government regulations mandating citizen involvement in environmental
policy decisions such as the National Environmental Policy Act (NEPA)
originally passed in 1969. NEPA requires that an Environmental Impact
Statement (EIS) evaluating the significance of an environmental hazard and
assessing the potential impacts of alternative cleanup actions be prepared
and made available for public comment at least forty-five days before any
action is implemented (40 C. F. R. 1500–08). Susan Mallon Ross (1996)
argues that efforts to seemingly involve members of the public by making
them more fully aware of an impending policy, such as distributing copies of
EISs to citizens before the policy is implemented, are little more than pla-

cating measures. The "EIS process historically has dealt with public concerns in a pro forma fashion: recording and appending them, but not seriously considering them" (p. 186). Drawing from Killingsworth and Steffans (1989), Ross further argues that EISs are seen by government agencies as an attempt to defend decisions already made and to ward off lawsuits rather than an attempt to solicit citizen response (p. 179). While these governmental laws originally may have been put in place to invite citizen participation, the wording of the mandates often works to preclude anything other than the most superficial public response.

Environmental Protection Agency (EPA)

While the rules and procedures of risk assessment and governmental law work to inhibit significant participation, the practices of the EPA also can pose obstacles for citizen involvement in the decisions of public policy. The EPA's process for conducting risk communication illustrates its assumptions that knowledge and power lie with the experts. The agency's model implies a one-way flow of technical information that positions members of the public as consumers and entities to be managed. Milton Russell, an EPA administrator for policy, planning, and evaluation, characterizes the risk communication process in terms of a metaconduit model:

> Let's imagine risk reduction as a consumer-driven production and distribution process. Scientists, who assess the severity of the risks, are the manufacturers. Government regulators, who make risk management decisions, are the wholesalers. And professional communicators—network and newspaper journalists—are the retailers. We government regulatory wholesalers use risk characterizations from the scientists to explain the reasons for our decision. Then journalistic retailers pick up our product on the loading dock. . . . [and] they present the news of the day. Based on those presentations consumers of the news decide to buy the news or not, use it or misuse it, and change their behavior or demand that public officials change theirs. . . . If citizens misjudge risk, their orders will still come through, and the government machines still delivers, but the results don't necessarily leave citizens better off.[5] (qtd in Stratman, Boykin, Holmes, Laufer, & Breen, p. 10)

This model resembles, in many ways, the Shannon and Weaver model of communication where knowledge is constructed prior to communication, and miscommunication is attributed to "noise" (or irrationality) along a one-way, linear channel. Knowledge is produced separately by experts, then communicated to citizens, who are seen as end users of the policy, devoid of any knowledge that might prove useful for producing the policy itself. (Further implications of the still prominent Shannon and Weaver model of communication are discussed in later chapters).

According to Porter (1998), communication of this type that positions the audience members as "passive receivers" of a predetermined message, and that persuades the audience to accept a predetermined point of view, is a "rhetoric of domination" (p. 94). It is only when the audience is considered capable of participating in the dialogue, and of constructing knowledge that the communication become a "rhetoric of democratization" (p. 94).

To see the transfer of information in terms of problems of knowledge, and furthermore, to see knowledge as something produced separate from audiences by a select few experts, fails to adequately conceptualize the complexity of the *construction* of knowledge in complex situations. By failing to see knowledge about a policy as socially constructed, this view positions audiences as entities to be persuaded, not as participants in the construction of policy. Further, such a view does not account for the practices of power in risk assessment and communication. In order to participate in the development of risk policies, the public must be seen as capable of contributing knowledge to the process and brought in early enough in the design phase to actually affect the policy.

Because understanding how the public is excluded from significant participation through local manifestations of risk assessment, government law and agencies may reveal a space for productive change, this book examines in more depth these institutions as well others that restrict public participation.

This case approach is a way to develop heuristics for risk communication practices by challenging the long-held belief that citizens cannot be significantly involved in the decision-making process of risk policies. The cases I investigate involve the decision-making process of a risk policy by regulatory agencies, local government, citizen activist groups, and other members of the public. I examine these cases in an attempt to understand how public participation occurred in this particular situation by questioning who participates, who is left out, who is allowed to speak, who listens, and how these voices are integrated into the resulting policy.

EXAMINING CIVIC DISCOURSE IN TECHNICAL POLICY DEBATES

While much research has been done on providing government agencies with strategies for effective communication (Morgan, 1992; Hance, Chess, & Sandman, 1991; Sandman, 1990), much less has been done with helping citizens develop those same strategies (exceptions include Cantrill 1996). Wartella (1994) asserts that "by not serving the public at large with our research we leave ourselves vulnerable to the accusation that we are wittingly or unwittingly supporting the status quo and the society's dominant institutions" (p. 58). Rather, she claims we should direct our research to the "public at large and not just to policymakers or institutional elites" in an effort to "empower the disempowered with knowledge and understanding" (p. 59).

If we hope to respond to this call, we need to observe the decision-making process through the lens of citizens in an effort to theorize how citizens can be more significantly involved. By examining when and how citizens are allowed to become involved, when, why, and how an activist institution decides to become involved; and how governmental agencies respond to this involvement, we can locate new spaces for significant participation from all involved parties.

Power relations are more readily apparent from the perspective of the less powerful because they are the first to be denied access to decision making. Drawing from Haraway, Dautermann (1996) asserts that studying less powerful groups—those who do not necessarily occupy positions that enable them to participate in the development of policy matters—"may open our work to the counterdiscourses that also inform an institution's climate and affect the work of those more commonly studied" (p. 244). Such a perspective, she argues, may reveal class, gender, institutional power, and social interaction issues that would otherwise not be apparent (p. 243). Cantrill (1996) further asserts that the best place to observe the "discourses that oppose the dominant social paradigm" of environmental controversies is in the rhetoric of activist groups, because "small grassroots alliances may exhibit the greatest rhetorical alienation exactly because they often are marginalized by more dominant cultural groupings" (p. 168). It is impossible to know who was not allowed to participate, if you do not know who wanted to participate. While no perspective could illuminate all those who wanted to participate, a citizens' group offers a useful perspective in that regard. Focusing on the power relations that constitute specific risk communication practices and the resulting degree of participation that those practices make possible reveals much about the current decision-making processes. While I focus on the procedures and practices of the institutions regulating the decision and public participation in the decision, I look to the citizen groups to provide multiple perspectives on the process. I also consider how each citizen group's own procedures and practices played a part in the decision. I am particularly interested in how the different groups intersect and conflict in the chemical weapons disposal decision at the Newport Chemical Depot. The groups on which I focus include the state and federal agencies involved with the Newport Chemical Depot, a state-wide citizen organization, and a local citizen group in Newport.

The Newport Chemical Depot, located thirty-two miles north of Terre Haute, currently houses 1,269 tons of the nerve agent VX (*Journal and Courier*). A multinational Chemical Weapons Convention treaty requires all VX agent be destroyed by April 2007. But the U.S. Congress ban on the transportation of the nerve agent required a plan for disposing of it on site. In 1997 the Army proposed to build an onsite facility to neutralize the stored nerve agent then discharge it into the Wabash River—but the Army's battle with area citizens over the VX disposal process began nearly ten years before. In 1988 the Army held a public meeting near the Newport Chemical Depot to inform the community that it intended to destroy the VX stockpile at Newport by incineration. Because this plan met with strong opposition from the state government, state and local citizen groups, and individuals in the Newport community, the Army eventually investigated disposal methods other than incineration. The Army proposed an alternative method of VX disposal with plans to investigate this method in an EIS and in July 1998 distributed an EIS examining the possibility of neutralization/supercritical water oxidation. It was at this point that I began attending the public meetings and gathering information regarding the environmental decision at the depot. Agencies involved with the chemical weapons disposal decision at the Newport Chemical Depot announced public meetings in local papers with statements asserting that public participation was a goal of the meetings (see appendix A). I would soon find, however, that the definition of public participation could vary widely.

The Midwest Environmental Group[6] (MEG) is a nonprofit, statewide environmental organization that works toward alerting and educating Indiana citizens to environmental and human health concerns within the state. Based in Indianapolis, MEG brings together Indiana citizens to initiate court action against potential threats to environmental and human health. For example, MEG brought suit against an incinerator owner resulting in the owner being required to reduce the amount of toxins the incinerator releases into the air. The group solicits volunteers to participate in its activism primarily by writing letters to Congress and state legislators and attending public meetings and hearings (http://www.hec.org, 11.15.98). MEG was involved in the early stages of the chemical weapons disposal decisions at the Newport Chemical Depot but became less active after the decision to pursue disposal methods other than incineration was announced. Historically, the lack of publicity of public meetings has prohibited many citizens from even being made aware of environmental health issues and decisions. The Midwest Environmental Group, however, includes as part of its mission alerting and educating citizens about environmental health concerns in their area. A section of the MEG web site is devoted to listing information about upcoming public meetings.

It was through my discussions with MEG that I became aware of another citizen group involved in the chemical weapons disposal decision at the Newport Chemical Depot. During conversations I had with Tyler Mayes, a longtime and active member of MEG, about the Newport Chemical Depot, I learned about the Newport Citizens against Incineration. This grassroots Newport-based citizen group was comprised of between eight and ten individuals in the Newport community who took issue not only with incineration but also with not being allowed to participate in the chemical weapons disposal decision at the Newport Chemical Depot. The Newport Citizens against Incineration also worked with, and often received support and advice from, the Chemical Weapons Working Group—a national citizen group opposing incineration of chemical weapons at U.S. Army installations.

The Newport Citizens against Incineration organized in 1988 when the Army announced to the Newport community its intentions to incinerate the VX agent stockpiled at the depot, and has remained active in the process, even now continuing to monitor the actions of the institutions overseeing the Newport Chemical Depot. The spokesperson for the group, Sybil Mowrer, provided invaluable examples of the obstacles the public faced in trying to participate in the decision-making process. Further, she was able to illuminate aspects of the decision-making process that were not documented. Mowrer's information often provides interesting points of conflict with information obtained from the federal agencies regarding the chemical weapons decision at the depot.

Theorizing a new framework for risk communication practices and environmental policy decision making requires that theory be grounded in the practices of actual communication processes. Observing the practices of multiple citizen groups and institutions within a risk communication situation provided different lenses on risk communication practices and established for me a point from where a new framework could begin. The institutions regulating the Newport Chemical Depot (the federal agencies, regulations, and programs) reveal the established procedures and practices of public participation in decisions of environmental risk. MEG focuses on the interests of an organized institution occupying the space of the public on multiple cases, while Newport Citizens against Incineration illustrate the interests and actions of a group organized for the sole purpose of opposing a particular environmental action.

While the results of this multiyear study of public participation at the Newport Chemical Depot cannot be generalized beyond that specific context, these in-depth firsthand cases, coupled with the historical cases, reveal patterns of institutional control and denied participation. Examining a range of examples through multiple methodologies can inform a framework for evaluating whether risk communication practices (and environmental policy decisions in general) actually do encourage the kind of active participation by all affected that results in just and appropriate environmental policies. While I use risk communication cases as examples of environmental decision making, I believe this project has broader relevance beyond risk communication. The examples help me to develop a theory for democratic and ethical public involvement and offer a model of public participation that grants citizens more power in decision-making processes. Yet this theory and model are applicable to other environmental issues, such as natural resources and water and land use, which include many of the same concerns with public involvement (Blyler, 1994; Cantrill, 1996; Graham, 2004; Karis, 2000; Ross,

1996). In fact, I believe the critical rhetoric approach I develop is applicable to most environmental policy decisions.

TOWARD A RHETORIC OF ETHICAL PARTICIPATION AND JUST POLICIES

A rhetoric of ethical participation and just policy debates must address ways to (1) identify and bring to the forefront the unequal power relations that currently work to marginalize public involvement, (2) see the public as capable of contributing useful knowledge to the decision-making process, and (3) offer ways to include the public earlier and more significantly in the decision-making process. Yet developing such a framework requires that we better understand the multiple ways that the multiple individuals affected by a decision engage in discourse with one another about that decision.

For some time now researchers in rhetoric and professional writing have studied communities outside the classroom. Often that research has focused on writing by one community within one institution. Yet this approach to research runs the risk of essentializing the institution with a single vision of the way writing functions in the culture. Envisioning an institution through a single lens does not leave space for locating conflicts among groups who have competing views of what writing should and could accomplish.

I want to rethink this approach to nonacademic writing research by examining how different communities perceived the ways in which public discourse affects how policy is written on chemical weapons disposal. Because the discourse each group used focused on its own expectations but did not meet the expectations of other communities, the public discourse often failed. Examining the actions, experiences, and perspectives of these different groups may allow us to better understand the conflicts that derail significant public involvement.

Charles Arthur Willard (1996) and public policy scholar Frank Fischer (2000) assert the need for studies of actual policy debates that focus on "the specific relationships of different types of information to decision making, the different ways arguments move across different disciplines and discourses, the translation of knowledge from one community to another, and the interrelationships between discourses and institutions" (Fischer, p. 256). Yet, according to Fischer, "despite the contemporary emphasis on citizenship, democratic theorists largely remain distant from the level of citizen ... such theorists mainly labor at the abstract level of nation-state and, in doing so, neglect the everyday aspects of deliberative politics, especially as they relate to ordinary people" (p. xi). By focusing on specific discourse practices of institutions and citizens in environmental debates, we can illuminate complex problems with current decision-making processes that discussions at the level of the final policy often overlook. To investigate how citizens are allowed to participate in environmental public policy decisions, we must consider not just whether spaces for public participation exist but also how the institutions involved navigate those spaces and how significantly they value the public's participation. As a result, this book addresses the following questions:

- What risk communication practices discourage democratic citizen participation?

- In what ways does the discourse of existing federal regulations inhibit significant public participation in environmental public policy? And what are the ethical, political, and economic ramifications of limited public participation?

- How do different publics and institutions affected by a decision construct their knowledge and arguments about a policy? How do the different discourses intersect and conflict in the decision-making process?

- What literacy/discourse practices are necessary to actively participate in collaborative, complex, and technical decision making? What practices might help integrate both "expert" and public knowledge in an attempt to develop more appropriate policy?

- In what ways does the public's knowledge and ability to contribute to a policy challenge existing regulations and notions of public participation?

- What strategies might policy makers employ to ensure just decision-making and policies?

- How might rhetoricians and technical communicators intervene in decision-making processes to encourage a more democratic environment?

Within each historical and firsthand case, this book examines the following:

- Who is included in the decision-making process? (And who is left out?)

- Who is considered the public (who is alerted to town meetings and sent draft environmental impact statements)?

- How and when is the public involved in the decision-making process?

- What is the status of members of the public as decision makers?

- What changes are made in the drafts and final versions of the policy?

- How are the public's contributions reflected in the resulting policy?

Examining these issues of participation and power required multiple and varied examples of writing and discourse used to shape the decision making including the following:

- interviews with members of citizens' groups and Army Public Relations,

- observations of public meetings,

- transcripts of official town meetings, and

- government documents such as

    — legislation concerning the issue in question,

    — EPA/Federal regulations,

    — meeting handouts,

    — institutional definitions of public participation from policy documents,

    — Environmental Impact Statement (draft and final version).

DATA ANALYSIS

I am most interested in points where institutional texts intersect and conflict with citizen texts and responses. Specifically, I am interested in the institutional texts that represent and determine the risk and risk communication practices (e.g., definitions of risk, definitions of risk communication, governmental regulations, minutes from town meetings, policy drafts and final versions, etc.) and compare those with the texts in which the activist groups react to and resist the subject positions and decisions placed on them by the risk communication practices and the policy (e.g., my notes from town and activist meetings, interviews with activist groups and/or individual citizens, letters written by the groups to local newspapers or legislators, concerns/questions voiced by activist group members, etc.) in order to study points where public participation intersects/conflicts with institutional practices.

A number of other methodologies and theoretical lenses informed my research, including mapping, ethics, and Scandinavian participatory design. Mapping (Soja, 1989; Sullivan & Porter, 1997) is an important methodology for making visible the assumptions, values, theories, and positions of those involved in risk communication practices. Sullivan and Porter assert that "mapping is one tactic for constructing positionings of research that are reflexive—a key to developing postmodern understanding of research [. . .] postmodern geographies recognize the significance of the construction of space. Space provides a frame of reference for the physical world" (pp. 78–79). Specifically, mapping is a strategy for illustrating theoretical positions of other researchers, for positioning myself in relation to these theoretical positions, for representing difference, and for locating spaces/gaps where research is needed.

For example, if we take the views or assumptions on risk decisions and risk communication as expressed in the quotes from representatives of institutions involved in risk communication (risk assessment, governmental law, and the EPA), we get one snapshot of what several institutions value in determining environmental risk decisions. Mapping those assumptions on two continua—one a continuum of the type of factors considered in the decision-making process (from technical to nontechnical), and one a continuum of how contextualized and nonhierarchical the approaches to determining a policy were (from decontextualized to contextualized)—would reveal the approaches most valued by institutions in determining a policy. For this map, positivistic represents a decontextualized view of risk that assumes risk decisions are best made by technical experts, while the critical represents a more situated or contextualized view of a risk situation that assumes decisions are best made through discourse by all affected. The technical end of the other continuum suggests that only technical aspects are factored into the environmental policy, while the cultural end suggests that more social, economic, and political aspects guide the decision. In this case, mapping reveals that risk communication practices currently value a positivistic approach to determining risk and further illustrates that institutional approaches to incorporate more critical and cultural aspects into risk communication are currently absent from risk communication practices (see figure 1.1). While considerations of both cultural and technical aspects are necessary for a just policy, more ethical risk communication approaches would be positioned nearer the middle of the continuum between the cultural and the technical on the critical side of the quadrant.

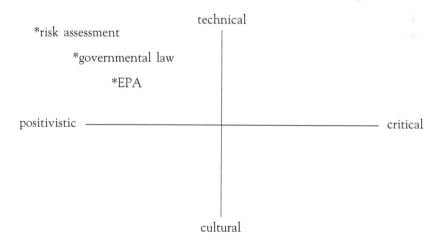

Figure 1.1: Institutional Assumptions That Perpetuate Risk Communication Practices

Multiple theoretical lenses are necessary to address the questions posed for this project. The proposed ethical framework for encouraging significant participation by all involved parties draws largely from Young (1990), Benhabib (1992), and Porter (1997). One of the assumptions of my project, informed by both feminist and participatory design theory, is that the decision-making process should be decentralized and that members of the public should be included in the decision-making process—not only because individuals have a right to be involved in the process of making decisions that affect them, but also because they are capable of contributing useful knowledge to the risk policy. Here I draw primarily from the work of Ehn (1988), Winograd & Flores (1986), Winograd (1995), Winner (1995), and Johnson (1997). Paying special attention to the ways institutions constrain or marginalize citizen participation, we can begin thinking about ways to resist and modify those constraints to actually encourage participation. A historical purpose of rhetoric has been to help citizens participate in public discussions necessary for democratic government. By expanding the boundaries of rhetoric and technical communication to include public policy, we help prepare our students and our community to be responsible, active citizens.

THE STRUCTURE AND ARGUMENTS OF THE BOOK

Chapter 2 examines a range of cases of public participation in environmental policy drawn from political science, technical communication, urban planning, sociology, and risk assessment texts. Examining citizen participation in historical cases of environmental public policy reveals the marginalized status of the public in environmental decisions. The citizens' status is marked by low interaction with the technical experts as well as little power in influencing the final policy. Public participation practices focused on either (1) bombarding the public with a one-way flow of information in an effort to bring its perceptions about an issue into conformity with the technical experts or (2) holding public meetings and allowing public comments that attempt to placate the public but that do not influence the final policy. According to the cases examined, publics often react, not to the technology chosen, but to not being involved in the decision-making process (Belsten, 1996, Katz and Miller, 1996). These cases suggest that current models of risk communication are ineffective for involving the public in the decision-making process.

Chapter 3 emphasizes the sites where risk communication practices take place and the power operations involved in and around those sites. For example, the chapter illustrates that the manner in which public comments are recorded at one public meeting reflects both the extent to which the public will offer comments and how significantly those comments can affect the policy. Based on interviews, firsthand observations, and public record documents, the stories emphasize the communication procedures and discourse practices of the institutions regulating the decision as well as two citizen groups protesting many of those decisions. Examining multiple group viewpoints on the same decision-making process revealed complex conflicts that were not apparent from the policy itself. Observing the actual practices illuminated additional insights into the ways in which institutions inhibit the public from contributing significantly to a policy and revealed spaces where current public participation practices could be modified to better encourage participation.

In Chapter 4, I analyze the institutional approaches to public participation in terms of risk communication models—looking at spaces where the public might be involved and how each institution navigates those spaces. I show that the discourse surrounding policy discussions is often more complex than models can suggest. Drawing from participatory design theories, I focus on two factors: how much power the public had in influencing the final policy and the level of interaction with decisions makers the public was granted. Based on this analysis, a new framework of public participation is needed to dissolve the separation of technical decisions from public discourse and to locate epistemology within the process that involves the public. Participatory design—a form of usability research used by rhetoricians and technical communicators—becomes a useful approach for this new heuristic/framework.

Based on the institutional critique of firsthand and existing cases of public participation in policy decisions, Chapter 5 presents a framework for a more appropriate and ethical approach to public participation that encourages significant democratic citizen participation in the decision-making process. This framework focuses on particular aspects of policy debates—participation, process, and power relations—as a way to consider whether a particular policy debate is ethical and appropriate and provides strategies for policy makers, community groups, and rhetoricians to encourage more active public participation.

Building from the framework developed in Chapter 5 for ethical debate, Chapter 6 examines firsthand a community-based project to illustrate how rhetoricians can identify oppressive power relations and intervene in the decision-making process to bring about a more democratic environment. This section also reveals how the participatory framework might inform community-based projects and classroom service-learning projects.

The epilogue revisits the environmental decision to destroy VX at the Newport Chemical Depot three years later, in 2003, and examines how the attacks of September 11 prompted the Army to declare the depot a terrorist target and reopen the decision. Finally, this chapter examines the continued need for a civic rhetoric for policy decision making now that public participation has been made even more complicated by issues of national security.

CHAPTER TWO

CITIZENS INVOLVED: MAPPING PUBLIC
PARTICIPATION AND POWER IN
RISK COMMUNICATION PRACTICES

As a starting point for considering risk communication approaches that more significantly involve the public, and consequently, are more just, this chapter examines risk communication and public policy debate practices. Focusing on ways in which citizens have been encouraged to, or inhibited from, participating in the decisions of public policy and on the actions and nonactions of institutions implementing environmental policies, this chapter works to make visible institutional assumptions about citizen participation in environmental risk policies. Mapping the degree to which citizens are allowed to contribute to the actual development of a policy can reveal the public's marginalized subject position and powerlessness in current risk communication practices and be a starting place for theorizing a more ethical approach. As discussed in chapter 1, by examining institutions and the way they exercise power, we can work toward changing those practices that prevent significant citizen participation.

SITUATING PUBLICS IN RISK COMMUNICATION PRACTICES:
STUDIES OF CITIZEN PARTICIPATION
IN ENVIRONMENTAL POLICY

Much has been written about risk communication, but a look at studies focusing specifically on public participation in particular situations, and on institutional notions of citizen participation, proves most useful for rethinking a framework that encourages significant participation of all involved parties. While this chapter focuses on public participation in recent *published*

25

studies, chapter 3 will detail findings of citizen participation from my own observations of the decision to dispose of the VX nerve agent at the Newport Chemical Depot in Newport, Indiana, through the discourses, documents, and interviews of a state-wide citizen activist group, a grassroots Newport-based citizen group against chemical incineration, and federal and state agencies. Those firsthand observations, along with these historical accounts, suggest that if we believe the public has knowledge to contribute to environmental decisions that affect their own lives, the procedures for public participation in environmental policy must change.

Arguing that good policy decisions require both scientific knowledge and social justice, Kathy Rowan (1994b) suggests that an ethical framework, or approach, for risk decision making is needed to ensure that both are reflected in a policy (p. 304). However, current approaches to studying risk communication have not pursued such a framework. Most risk communication research concerning public participation has focused on either providing theoretical models to *predict* citizen perception/participation or describing public participation in a particular risk situation via qualitative studies. Examining the assumptions of the predictive models—psychometric scale studies—can illustrate the marginalized subject position of citizens in risk communication practices. Further, while most risk communication research does not specifically examine the roles institutions play in regulating public participation, an examination of the descriptive studies that focus on public participation in a particular situation could be a starting point for illustrating how citizens are traditionally positioned in the decision-making process.

WHY CURRENT RISK COMMUNICATION MODELS AND PSYCHOMETRIC STUDIES DO NOT WORK

While the most useful examples of public participation practices can be gleaned from descriptive studies, it is important to understand the limitations of psychometric studies. Theoretical models have been developed primarily by those in risk assessment and cognitive psychology. When researchers in risk analysis began to realize that the public rarely perceives risk the way risk assessors do, they began working with researchers in cognitive psychology to explain the discrepancies between "expert" analysis and "public" perception of risk. As Barbara Mirel (1994) explains,

> Because psychological theorists of risk see that an individual's outrage is generated by cognitive reactions to social and ethical interests, they argue that the goal of risk communication must not be to educate citizens in expert "facts" to change their opinions but rather to evoke dialogue through a focus on the sources of a particular audience's outrages and fears. (p. 45)

Together, the scholars in risk analysis and cognitive psychology have adapted a psychometric scale to predict how lay audiences would react to specific risks. Psychometric scales ask people to rate the "riskiness" of different hazardous activities and to indicate how strongly they believe that these hazards should be reduced or regulated. According to Slovic, "these global judgments have then been related to judgments about the hazard's status on various qualitative characteristics of risk" (p. 408). Risk communicators currently use psychometric risk factors to determine how best to adapt their initial message to the public and how to negotiate the decision-making process. However, these factors focus primarily on the risk itself, not the citizens. For example, a person might be asked to rank the hazard of living near a chemical company that produces toxic chemicals on a scale for nine different attributes. Attributes include how well known the hazard is to the person; how harmful the effects of the hazard would be; how frightening those effects are; how easily those effects can be controlled; how easily the hazard itself can be avoided, and so on. Based upon these attributes, a risk is characterized as a specific type. Health assessors consider these risk types static and universal perceptions. As a result, they often approach similar risk types in a similar manner in all communities, often leading to inappropriate policies and hostile reactions from involved lay persons (see Ross, p. 176). Slovic argues that one of the generalizations that can be drawn from psychometric studies is that "perceived risk is quantifiable and predictable. Psychometric techniques seem well suited for identifying similarities and differences among groups with regard to risk perception and attitudes" (p. 408).

These generalizations pose a problem for risk communication and public participation practices because these labels, which try to provide objective estimates for the public's "irrationalities," often take on ontological status and do not account for cultural differences across communities. Public participation should be determined by real and localized situations, not hypothetical, decontextualized questions of the psychometric scales. Mirel (1994) argues similarly that such psychological theories are too limited for risk communication because they focus on outrage factors of individuals and fail to consider social and cultural influences. She asserts that the social and cultural structures and relationships should be the unit of analysis, rather than the individual, because risk perceptions are constructed not by individuals but by social and cultural groups (p. 45). While investigating factors that affect the public's perception of risk could be useful, the psychometric scale alone is inadequate because it not only decontextualizes the risk but decontextualizes the public as well.

Drawing from Douglas and Wildavsky's theories of social dynamics that influence attitudes about environmental risks, Mirel (1994) claims that the "real debates going on in risk controversies are over institutions that different groups set up as decision processors [. . .] In risk debates, questions over the acceptability of potentially dangerous technologies are actually questions about the distribution of power, the credibility of authority, and the legitimacy of decision-making practices and procedures" (p. 47). The approaches to risk communication research advocated by risk assessment and cognitive psychology seek to understand public *perception* in order to incorporate those perceptions in communications about the risk but deny citizens any real power in determining what factors should shape the risk policy. Further, research goals of psychometric studies do not include *increased* participation or betterment of the community, but rather a less hostile environment for the risk assessors themselves.

HOW CURRENT PUBLIC PARTICIPATION PRACTICES MARGINALIZE THE PUBLIC

While the quantitative approaches to studying public participation adapted from cognitive psychology tend to be arhetorical and decontextualized in their approach to citizen involvement in policy decisions, there are a number of case studies that describe a particular risk situation, what communication model was used, what worked well, and what did not and end with a call for a more rhetorical approach to risk communication. These studies are important for developing a new framework for more ethical decision making in that they illustrate some of the factors that encouraged as well as discouraged active participation in actual environmental public policy decisions. The examined literature is interdisciplinary, drawing from rhetoric and composition, technical communication, sociology, participatory design, and risk assessment studies. These particular studies were chosen because they focus specifically on the ways in which citizens were allowed to participate in environmental public policy and question what encouraged or discouraged that participation. This section reviews a number of studies of public participation in environmental policy as a way to illuminate the assumptions of institutions about risk communication and public participation in policy decisions. Collectively, these examples show patterns of power and participation that are often employed in environmental policy decision-making processes.

One of the earliest risk communication studies to question the lack of significant citizen involvement in environmental policies—and to use a case study approach—Plough and Krimsky (1988) argue against policies based solely on technical factors determined by government agencies and health officials. Focusing on the cultural and historical aspects of risk communication practices they examine five different "risk communication events" including an ethylene dibromide (EDB) pesticide controversy in 1983–1984. Using data they gathered from media reports, messages from federal agencies to the public, communications among federal and state agencies and industry, and communications from interest groups and citizens, Plough and Krimsky examine public participation in the debates over the use of the pesticide

EDB on and in food. They found that while there were public congressional hearings on EDB, Congress also held "secret meetings with industry officials" and that "all of the important decisions are made in private meetings where the public is not present" (p. 27). According to Plough and Krimsky, the debates and ultimately the policy were "the responsibility of the elites" (p. 303). The citizens' marginalized position in this case is clear. Not only were citizens not encouraged to participate in the decision-making process, but they were not invited to the meetings where the actual decisions were made.

Drawing from multiple cases, Plough and Krimsky assert that current models of decision making in environmental policy often employ a "technical" model that assumes "risk can be studied independent of context" (p. 305). In their technical model, risk assessors strive to educate the public into thinking about risk the way experts do. Public perception must be brought into conformity with scientific rationality. In the technical model, citizens' responses to "risk are important only in understanding the extent to which ordinary people's ideas deviate from the truth" (p. 305). Plough and Krimsky argue that this model establishes hierarchies based on expert status and assumes that risk policies can be determined by a defined set of principles and scientific norms independent of citizen input. This exclusion of citizens denies that risk is socially constructed and that citizens are capable of contributing useful knowledge to the decision-making process. By excluding members of the public, and their knowledge of how a policy will affect them, from the decision process, scientists diminish the likelihood of constructing a policy that is considered just by all parties involved.

The EDB case illustrates citizens' most marginalized position in the decision-making process. When citizens are regulated to spectators in the decision-making process, or "educated" into agreeing with agency decisions, they fit Young and Gaventa's definition of powerless. While some risk communication practices have evolved to better involve the public in the years since Plough and Krimsky's study, the following case studies illustrate that too many public policy decisions deny citizens the ability to actively participate in the decision-making process.

Steven Katz and Carolyn Miller (1996) look at the level of citizen participation in the decision-making process of a low-level radiation waste facility siting controversy and critique what they call the "elitist participation" model of risk communication employed by the North Carolina Low-Level Waste Management Authority (the Authority). By examining the documents and testimony of the institutions and parties involved in the decision-making process, Katz and Miller found that the risk communication practices reduced public participation to passive reception and turned dialogue into a public relations campaign. Drawing on studies by Kasperson and Fiorino, they assert that while public meetings are the most common form of public participation, they may be the most "ineffective and alienating" because they are often dominated by groups that prevent those most affected by the risk from being heard (p. 118). Katz and Miller found that even though there was a "public participation plan" in place, the Authority maintained control of every aspect of the decision-making process: they set the agenda to which the public was allowed to respond, they decided when and if the public spoke, they allowed the public to comment at few points in the decision process, and all but excluded those comments from the final policy (pp. 123–124). Public comment, they further note, was not allowed until the end, when the official business was completed—often *after* the Authority voted on citing issues (p. 128).

Pointing out how the slight rewording of the hazardous waste bill by the North Carolina legislature also worked to exclude the public, Katz and Miller note, "The North Carolina legislation also requires the Authority to develop procedures and criteria for selecting a site, procedures that are to be 'developed with, and provide for, public participation' [. . .] The original version of the hazardous waste bill read: 'the procedures shall be developed through public participation' " (p. 119). Here the discourse of institutional procedures allows the Authority to maintain power in the public participation process.

Katz and Miller assert that the actions of the Authority are characteristic of risk communication: complete control of the decision process; a trust in the power of information and education; and a limited understanding of communication (p. 123). This model of public participation focuses on the product, not the process of decision-making, and assumes that experts, with their specialized knowledge, can act in the best interest of the citizens.

While citizens were not completely excluded from the decision-making process, they still were powerless to actively contribute and shape the decision. Citizens are allowed to participate but only in ways that the experts can control. Iacofano, Moore, and Goltsman (1990), urban planners and scholars in participatory design, call this "pseudo participation." Pseudo participation, they assert, is a strategy used by those in power to "present the illusion" of participation (p. 198). Further, they note that, "policies may have already been made and public programmes are devised so as to make participants feel that they had a useful role in creating them" (p. 198). Here, participation is only a strategy for placating potentially hostile reactions from citizens.

This approach to public participation is especially oppressive for citizens because they are manipulated into accepting the policies determined by the institutional elite. Sanoff (1990), in his discussion of the complexities of involving the public in city planning decisions, quotes Arnstein's discussion of the powerless, asserting, "Participation without redistribution of power is an empty and frustrating process for the powerless. It allows the power holders to claim that all sides were considered but makes it possible for only some of these to benefit" (p. 6).

In cases where citizens are completely excluded, such as the EDB case, citizens can, and often do, appeal to Congress to change the policy. While this redesign is rarely satisfactory to any of the involved parties because it is not a negotiated policy, but rather an appeasement for the loudest voice, it is still influenced by citizens. In the approach used by the North Carolina Low-level Radiation Waste Management Authority, public outcry is contained within the controlled setting of an institutionally arranged public meeting.

Belsten (1996) argues that often citizens in a community choose not to participate, not because the issue does not interest them, but because they see public meetings as a "decide—announce—defend" event designed to generate an administrative record that the public was consulted (p. 36). She maintains that this approach to environmental risk communication "has failed miserably," often resulting in significant opposition from the public that delays policy decisions (p. 31). Arguing for a theory of "community collaboration," she asserts that a truly open forum for discourse, one that is inclusive and respectful of all involved parties, is needed in order to encourage citizen participation. Illustrating her argument, she details a case study of a hazardous waste incinerator siting in Kimball, Nebraska. Like the North Carolina low-level radiation waste facility case, the community in Kimball was faced with building an incinerator that would accept hazardous waste from out of state. However, the decision process was quite different. In this case, the director of community involvement for the company responsible for siting the incinerator maintained that the facility would be built only if community members determined that they wanted the incinerator. Further, the director met informally with many individuals from the community, providing them access to reports and videos describing the potential hazards of incinerators. Belsten maintains that this incinerator siting was one of the most successful in terms of citizen approval, not because the citizens were unconcerned about the risks, but because of the positive risk communication and public participation practices employed by the director of the waste company. Belsten argues that an open forum—necessary for just decisions— was encouraged by five strategies: (1) the decision to build the incinerator was left to the community; (2) the decision-making process was "open and inclusive"—attended by local officials and lay citizens whose comments, according to Belsten, were valued equally; (3) the director freely offered both advantages and dangers to building the incinerator in the community; (4) "the process was interactive" in that the director listened as much as he talked and "incorporated the community's suggestions into the final design" (p. 40); and (5) the community was included in the decision from the beginning (p. 40).

This approach to citizen participation values the contributions by all parties, by involving those affected early and in ways that allow them to shape the resulting policy. Iacofano, Moore, and Goltsman characterize the type of citizen involvement that Belsten describes in the Kimball incinerator case as "full participation." They assert that full participation occurs "when each individual member of a decision-making body has equal power to determine the outcome of the decisions [. . .] Power is decentralized and proposals or recommendations generated by citizen groups will be implemented" (p. 198). From Belsten's description, we see that power was decentralized in the Kimball incinerator case. There were no documented instances of a power struggle between the community and the company siting the waste facility. I think that it is interesting to note that the involvement of institutions in the Kimball incinerator case was at a minimum. While the presence or absence of institutions does not dictate whether the public will have access to the decision-making process, it may be that the power afforded many institutions because of legislated procedure may work to prevent citizen participation.

While encouraging, the approach adopted by the Kimball incinerator case does not appear to be the norm in risk communication practices. Like Belsten, Ross (1996) argues that an open forum, inclusive and respectful of all involved parties, is needed before policies are decided in order to avoid hostile reactions from excluded parties. Unlike Belsten, however, Ross bases her argument on two case studies where this open forum did not occur as part of the risk communication practices. Ross, in her examination of the decision to place a landfill less than a mile from a Mohawk Indian reserve, argues that efforts to seemingly involve the public in the decision making are often little more than placating measures. As an example, she notes that when the Mohawk tribe opposed the siting because the proximity of the landfill would negatively affect their water quality, they were told that their comment was placed in the "public opposition" category and that public opposition was not a criteria in the decision to place the landfill (p. 176). With the power to classify comments into categories that could be dismissed, the institutions in charge of siting the landfill illustrate that all involved parties did not have equal power in determining the outcome of the decision. Ross' example brings to light another issue. The public is made up of individuals with different perspectives, cultures, and values. The Mohawk tribe values teach a different relationship to Mother Earth than other cultures. Often, however, different perspectives are lost in the public participation process because experts see the public as a unified group and dismiss any differences among them. This dismissal oversimplifies the complexity of public debates and results in a decision that privileges a select few.

Drawing from Habermas and Benhabib, Ross asserts that if the "oppressive dynamics of current environmental policy making" are to be avoided, the "privileging of science and dogma" in discourse must be replaced with inclusive debate (p. 180). Discourse focused only on technical aspects of risk or on one public perspective often denies those affected the opportunity to participate in environmental policy making—and as will be illustrated in the Newport case in chapter 4, often results in inappropriate, or even unsound, policies. Further, like Belsten, Young, and Gaventa, Ross argues that decisions are only ethical if all involved parties are allowed to participate.

Craig Waddell (1996) argues that under certain conditions citizens can more fully participate in policy decisions. In his study of public participation in the International Joint Commission's Great Lakes Water Quality Hearings, he asserts that the public "had considerable influence" on policy recommendations, especially when they used emotional appeals to persuade the commissioners of the hearings (p. 153). He maintains that when the commissioners employed a "social construction model" of risk communication there was an "interactive exchange of information" by all participants (p. 142). However, drawing from his accounts of hearing testimonies, public discourse and scientific discussions are often separated. Waddell states,

> in at least some cases, the commissioners pursued an issue on the basis of public testimony, sought the support of their scientific advisory boards before committing themselves, and then, having received such support, genuinely perceived subsequent comments on this issue from the public as simply confirming their scientifically based beliefs. Thus, although the commissioners have found it politically expedient to cite public support when presenting their recommendations to legislators, they have found it politically inexpedient to suggest that their recommendations *derive* from public (as opposed to scientific) testimony. (emphasis in quote, p. 153)

While the public is allowed to suggest directions, the power lies with the scientific advisory board, who must be consulted before the commissioners will "commit." These institutional actions suggest that legislators value scientific over public discourse. While scientific information is essential to the development of an environmental policy, technical experts often do not have the local knowledge about how a particular policy would affect a particular community. Public discourse influenced technical decisions, but only when scientific advisory boards supported the public contributions. This separation of public discourse and technical decision-making denies the public epistemological status.

Katz and Miller (1996) illustrate a specific example of this separation in their critique of the ways in which public contributions were diminished because the technical experts claimed that "siting procedures and criteria...should be based on the technical language of a specific promulgated regulation and not on the interpretative layman's language which it includes" (124–125). Katz and Miller assert that this motion resulted in requiring the public to use technical language rather than the explanatory language used in documents designed specifically for the public to read regarding the siting issue. In this case, the information the public was given by the experts did not provide them with the technical language to participate in the decision-making. (See also Beverly Sauer (1993) and (2002) for examples of power structures in scientific coal mining debates and documentation that control discourse and prevent non-expert voices from being heard even when those voices offer sensible coal mine safety recommendations.)

Arguing for a rhetorical approach to decision making grounded in part in the Aristotelian concept of ethos, Katz and Miller assert that a process based on equal participation and mutual respect will result in more ethical decision-making (133–135).

Like Waddell, Griggs (1994) believes that environmental policies are and should be considered social constructions. She asserts that while interaction occurred among writers at hearings and meetings for a state water quality standards administrative law, the participation of the lay audience was constrained (p. 154). She details three attempts citizens made during the rulemaking to lobby the government officials with petitions that received no response from the officials and describes the public hearing procedure where citizens gave "testimony" to silent government officials. She notes that most citizens were actually representatives speaking on the behalf of companies or organizations (a finding that even further complicates the already problematic notion of citizen or public). While citizens succeeded in delaying the water quality standards ruling, they were prevented from contributing significantly to the policy itself due to a series of what I would call mundane institutional procedures. For example a ruling had to be passed by a particular date whether or not there was consensus among the involved parties. This procedure resulted in officials passing the decision even though citizens had maintained they were opposed to the current policy. The distance citizens had to drive in order to attend public meetings—as much as eight hours—restricted the number of citizens who were able to attend and participate in the meetings—and the low-level technology used to inform the citizens about the meetings and decisions often resulted in citizens not alerted to meeting times and places. Yet, as illustrated in the case of the VX nerve agent disposal in chapter 4, even the use of high-level technology such as web sites to announce meeting times is of little benefit if the web site is not updated regularly to reflect upcoming meetings. Both Waddell and Griggs illustrate that federal procedures and practices can diminish the citizens' power to actually contribute to the resulting policy.

For example, Stratman, Boykin, Holmes, Laufer, and Breen (1995) illustrate in their examination of an Aspen town battle with an EPA remediation proposal, the EPA's legal power and authority make it difficult for the agency to appear sincere in its attempt to consider public concerns in its risk decisions. Stratman and colleagues note,

> Once an EPA risk assessment and remediation plan is set in motion, there is much uncertainty and conflict as to how far an EPA field representative may go in sincerely listening [. . .] Indeed, it is hard

for EPA to genuinely listen when [. . .] EPA continues to retain final ownership of risk determination expertise—if not explicitly by law, then by the prejudice of power and incumbency. (p. 10)

They assert that the EPA policy guidelines actually work to feed the perceptions that citizens are coerced into a policy and that the EPA has a hidden agenda (p. 23). For example, they note, "Although the public can request a preliminary assessment, at no time until the EPA completes the RI/FS [remedial investigation/feasibility study] and issues the ROD [record of decision] identifying the remedy can the public participate in determining, even through additional experts, the nature and extent of the contamination or what the remedy should consider and include" (p. 25). While citizens could influence the policy, the institutional procedures granting the EPA final power made it difficult to involve the citizens in ways that advocate a just policy. The study by Stratman and others suggests a more in-depth look at the role institutions play in restricting public participation. Gaventa (1980) asserts that the exercise of power does not have to be present to affect participation. The mere reputation of power, he argues, is enough to inhibit citizens from participating in policy decisions. This theory seems to be at work in the Aspen case. The citizens, aware that the final decision rests with the EPA, resent the attempts of the EPA to act otherwise and react against the EPA's proposed decisions.

This uneven power relation between the EPA and area citizens is not a situation limited to the Aspen case. Plough and Krimsky (1988), in their case study of risk communication practices involved in a copper-smelting plant releasing toxic arsenic emissions, examine the EPA's self-professed attempt to "open up its standard setting to the community" (p. 182). This attempt led the EPA to arrange a series of workshops for the Tacoma community designed to explain proposed arsenic regulations and to solicit comments from the community. At the time of the study, while the copper-smelting plant in Tacoma, Washington was responsible for 25 percent of arsenic emissions in the United States, it was also the major employer in the area. According to Plough and Krimsky, the EPA "carefully orchestrated the agenda" (p. 203) of the workshops and "retained its final decision-making authority" (p. 182) in determining arsenic emissions regulations. As further evidence of their power, the EPA had security personnel present at one meeting, though there were no reports of prior or potential need for crowd control (p. 203).

As Gaventa points out, this mere presence of power can work to prevent citizens from participating. On the one hand, the EPA is asking for comments on their proposed regulation, yet on the other hand, they are calling in the police to ensure that control is maintained. It is little wonder, then, that the citizens were not wholly satisfied with the level of citizen participation adopted by the EPA. According to Plough and Krimsky, "to the environmental regulators, citizen participation means input into a process defined by officials in technical terms. For the public, participation often means gaining greater control of both the process for making decisions and the language of risk" (p. 222). When citizens realize that ultimately their comments are not valued equally with those of the EPA, that they are validating, not developing, a policy, and that there may even be repercussions for voicing their concerns, they are not only relegated to a powerless position but also threatened into not speaking at all.

It is tempting to hope that public participation practices have evolved over time to better integrate the contributions of all affected in the decision-making process. And indeed some agencies have begun to employ a "consensus" model of participation where stakeholders are characterized as "equal with everybody having the chance to speak up and be heard" (Wills-Toker, 2004, p. 186). This model seems based on the Habermasian approach to public deliberation where equals will attempt to understand each other. Yet this model does not account for the unequal power relations that are more reflective of actual technical policy debates. As Amy (1987), notes, "environmental participation is not simply about communication. It's also about power struggles. It is not only about horse trading but competition between conflicting values and different moral visions" (as cited in Wills-Toker, 2004, p. 198). Drawing from her examination of the Georgia Port Authority's decision to employ a "consensus-based Stakeholder Evaluation Group" to address public opposition to a harbor deepening project, Wills-Toker argues that such models often "cover up" and "smooth over recognition of inequality and control" (p.197). For example, she found that despite the vocabulary of consensus among equals and "common good," the technical elite would categorize issues that the public brought to light in ways that diminished their importance by framing past public comments as "historical issues" and refusing to discuss those unresolved issues in meetings. I argue then, in order to achieve ethical and appropriate policies, we must examine not only whether the public is allowed to participate in environmental decisions, but also whether they are granted the power to directly influence the decision.

EXAMINING PARTICIPATION AND POWER
IN ENVIRONMENTAL POLICY DECISION MAKING

Examining the previous cases, we see a variety of risk communication practices and a range of citizen participation within those practices. A number of theorists from disciplines including risk assessment, sociology, rhetoric, and public policy have characterized the most common models of risk communication practices based upon the level of public involvement (Krimsky and Plough, 1988; Waddell, 1996; McGarity, 1998). While each theorist assigns a slightly different name to each model, they all identify four typical models of risk communication or public participation in environmental decisions: (1) no public involvement, (2) one-way flow of technical information to bring public perception of risk into conformity with scientific perception, (3) superficial participation to placate public, and (4) a wished-for negotiation model. One set of characteristics about risk communication approaches that I find especially useful is Iacofano and colleagues' (1990) discussion of public participation that focuses not only on the level of participation but also on the degree of power afforded affected parties.

In figure 2.1, I map the degree to which citizens were involved in the actual decision-making process in these example cases as a way to reveal the public's marginalized status and powerlessness in current risk communication practices. In order to map levels of participation and power, I borrow a framework and map design from Iacofano and colleagues' (1990) work in participatory design research. In their discussions of public participation in urban planning, Iacofano and others argue, in close alignment with Young, Gaventa, Belsten, and Ross,

> Public participation in agency decision-making implies a sharing of power, but within a given situation the desire on the part of public agency staff or elected officials to share or seek power varies. Simply inviting citizens to comment at public meetings on environmental planning proposals will not ensure that their concerns are readily embraced by planners and taken into account in agency decision-making. (p. 197)

Again, we see that all participation is not equal. They note that public participation in policy decisions is based on two dimensions: "the degree of political decentralization or shared power" and "the degree of desired participant interaction" (p. 197). While Iacofano and others are not mapping cases of risk communication—in fact, they are not mapping any case, but rather illustrating the possible dimensions of public participation in urban planning—their approach is useful for considering public participation in risk communication cases. Using each dimension as a continuum on an axis, they indicate that the spaces between the axes are made up of four possible approaches for interactive decision making: pseudoparticipation, consultation, partial participation, and full participation. Because their model assumes some level of interactive participation (which was absent in the EDB case), I have modified my adaptation of a participation map to indicate strategic action rather than consultation.

Drawing from Habermas' theories of discourse ethics, I see a strategic action approach to risk communication practices as one in which the technical experts try to bring public perception into conformity with scientific rationale, believing that with enough technical information the public can be influenced into thinking about risk the way the scientists do. According to Habermas, strategic action occurs when one "seeks to influence the behavior of another by means of the threat of sanctions or the prospect of gratification in order to cause the interaction to continue as the actor desires" (p. 58). It is in this type of communication, Habermas asserts, that the communicators are "interested solely in the success, i.e., the consequences or outcomes of their actions, they will try to reach their objectives by influencing their opponent's definition of the situation, and thus his decisions or motives, through external means by using weapons or goods, threats or enticements" (p. 133). Here the communicator is more interested in succeeding, or winning the argument, than in reaching an understanding with the other parties (p. 134). Aligning closely with Krimsky and Plough's description of the technical model of risk communication, the strategic action approach sees citizens as entities to be managed, incapable of contributing to the development of the policy.

A pseudoparticipation approach to risk communication practices is often adopted for the purpose of *appearing* to actively involved citizens when a policy has already been determined by a smaller group (p. 198; see examples in Katz and Miller; Ross; Waddell; and Stratman et al.). The motivation for this approach may be to placate hostile citizen groups by making them believe that they have played a part in the development of a policy (Iacofano et al., 1990).

According to the framework of Iacofano and colleagues, partial participation occurs when the involved parties "can influence each other, but the final power rests with one party only" (p. 198). They argue that this is often the approach adopted in cases where citizen participation is the requirement of a federal regulation. As illustrated in the Aspen EPA case (Stratman et al.), because the final decision is ultimately that of the federal agency, the public participation activities are often a strategy for fulfilling regulation requirements. Iacofano and others warn that this type of approach can easily "denigrate towards pseudo participation" (p. 198).

Full participation, Iacofano and others assert, occurs when "each individual member of a decision-making body has equal power to determine the outcome of decisions" (p. 198). In this case, power is shared and citizens are involved in ways that encourage them to actively contribute to the development of the environmental policy. While few risk communication cases achieve full participation (Belsten's description of the Kimball incinerator case appears to be an exception), this approach seems to be aligned with the theories of ethical debate advocated by Young, Gaventa, and Benhabib. Mapping these representative cases to illustrate the degree of power and interaction citizens were granted in each case suggests that in most cases citizens were afforded little power (see figure 2.1). Perhaps the most disconcerting aspect revealed by the map is the high number of cases that fall into the pseudoparticipation quadrant—where citizens are placated with a high number of public meetings suggesting that their concerns are being considered in the decision-making process but where their input is granted little power in influencing the final policy.

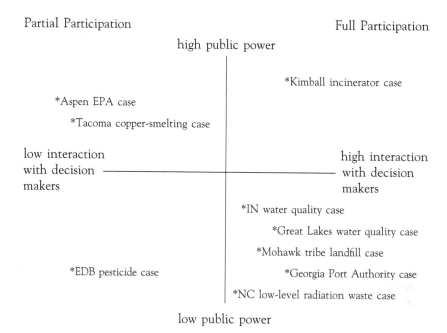

Figure 2.1: Citizen Participation in Cases of Environmental Public Policy

Citizens' Marginalized Status in Definitions of Risk Communication

Examining the prominently accepted definitions of risk communication advocated by institutions that regulate environmental risk in terms of the same participation framework of power and interaction can reveal how their assumptions about risk communication might work to perpetuate the marginalized status of citizens in the decision-making process. While the earliest definition of risk communication was "[a message] which would furnish the lay public with information to convince them to agree with the experts" (Baker, p. 343), the earliest accepted, and still predominant, view on risk communication by those in risk assessment is Covello, Winterfeldt, and Slovic's (1986) assertion that risk communication is "any purposeful exchange of scientific information between interested parties regarding health or environmental risks" (p. 222). This definition assumes that the power and knowledge about a risk, and how to deal with that risk, should remain with the technical experts. Exchanges are limited not only to scientific information but also to what those in power consider "purposeful." Citizen knowledge is not considered.

Later in 1988, Covello and Allen reworded the original definition for their book, *Seven Cardinal Rules of Risk Communication*, which became the basis for the EPA's risk communication practices (Stratman et al., p. 8). In this version, risk communication is defined as "the act of conveying or transmitting information between interested parties about levels of health or environmental risks; the significance or meaning of such risks; or the decisions, actions or policies aimed at managing or controlling such risks" (p. 112). Still, this definition privileges technical information and assumes knowledge about the risk is determined by experts in isolation of context or citizens and then transmitted to affected parties.

In 1992, Covello again reworked his definition, redefining risk communication as "the exchange of information among interested parties about the nature, magnitude, significance, or control of a risk" (p. 359). Yet, he still relies on the assumption that with enough information regarding risk, all parties will conform to the same conclusions about a given risk.

In response to criticism by social scientists that Covello and others' 1986 definition excluded all but technical information, the National Research Council (1989), in its book, *Improving Risk Communication*, presents another definition, asserting that risk communication is "an interactive process of exchange of information and opinion among individuals, groups and institutions. It involves multiple messages about the nature of risk, and other messages, not strictly about risk, that express concerns, opinions or reactions to risk messages or to legal and institutional arrangements for risk management" (p. 21). While this definition recognizes nontechnical information as important criteria in the decision-making process, it still relies on the power of information to bring all views into conformity.

Further, while the National Research Council argues that risk communication is a "particular instance of democratic dialogue" (p. 21), its definitions of other aspects of risk communication practices suggest otherwise. Claiming that "risk communication practitioners and researchers and the general public often confuse key distinctions such as [. . .] that between risk communication and risk message" (p. 321), the authors offer additional definitions of "risk communicator/message source" and "audience/recipients." They define *risk communicator* as "the individual or office sending a risk message or interacting with other individuals, groups, or organizations in a risk communication process; may also be the risk manager, risk message preparer, risk analyst, or other *expert*" (emphasis mine, p. 322). *Audience*, they define as "the recipient(s) of a risk message; almost never a homogeneous group; can include the recipients intended by the preparer of the message as well as others who receive it even though addressed elsewhere" (p. 322). With these definitions, the National Research Council suggests that while citizens may be present, even speak, during risk communication practices, they are not responsible for constructing risk messages but rather being the recipients of risk messages constructed by experts. The possibility of a socially constructed risk, which is suggested by the Council's definition of *risk communication*, cannot be fulfilled with its belief that risk policy epistemology is limited to experts.

A 2002 NRC online document entitled, *Risk-based Decision-making Guidelines*, reveals a revised definition that states risk communication is: (1) "an interactive process," (2) "an exchange of information and opinion," (3) "a process that involves individuals, groups, and institutions, and (4) a process that concerns the nature of risk (section 1 of Principles of risk communication). On the surface, this definition seems a step in the right direction. However, a closer look reveals that the attitudes toward the public have changed little since the earlier definitions. For example, the supplementary information for the second category states "The goals of this information exchange include (1) improving people's understanding and (2) changing impressions, attitudes, and behaviors" (section 1 of Principles of risk communication). A section entitled, "Risk Communication in the Risk-based Decision-making process" states "A balance of stakeholder involvement is required, though. Involving too many stakeholders in all aspects of the risk-based decision-making process can be overwhelming to the stakeholders and counterproductive to the decision-making objectives" (section 2 of Principles of risk communication). A list of "dos" and "don'ts" warn the risk assessor to "Be responsive, but maintain control. Do not lose your cool with a questioner who seems pushy or technically uninformed" (Section 7: Working with the media). The document still includes the "Seven Cardinal Rules" and still separates discussions of risk communication from discussions of risk assessment and risk management. The revised definition may be advocating a process, but the underlying attitudes and assumptions that marginalize the public are still present.

None of the generally accepted definitions of risk communication indicates a negotiation process where each affected individual's contribution is valued equally in the decision-making process. Yet what I find most interesting in the series of definitions is that three of the four accepted and cited definitions are by the same group of people, Covello and colleagues. While numerous individuals and groups have characterized risk communication, only Covello and the National Research Council have been granted definition status. Indeed, these definitions dominate risk communication literature. Yet each of these definitions represents only the technical expert's view of risk communication. And only the definitions of risk assessors are cited and accepted. Also interesting is that by and large, the cases see what is called for by the definitions (see figure 2.2). Until institutional assumptions and procedures of risk communication are modified to value the knowledge citizens can contribute to the policy, the public will retain its marginalized status in the decision-making process.

While the existing cases of public participation in environmental policy provide useful descriptions and critique of currently employed approaches to public participation, most stop short of examining the institutions that work to perpetuate the traditional models of risk communication and of offering a new framework, or heuristic, for a more ethical model. Chapter 3 examines

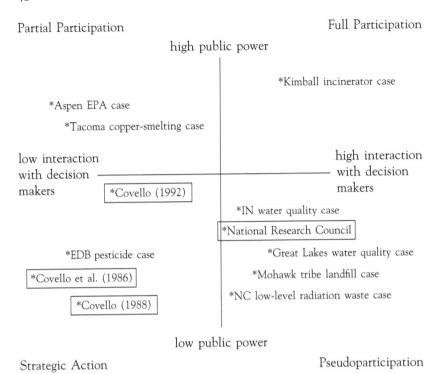

Partial Participation   Full Participation

high public power

*Kimball incinerator case

*Aspen EPA case

*Tacoma copper-smelting case

low interaction   high interaction
with decision   with decision
makers   *Covello (1992)   makers

*IN water quality case

*National Research Council

*EDB pesticide case   *Great Lakes water quality case

*Covello et al. (1986)   *Mohawk tribe landfill case

*Covello (1988)   *NC low-level radiation waste case

low public power

Strategic Action   Pseudoparticipation

Figure 2.2: Institutional Definitions of Public Participation in Risk Communication and Cases of Environmental Public Policy

risk communication and public participation practices in the U.S. Army's decision to destroy nearly two thousand tons of VX nerve agent on site through the discourses, documents, decisions, and interviews of a state-wide citizen activist group, a grassroots citizen group against incineration, and state and federal agencies—paying special attention to the power relations and institutional constraints that work to prevent active public participation. By combining and comparing the extended examples of my observations with the accounts from literature, I seek to illuminate a range of examples of specific risk communication practices that will allow me to theorize about why significant participation is often not possible and the ways in which citizens could more significantly participate in the decisions of environmental policy.

CHAPTER THREE

A CASE OF INSTITUTIONAL POWER: PUBLIC PARTICIPATION IN DECISIONS ABOUT VX NERVE AGENT DISPOSAL AT THE NEWPORT CHEMICAL DEPOT

What role does the public play in technical policy decisions? On December 3, 1999, with no visible public opposition, the U.S. Army was granted approval to destroy one-third of the 1,269 tons of stored VX nerve agent—the deadliest substance known—at the Newport Chemical Depot in Newport, Indiana, and was granted a license to dispose of the effluent from the neutralized agent into the nearby Wabash River. Despite at least five public meetings (specifically regarding the proposal to dispose of the VX agent by neutralization), no public comments affected the revision of the final environmental impact statement, nor did any public comments affect the licensing permit.

On the surface, indeed, on the record, the public was represented as being either in agreement with the proposed plan or apathetic toward it. However, a closer inspection of the events revealed that in a number of ways, the public had been prevented from participating in the discussions where the policy was actually constructed. In this case institutions and the procedures in place to ensure public participation often actually worked to prevent significant participation. While the institutions involved in the VX decision-making process repeatedly stated the importance of public participation, there were numerous and frequent obstacles that prevented the public from contributing to the decisions about VX disposal in any but the most superficial of ways. Not only is this denied participation unethical, but it can result in inappropriate policies. Yet if public participation is

43

to become more significant in public policy decisions, the process for decision making must change.

This chapter examines public involvement in the decision to destroy
1,269 tons of VX nerve agent at the Newport Chemical Depot. By exploring
the discourses, procedures, and documents of the state and federal agencies
and two citizen groups involved in the decision, I examine how institutions
determine risk communication practices and how those practices work to
encourage or inhibit significant public participation in contributing to an
environmental policy. Paying special attention to the ways institutions constrain or marginalize citizen participation, we can begin thinking about ways
to create spaces for more significant public discourse in environmental policy
decisions. This chapter focuses on the institutions directly involved in chemical weapons disposal decisions at the Newport Chemical Depot, considering
each institution's expectation about public participation as evidenced by its
procedures for public involvement and offering examples of public involvement with each institution. One such procedure is the environmental impact
statement (EIS). Many studies on public participation in environmental policy
have examined the EIS as a genre of public decision-making discourse (Dayton, 2002; Killingsworth and Palmer, 1992; Killingsworth and Steffans, 1989;
Miller, 1980; Rude, 1995). Yet, with this study, I want to show that while
the EIS is a critical part of the decision-making process that often precludes
public involvement, evaluating public decision making must also include
examining other, more seemingly mundane institutional practices to determine whether or not citizens are allowed to participate in significant ways as
well as whether the environmental decision is just. Foregrounding these
institutional power and discourse practices brings to light practical and complex problems that discussions at the level of policy itself often miss. Such
a focus is important if we hope to understand and change current decision-
making practices that marginalize civic discourse in policy issues. Chapter 4
further examines the institutional procedures for public participation by focusing on two factors: how much power the public had in influencing the
final policy and the level of interaction the public was granted with the
actual decision makers of the policy before considering how a participatory
design approach to environmental policy decisions might grant citizens more
power and interaction. In order to change models of public participation that
deny significant participation, we must understand the various ways in which
public participation is currently allowed to influence policy, and we must
recognize the power structures in place that work to prevent participation.
We must also understand the discourse practices that enable resistance to
those power structures by analyzing the institutions that govern the policy-
making processes.

Drawing on Frank Fischer's (2000) call to examine the discourses of
public policy debates; Young's (1990) connection of decision-making practices with power relations; Gaventa's (1980) call to link power with partici-

pation; and Foucault's (1982) view of institutions as sites of power, examining the discourses of a public policy debate in its institutional settings reveals spaces where citizens are denied significant participation as well as spaces where citizens might be encouraged to participate more significantly. The case of VX nerve agent disposal at the Newport Chemical Depot is especially useful for illustrating specific barriers set up by the institutions involved. In some instances, citizens did influence events, but to a large degree only because they resisted the existing institutional power structures and institutionally established model of decision making by adopting alternative literacy and discourse practices that granted them agency to participate in the decision-making process.

By entwining narratives about the public's participation from the point of view of representatives at the Chemical Depot, citizens' groups, and my own observations, both chapters present multiple perspectives on the decision-making process in an attempt to tease out institutional positions on public participation. The additional evidence that traces institutional power in the disposal of VX nerve agent at the Newport Chemical Depot comes from federal and state regulations, environmental impact statements, public notices, fact sheets compiled by the program manager for the chemical demilitarization section of the U.S. Army, documents, descriptions, and interactions from public meetings. The discussions surrounding the decision to dispose of the VX nerve agent at the Newport Chemical Depot date back to 1988—nearly ten years before I began investigating public participation practices. As a result, I rely on public records and especially on interviews with the spokesperson for a grassroots citizen group, a representative from the depot, and a spokesperson for a state-wide citizen group—all of whom were involved in the earlier stages—for their perspectives of the public participation practices that occurred before 1998.

While examinations of existing case studies of public participation as discussed in chapter 2 are useful for seeing that the public is often denied significant participation in the development of an environmental policy, they have not illuminated important aspects of the decision-making process such as the institutional power constraints that dictated who participated, who was left out, who was allowed to speak, who listened, and how these voices were integrated into a public policy. With the case of chemical weapons disposal at the Newport Chemical Depot, I hope to illustrate the complexity of the institutions involved and the multiplicity of the risk communication models employed. Studies of public participation often suggest a dichotomy of players—experts and citizens. In the case of the VX nerve agent disposal decision, a multitude of agencies, institutions, citizen groups, and individuals—and their view of the purpose and functions of public participation—complicate this dichotomy. While many of the existing cases on public participation in environmental issues suggest that each case employs a single model of risk communication, the VX nerve agent disposal case illuminated that, in many situations, multiple approaches to public participation are employed, even by the same agency, throughout the process of implementing a policy. Understanding the complexity of institutions and their disparate public participation procedures is important for considering what inhibits or encourages significant public participation.

By focusing on localized sites, then combining and comparing the extended examples with accounts from existing literature on public participation, a range of specific communication practices reveal what conditions are necessary for citizens to participate in environmental decisions more significantly. From these instances much can be learned about civic discourse and public involvement in environmental policy.

The Newport Chemical Depot, formerly the Newport Army Ammunitions Depot,[1] located thirty-two miles north of Terre Haute, currently houses 1,269 tons of the nerve agent VX (*Journal and Courier* 1998). A brochure distributed by the Newport Chemical Depot at public meetings describes VX as "similar to present day pesticides [. . .] that affects the nervous system by interfering with the signals sent from the brain to the vital organs and other parts of the body" ("Questions and Answers") (see appendix F). Yet other sources describe VX as posing a significantly larger threat than most present day pesticides. The draft EIS for the disposal project at Newport asserts that "exposure to high doses can result in convulsions and death because of paralysis of the respiratory system. Death from agent VX can occur quickly, often within 10 minutes of absorption of a lethal dose" (p. 2–2). Considered to be the deadliest substance known (*Journal and Courier*), VX was first produced in 1962 for use as chemical warfare at the Newport Chemical Depot. According to the "Fact Sheet" distributed by the Army, all VX produced for U.S. defense stockpiles was manufactured at the Newport Chemical Depot (p. 1). Approximately 4 percent of the stockpile of total chemical agent, and the largest stockpile of VX agent, is stored at the Newport Chemical Depot[2] (NECD EIS Record of Decision on Program Manager for Chemical Demilitarization web site).

In 1985, at the Geneva Summit, President Reagan and Soviet General Secretary Gorbachev agreed to support a ban on chemical weapons. In 1986 Congress passed the Department of Defense Authorization Act (Title 14, Part B, Sect. 1412 of Public Law 99–145, as amended in public Laws 100–456, 102–190, and 102–484) (50 U.S.C. 1521)), requiring the destruction of the U.S. stockpile of lethal unitary chemical agents and munitions. In 1997, the United States and eighty-seven other nations ratified the Multilateral Chemical Weapons Convention Treaty mandating that the United States and other participating nations would destroy their entire chemical weapons stockpiles by December 2007.

A U.S. Congressional ban on the transportation of nerve agents (Hazardous Materials Transportation Act of 1994, [49 U.S.C. § 5101 et seq.; 49 C.F.R. § 107.601–620]) prompted the Army to consider a plan for disposing of the VX agent on-site. In 1988, the Army proposed to incinerate the VX agent. In public documents, the Army argued that incineration "has been evaluated as a safe and effective method" of chemical agent destruction (Program Manager for Chemical Demilitarization web site) and that the "only proven technology, adopted by the Army, that has successfully destroyed chemical agents is incineration" (NPDES Permit Application for Newport Chemical Depot). However, the VX agent at the Newport Chemical Depot was never incinerated.

In June 1997, nearly ten years after the Army proposed incineration, the Army proposed another plan for disposing of the VX agent on site. This new plan included building a facility on site in order to first neutralize the stored nerve agent then destroy it by means of supercritical water oxidation. In this two-step process, the VX nerve agent would be added to a reactor vessel containing sodium hydroxide and water. The reaction that occurs produces a liquid solution composed of water, sodium hydroxide, phosphorus, and sulfur organic compounds. This solution is mixed again with sodium hydroxide. The final product is a solution of water and industrial salt (consisting of potentially hazardous heavy metals), which would be disposed of in a landfill licensed to accommodate hazardous waste, and the water solution would be sent through the depot's wastewater treatment facility before being discharged into the Wabash River. This method of disposal had never been conducted on a large scale, and the Newport Chemical Depot would serve as a site for pilot testing this new technology.

The new proposal was attributed in part to strong public opposition to incineration. A public affairs officer and spokesperson for the Newport Chemical Depot, Adrian Thompson,[3] noted in an interview that when the plan to incinerate the stockpile of VX agent was announced, the area residents "demanded" public sessions to discuss the decision. Thompson has been involved in all action plans regarding the chemical weapons decision at the Newport Chemical Depot since 1988.

Prior to the public's insistence on more meetings, only one information session was scheduled where, according to Thompson, "the Army cruised into town, announced 'here's what we are going to do to the VX stockpile— by the way, did you folks know there was a VX stockpile here?—We're going to burn that stockpile. Trust us, this is safe'" (Adrian Thompson, personal interview, April 27, 2000). This approach to risk communication is another example of what Belsten calls the "decide-announce-defend" approach (see chapter 2), where decisions about policy are already made by the technical experts and brought to the public under the assumption that with enough information the public will agree with the decision. With this approach, the Army assumed that the public was a group to be managed, to be informed, not capable of contributing useful knowledge to the decision-making process.

In this case, however, the public resisted that passive role. According to Thompson, one of the "demanded" public meetings had to be moved from its original location to a large auditorium because nearly three thousand protesters were present. The meetings, according to Thompson, were "hostile" at best, with the "Army, standing in front of the citizens in suits defending their decisions" (Adrian Thompson, personal interview, April, 27, 2000). However, Thompson notes that the "citizens yelled until we finally listened."

According to the *Pilot Testing of Neutralization/Supercritical Water Oxidation of VX Agent at Newport Chemical Depot Environmental Impact Statement (EIS)*, "as a result of interest in alternatives to the baseline technology (high-temperature incineration)," Congress passed Public Law 102-484 requiring that the Army consider technologies other than high-temperature incineration at certain storage sites, including Newport (EIS, April 1998). Just whose "interest" prompted this law is not included in the EIS. Incineration of chemical weapons was proposed for the eight other Army installations, and public opposition was noted at six of them, including Alabama, Arkansas, Colorado, Kentucky, Maryland, and Oregon (Chemical Weapons Working Group web site). While it is likely that public outcry did influence the decision about chemical disposal at Newport, it is important to emphasize that it was not the Army's intention or plan to involve the public so significantly in the decision-making process. Rather, the influence was a result of strategic, often subversive, moves by groups of citizens to affect the decision. In this case, all stakeholders were not working together to determine the most appropriate decision for all involved, but rather working against other stakeholders. While the decision against incineration ultimately may have been considered appropriate by all parties, the risk communication practices adopted by the Army were not.

Even though the final disposal policy required an alternative to incineration and gained approval from the Army, the public, and the State Environmental Department, Army representatives and citizens alike maintained that they were unhappy with the eleven-year decision-making process and resulting continued hostile interactions among the Army, the citizens, and other involved parties. In observations of public meetings, interviews with citizens and Army officials, and review of the case, I found that the procedures in place to allow for public participation actually worked to prevent citizens from significantly contributing to the decision-making process.

PUBLIC MEETINGS AND OTHER DISCOURSE OBSTACLES

Before focusing on the specific institutions' procedures that guided public participation in the decision to dispose of VX nerve agent at the Newport Chemical Depot, a brief narrative of the public meetings held to discuss the proposed plan to build a facility to dispose of the stored VX nerve agent by supercritical water oxidation may be helpful for contextualizing the situation. For example, a "public scoping meeting" was held in June 1997, to discuss replacing the original plan to incinerate the VX agent

with the new plan to neutralize the VX through supercritical water oxidation. The purpose of the scoping sessions was to allow the public the
opportunity to express issues they believed should be addressed in an EIS.
The National Environmental Policy Act of 1969 (NEPA), requires any
federal agency that is considering a major decision that could significantly
affect the environment to "prepare a detailed explanation of the environmental consequences of its actions, and to make that report available to
higher-level agency officials, other agencies, and the public" in an EIS
(Findley and Farber, p. 26). The process of preparing an EIS includes a
draft EIS, a comment period, and a final document that is supposed to
address the concerns voiced by other agencies, stakeholders, and the public
during the comment period. Yet there is no guarantee that these concerns
will be reflected in the final EIS.

One indication of how significantly members of the public are allowed
to participate in the decisions about environmental risks is how their concerns are reflected in the documents used to make the decisions. The public
comments gathered during the scoping meeting for the proposed neutralization project at the Newport Chemical Depot only appeared in an appendix
of the draft EIS and were summarized (in other words shaped) by the Army.
No actual comments made by the public were included.

Despite the summarized public concern over the impact of the facility
on the health of the public and workers, the draft EIS devotes only twenty-
three paragraphs to discuss potential human health impacts resulting from
the construction, routine pilot testing, and accidents, represented less than
six pages of the 283-page draft EIS. In this case the letter of the law was
followed—the public was allowed to voice its concerns, yet these concerns
were not significantly reflected in the scope of the EIS.

Citizen comments were similarly marginalized in a web site maintained
by the U.S. Army that posted summaries of public meetings over the course
of the VX disposal decision. These summaries rarely focused on the public
input. For example, the summary of a meeting on January 22, 1998, indicates
that the meeting consisted of two poster sessions that offered the public an
opportunity to meet the technical experts and ask questions about the application process for the onsite disposal facility. While the summary indicates
that a stenographer was available to record public comments and that "two
citizens had their comments recorded for the record," those comments are
not even posted in the summary (Program Manager for Chemical Demilitarization web site). This time public comments were not taken seriously enough
to warrant placing them in the summary at all. Claiming to have allowed
public comment seems to have replaced the importance of the comments
themselves. A problem with this omission is not only that citizen contributions are not considered in the decision-making process but also that citizens
realize that their participation at meetings is not valued, often resulting in
hostile attitudes among the citizens and agency officials.

Over the course of the VX disposal decision, public meetings seemed to focus on making certain the public's understanding of the VX disposal was aligned with the "experts" rather than creating a dialogue where experts could describe a proposed process, and citizens could describe how the process would affect their community. In July 1998, a meeting was held to distribute draft EISs and to provide the public the "opportunity to speak one-on-one with Army technical experts in order to clarify any issues regarding the content of the Draft Environmental Impact Statement" (public notice, see appendix A). Under federal regulation in accordance with NEPA the public has forty-five days to submit comments regarding the findings and proposal set forth in the draft EIS. Yet efforts to seemingly involve citizens by making them more fully aware of an impending policy, such as distributing copies of EISs to them before the policy is implemented, are little more than placating measures, more to protect against lawsuits than to solicit citizen response (Ross, 179; see also Killingsworth and Steffans, 1989). While these governmental laws may have originally been designed to invite citizen participation, the wording of the mandates often works to preclude direct and significant public response.

What I think most markedly illustrates the power often denied citizens in public policy debates is the attitude toward citizen contributions expressed by some of the "experts." Prior to a public meeting to discuss a permit to allow the Army to dump the remains of the neutralized VX nerve agent into the Wabash River, the Indiana Department of Environmental Management (IDEM) sent a public notice to area residents indicating that this meeting would be devoted to "allowing the public to ask questions and learn how to better effectively participate in the permitting process" (IDEM public notice, see appendix A). It was during this meeting that the representative from the chemical company hired to build the neutralization facility told me that public participation in technical decisions went "against her way of thinking." As previously mentioned, she acknowledged that public response was required and told me the Army's plan where local residents were invited to a roundtable with two Army representatives familiar with the events at the Newport Chemical Depot. At this roundtable discussion, the residents were given free pizza and allowed to vent their concerns. "So that the residents don't feel intimidated," she reported, "their responses aren't written down, they are completely off the record." Yet, completely off the record precludes that any comments help shape the final policy or are even valued.

In a later interview, an Army spokesperson confirmed the purpose of the pizza roundtables. She explained that an Army commander and a Public Outreach and Information Office representative "sit down with the citizens and tell them what's going on." Further, she added, "to make people feel comfortable voicing their concerns, there are no notes or tape recorders." I asked if decision makers are made aware of the citizen concerns after the meeting. She replied that if someone voices a concern or question during the meeting, the Army commander outreach representative will ask for the person's address or phone number after the meeting in order to send that individual information about their concern. Yet sending information to citizens suggests that the experts wish to align the citizen's understanding with the expert information not encourage an exchange of information and perspectives about the issue. Throughout my observations, the institutional procedures of the public meetings became obstacles to civic discourse in the decision-making process.

In December 1999, the Army was granted approval to build the supercritical water oxidation facility onsite at the Newport Chemical Depot to pilot test the destruction of one-third of the stored VX nerve agent. At the same time, the Army was granted a license to dispose of the effluent from the neutralized agent into the Wabash River. A closer look at the institutions involved in the decision reveals that regulations and procedures in place to ensure public participation often prevented the public from participating in all but the most superficial ways.

INSTITUTIONS AND THEIR CONSTRAINTS ON PUBLIC PARTICIPATION

A complex web of federal regulations and federal and state agencies governed every procedure, indeed aspect, of the neutralization/supercritical water oxidation of VX agent project at the Newport Chemical Depot. The fact that the project involved a government facility, a stockpile of chemical warfare, and a proposed plan to disrupt the storage of the "deadliest substance known" ensured the involvement of a myriad of agencies, regulations, and subsequent programs.

As a way to illustrate how institutional procedures and power relations work to encourage or discourage public participation, I examine the institutions directly involved in the policy decisions at Newport Chemical Depot focusing on their view of public involvement and, as a result, how they affected public involvement. The primary agencies, including the U.S. Department of the Army (Army) as the lead agency, and the U.S. Environmental Protection Agency (EPA), the state of Indiana (specifically the Indiana Department of Environmental Management or IDEM), the U.S. Federal Emergency Management Agency (FEMA), and the U.S. Department of Health and Human Services (DHHS) as cooperating agencies (EIS 1998) were "corporate authors" of the EIS who both contributed information to and reviewed the EIS. And the institutional procedures of each of these agencies affected the public's involvement in the decision-making process. Additionally, five federal regulations governed the procedures for implementing the neutralization/supercritical water oxidation of VX agent project, as well as the public involvement, at the Newport Chemical Depot: the National Environmental Policy Act (NEPA), Department of Defense Authorization

Act of 1986, the Resource Conservation and Recovery Act (RCRA), the Clean Water Act (CWA), and the Clean Air Act (CAA). With the exception of the Army and the Department of Defense Authorization Act, these agencies and regulations are the ones most often involved in cases of environmental policy. The procedures and policies of all of these institutions present interesting intersections and conflicts. Many of the programs are part of a larger agency, but each program can implement its own approach to public participation as long as it does not preclude the guidelines set by the regulations. Figure 3.1 reveals the ways in which the different regulations, agencies, and programs with specific public participation procedures overlap. Rather than attempting to illustrate a clear picture of each of the institutions involved, this figure aims to indicate the complexity of the many regulations, agencies, and programs involved.

Most of the agencies and regulations provide for a limited role for the public in decisions about environmental issues, assuming that the public should be involved but not in such a way as to interfere with expert decisions. Provisions are made to ensure that the public is aware of a proposed

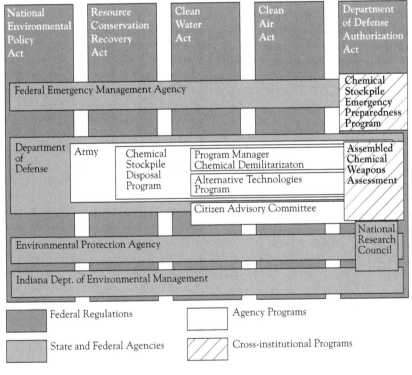

Figure 3.1: Web of Institutions Involved in Chemical Weapons Disposal at the Newport Chemical Depot

decision, and can offer its opinions on a proposed decision but not for en-suring that those opinions are considered in the decision-making process. Most of the agencies and regulations' expectations for public participation are for the public to grant approval for expert decisions. The public, as a collective group, is not considered capable of contributing useful knowledge but only of approving a decision already made. The one exception that I found in the Newport case was the Assembled Chemical Weapons Assess-ment (ACWA) created by Congress that required the Army to consider alternative technologies with the help of citizens. This group will be dis-cussed later in the chapter.

SEPARATING PUBLIC PARTICIPATION
FROM THE DECISION-MAKING PROCESS

The National Environmental Policy Act of 1969 (NEPA) imposes environ-mental responsibilities on all agencies of the federal government and dictates many of the procedures for public involvement in environmental issues. Because NEPA sets the precedent of public involvement in environmental issues, understanding NEPA's interpretation of public participation helps to illuminate other institutional interpretations of public participation since other institutions often build a public participation process that can be traced back to NEPA.

The procedural provisions of NEPA are implemented by regulations (40 C.F.R. 1500–1508) developed by the President's Council on Environ-mental Quality—a group of representatives from government agencies (EIS, p. 1–3). NEPA requires that the federal government "use all practicable means to administer federal programs in the most environmentally sound fashion" and "to take environmental factors into consideration when making significant decisions" (Findley et al., pp. 23, 25). To accomplish this, the statute requires any federal agency that is considering a major decision that could significantly affect the environment to "prepare a detailed explanation of the environmental consequences of its actions, and to make that report available to higher-level agency officials, other agencies, and the public" (Findley et al., p. 26). This detailed explanation, an EIS, examines, prior to implemen-tation, how a proposed action, along with alternative actions, would affect the environment. The process of preparing an EIS includes a draft EIS, a comment period, and a final EIS that is supposed to address the concerns that other agencies, stakeholders, and the public voiced during the comment period.

The purpose of the EIS is to provide the federal agency, other related agencies, and the public with enough information about the proposed action to make informed decisions about the action. However, the vague wording of the statute in regard to "detailed explanation," often works to defeat its purpose. According to Carl Bausch, a former Council on Environmental Quality (CEQ) member, the "insistence on great 'detail' in EISs, however, met with very predictable results—bloated, nonanalytical documents often exceeding 1,000 pages in length and costly delays in the decision-making process" (p. 236). EISs of this length were often impossible for most lay audiences to wade through in time to submit their concerns during the comment period before a decision was made.

In 1977, as part of a plain English movement fostered for public documents, President Carter directed the Council on Environmental Quality to issue regulations designed to "make the EIS process more useful to decision makers and the public" by making EISs clear and concise (p. 238). The regulation further mandated that EISs be prepared early in the decision-making process (p. 238). However, these regulations have done little to improve public involvement in the decision-making process. Even in the wording of the directive, the members of the CEQ separate the public from the decision makers, perpetuating the assumption that the public's role is to be informed. And while each of these two issues has the potential to positively affect public involvement in the decision-making process, neither has been enforced.

According to Killingsworth and Palmer (1992), EISs remain full of incomprehensible, detached prose, "high-density" graphics, and constant acronyms that render the EIS all but unreadable to most citizens. They note that the "expert" style of writing "limits access to the information of the EIS to those accustomed to reading and interpreting this form of discourse. Further they assert that the constant use of acronyms "increase[s] the density of information that must be absorbed in a short space. Because of this density, most EISs intimidate the average reader" (p. 174). And while they admit that high-density graphics are useful for displaying large amounts of data in small spaces, this too, they argue can cause information overload (p. 175).

In a directive aimed at preparing more concise EISs, the CEQ suggests that EISs not exceed 150 pages, yet this directive has been all but ignored. Few EISs meet the 150-page recommendation. In fact, the first EIS addressing incineration at the Newport Chemical Depot (as well as seven other similar installations) was distributed in three volumes that totaled over 1,000 pages. Even when another EIS was prepared specifically to examine the neutralization supercritical/oxidation of the VX agent solely at the Newport Chemical Depot ten years later in 1998, the draft EIS was 283 pages, and the final EIS was 317. And yet, despite the abundance of material included in the EIS, the material that is included is not often useful to anyone other than technical experts. For example, while the project proposes to destroy a stockpile of VX nerve agent, considered the deadliest substance known, there are only 2 paragraphs in those 283 pages that discuss in lay terms the effects of VX agent on humans (FEIS, p. 2–1).

While an EIS, under NEPA regulations, is required to include certain contents, these requirements would not preclude adding more information that would be of use to the public in making an informed decision about the disposal process. According to a pamphlet distributed by the Program Manager for Chemical Demilitarization, which is government speak for a program, not a person, an EIS must contain:

- Cover sheet

- Summary

- Table of Contents

- Statement of purpose and need for proposed action

- Alternatives, including the preferred alternative as well as no action

- Affected environment

- Environmental and socioeconomic consequences

- List of preparers

- List of agencies, organizations, and persons to whom copies of the statement are sent

- Appendices

- Index

The actual wording of NEPA's requirement for EIS contents found in the United States Code, however, focuses more on the affects of the decision than is stressed above. According to the regulation,

> every recommendation or report on proposals for legislation and other major Federal actions significantly affecting the quality of the human environment, a detailed statement by the responsible official on—(i) the environmental impact of the proposed action, (ii) any adverse environmental effects which can not be avoided should the proposal be implemented, (iii) alternatives to the proposed action, (iv) the relationship between local short-term uses of man's environment and the maintenance and enhancement of long-term productivity, and (v) any irreversible and irretrievable commitments of resources which would be involved in the proposed action should it be implemented. (42 U. S. C. 4321 § 4332)

The precise subject matter of the EIS, according to NEPA, is determined by a process called "scoping." "Scoping is intended to obtain early participation by other agencies and the public in planning the EIS, to determine the scope of the EIS, and to determine the significant issues to be discussed in the EIS" (Findley and Farber, p. 35). Under NEPA, the EIS is required to address issues that are gathered during a mandated scoping session.

Yet those gathered issues may or may not be what is actually addressed in the EIS. NEPA assumes a limited role for the public in decisions about environmental issues. NEPA's position toward public participation is that the public should be involved, but not in such a way as to interfere with expert decisions. Provisions are made to ensure that members of the public are aware of a proposed decision and can offer their opinions on a proposed decision, but not for ensuring that those opinions are considered in the decision-making process. NEPA's expectations for public participation are for the public to grant approval for expert decisions.

The Lack of Public Involvement in Environmental Impact Statements

The public comments gathered during the scoping meeting for the proposed neutralization project at the Newport Chemical Depot were reworded by the Army before being placed in the appendix of the draft EIS (see appendix B). According to the draft EIS appendix, the summarized comments from the scoping meeting were (1) "that any proposed uses of the NECDF after destruction of the chemical agent should be presented to the public for consideration and discussion and (2) "that the health and safety of the public and facility workers should be the first considerations in the design, construction, and operation of the facility" (draft EIS, p. B–2). Additionally a written comment "reiterated the concern regarding potential future uses of the proposed facility and the proposed site: that any future uses of the facility and land should be presented to the public for comment, and comments should be solicited at not only the local level but also the regional and state levels" (draft EIS, p. B–2).

Yet the comments and concerns had little impact on the issues addressed in the draft EIS. The concerns stated by the citizens comprise a total of twenty-three paragraphs comprising fewer than six pages of the 283-page draft EIS. For example, the draft EIS discusses in two paragraphs the "human health impacts" of constructing the proposed facility and all but dismisses the possibility of a risk: "No deleterious effects on the health of workers are expected from construction. The potential for human health impacts because of construction of the demilitarization facility would be limited to occupational hazards. Off-site impacts to human health are not expected" (draft EIS, pp. 4–6). In similar fashion, the draft EIS addresses the impacts to human health if no action is taken on the stockpile, that is, if the depot continues to simply store the VX agent, in five paragraphs, comprising less than a page.

The appendix states that the Army is always on the lookout for public comments and concerns during the decision process,

> the Army has noted any public concerns or comments that were expressed in these forums. Also, public comments on the Chemical

Stockpile Disposal Program in general and on incineration in particular were evaluated for their applicability to this EIS. The following outline summarizes the comments received during these public
involvement activities that were reviewed for their applicability to
the proposed NECDF" [Newport Chemical Disposal Facility]. (EIS,
p. B–2)

A bulleted list of citizen concerns follows, but without indication of
whether these issues are indeed addressed in the EIS, and if so, where. While
some of the issues are discussed in the draft EIS, many of them are not
even acknowledged.

While a review for applicability may be necessary, it also begs the
question, applicable according to whom. Assuming that some public concerns specifically about the proposed facility are not applicable reinforces the
belief that risk is not socially constructed but rather defined by the technical
experts. If the public's concerns match the experts' expectations about those
concerns, then the comment is deemed applicable. The current NEPA procedures for the EIS interpret public participation as a way to achieve acceptance for a decision made, not as a way to acquire new knowledge about the
decision. The public is relegated to audience, not part of the decision-
making process.

When the final EIS was issued seven months later, the final appendix,
appendix H, included public comments received on the draft version. According to appendix H, "The appendix displays copies of letters received
from agencies and the public commenting on the draft Environmental Impact Statement. All letters received by the Army during the comment period
(June 12 to July 27, 1998) are included verbatim" (final EIS, p. H–1) (see
appendix C). This appears to be an improvement over the draft EIS, which
only summarized the public's comments, except that often the comments
received by the citizens were handwritten and difficult to read because they
had been reduced to fit on one half of an $8\frac{1}{2}$" x 11" page. In the final EIS
the Army responded to each comment. According to the final EIS, appendix
H, "In each response, the Army states either that (1)the text was revised for
this Final EIS, (2)provides an explanation of why the text in the Draft EIS
was adequate and did not need to be revised, or (3) answers questions that
were asked by the commenter. If the response does not mention the text
revisions, then the corresponding text in the Draft EIS was not revised" (appendix H–1). The index for the comments and responses for the draft EIS lists
the names and affiliations of the sixteen people who submitted comments. Of
these sixteen, three were "private citizens," and one was on the behalf of
Newport Citizens against Incineration. None of the citizen comments resulted
in a revision of the EIS, and each received minimal comments.

The comments themselves deserve attention. One comment indicated
approval for the neutralization process and received the response "[T]he

Army appreciates the comment." Another citizen stated her position against incineration and that she was hopeful the neutralization process would be approved. This comment too received "[T]he Army appreciates the comment." While these comments may not have warranted a revision in the EIS, two other comments are quite different. On a piece of paper typed in memo format, not the common comment form issued by the Program Manager for Chemical Demilitarization, which had only thirteen lines for comment (the small size of the comment cards is an issue itself), a member of the Newport Citizens against Incineration submitted their response to the draft EIS with a list of five concerns. The memo appeared on one-half of a page of the appendix, divided into eight parts, with the Army's response to each of those parts on the other half of the page. Each concern, save the last, was of a technical nature, asking about monitors to check emissions on carbon filters used in the neutralization process, about incineration of those carbon filters, about disposal of the heavy metal salts and waste water, and about keeping the community "up to date during the construction of the facility" (final EIS, p. H–22). The Army addressed on that page a brief comment in response to the questions but indicated that the concern did not alter the information included in the EIS. Further, the text of the EIS contains information that would answer only one of those concerns (and this information was present in the draft EIS, so the concern itself did not prompt the inclusion of additional information). In fact, in response to one rather pertinent concern: "Monitoring and disposition of the waste water after leaving the NECD plant. We hope that the disposal of all wastes would be monitored during the process," the Army indicates it has not even been decided yet: "The monitoring requirements mentioned in the comment have yet to be determined by these agencies" (p. H–22) (see appendix C).

Two other citizens, expressing their position against incineration because the "vapors could cause problems in the air" (final EIS, p. H–23), received more of an admonishment. Defensive and bent on having the last word on the safety of incineration (the Army still maintains that incineration is a safe technology for disposing of chemical weapons), the comment states, "The Army appreciates the comment. It should be noted, however, that the baseline incineration process (which is not an alternative considered in this EIS) does not result in the release of atmospheric emissions (i.e., vapors) harmful to human health or the environment" (final EIS, p. H–23) (see appendix C).

The only revisions that were made to the EIS as a result of comments came from government agencies. Even when federal agency comments were similar to ones made by citizens, they received a different response from the Army. For example, an official from the U.S. Department of Interior commented:

> In addition, the RDEIS [Revised Draft Environmental Impact Statement] indicated that a monitoring program would be established in

order to determine contamination concentrations in the effluent, receiving stream, and aquatic biota. This proposed monitoring program for VX, VX breakdown products, and other contaminants has been dropped from further consideration and is not discussed in the current DEIS. We strongly recommend that monitoring occur, as was discussed in the RDEIS, for contaminants being discharged into the Wabash River [. . .]. (final EIS, p. H–13)

The Army's response to the Department of Interior was quite different from its response to the citizens' comment ("The monitoring requirements mentioned in the comment have yet to be determined by these agencies") (p. H–22). The Army's response to the Department of the Interior was,

> As part of the environmental permitting process, the Army has submitted monitoring plans in permit applications. The NECDF RCRA Part B permit application includes a Preliminary Assessment of Health Impacts (AHI), which uses toxicity data from bench scale tests to assess potential impacts to human health and the environment. A final AHI will be conducted as part of the Demonstration Test for the operational facility. This analysis will use samples and data collected during the Demonstration Test, which will be overseen by regulatory officials. (FEIS, p. H–13)

The different response to such a similar question suggests that the Army is more concerned with discussing its actions with another government agency, one with the immediate power to impede the proposed action, than with those most affected by the decision.

Moreover, while nearly illegible citizen comments were photocopied and included in the appendix H, some agency comments were "retyped for legibility (FEIS, p. H–27), further indication that agency comments were valued over the citizen comments. This action creates an even more obvious difference between the citizen concerns and those of the other federal agencies. Citizen comments appear unprofessional, even less credible printed on identifying comment forms when compared to the comments by federal agencies on official government letterhead (see appendix C). Both EISs illustrate that public comments are not valued on an equal level with those of federal agencies or more technical experts.

The Decide-Announce-Defend Approach of the EIS

Despite the 1977 executive order to prepare the EIS early in the decision-making process, most EISs are prepared after the responsible agency has decided what action to take, defeating the point of the EIS as an instrument to assist decision making. Bausch asserts that many agencies add the EIS requirement of NEPA onto the end of their existing decision-making procedures, which have a "very narrow, project-oriented focus" (p. 237). According to Bausch,

> Undertaking the EIS process in the later phases of agency decision making for projects in which substantial investments of resources may have already been made usually leaves little but "detail" to be developed in the document. Certainly, less environmentally degrading alternatives to the "proposed action" under study—consideration of which represents the heart of the EIS process—are pretty effectively eliminated at that point. (p. 237)

This approach brings to mind early usability testing used in computer design and software documentation where reviews of a document were often conducted near the end of product development. While this type of usability can yield more polished documents, it has come under criticism for its focus on the product rather than the user. Weiss (1988) asserts that "after-the-fact" usability testing is flawed because it all but eliminates the chance that the product will undergo significant design changes based on the users' responses (p. 175). This approach values the product and the designers' conception of that product over users and their needs. Further, it views users as end-of-the-line consumers without the knowledge to contribute to the design and implementation of the product (Johnson, p. 57). (How a broader notion of usability research could work to increase public input in decisions is addressed in chapter 4.)

Both the original EIS proposing incineration prepared for all eight installation sites and the EIS examining neutralization/supercritical water oxidation of the VX agent offer cases in point of this "after-the-fact" approach. For example, Futrell (1996) argues that the scoping meetings held by the Army at all stockpile sites in the mid 1980s were "after-the-fact meetings" to "satisfy the requirement of public participation in the decision making process by NEPA" (http://www.cwwg.org/, April 27, 2000). He asserts that the Army had already made the decision to use incineration for chemical weapons disposal and in the meetings asked local citizens "not for input into the choice of technology, but for input into whether agent should be incinerated on-site or transported" off site. Despite the citizens' concern with on-site incineration, the Army decided to build a chemical weapons incinerator at each stockpile site, citing safety hazards with transporting weapons off site (Ambrose, 1988 http://www.cwwg.org/, April 27, 2000).

An EIS requires the detailed consideration of an alternative action to the action proposed. In the EIS for *Pilot Testing of Neutralization/Supercritical Water Oxidation of VX Agent at Newport Chemical Depot*, the Army chose to discuss a "no action alternative" to VX disposal.[4] In this scenario, the VX agent would remain stored in containers at the Newport Chemical Depot. Yet, according to the Chemical Weapons Treaty Compliance Program and

Public Law 99–145, all chemical weapons must be destroyed, so the alternative action is precluded by law. Acknowledging this in the FEIS, the Army states that this alternative is included for the purpose of analysis. Yet the Army spends both time and money researching fully the impacts of an option that is not permissible by law. This choice of alternative suggests that the Army is not seriously considering an alternative but has already made its choice for chemical disposal and, by eliminating the alternative, controls the decision. These examples illustrate that rather than encourage public participation, the NEPA requirements often allow agencies to provide the illusion of public participation after the decision is already made.

In summary, *Pilot Testing of Neutralization/Supercritical Water Oxidation of VX Agent at Newport Chemical Depot* illustrates that the Army, the preparer of the EIS, all but controlled what was discussed in the EIS, and consequently, what action was taken in the decision to dispose of the VX agent with little regard for how the action would affect the area citizens.[5] The citizen comments concerning what should be included in the EIS were summarized in an appendix, but not necessarily included in the draft EIS. Citizen comments on what issues were still of concern to them after reading the draft EIS were relegated to the appendix and did not affect the revising of the EIS. Further, the comments that affected the revision of the EIS most significantly came from other Army agencies including the Army Corps of Engineers and the environmental coordinating officer of the Newport Chemical Depot, an internal Army official. In this case, the EIS did not function as a document to inform decision making, but rather as a document to justify a decision made.

As Killingsworth and Palmer (1992) note, EISs are often prepared after decisions have been made for "defensive purposes" to ward off legal action against the agency and have "little relationship to actual decision-making" (p. 189). Two extended quotes are warranted here to illustrate the ways in which they found the EIS to deny citizens power in the decision-making process. Drawing on Habermas' notion of "instrumental rationality" and Poster's (1989) notion of "steering mechanisms," they characterize the EISs as "instrumental documents" that

> have as their sole purpose the control of the document's readers. These writings may take on the appearance of traditional scientific papers whose purpose is to persuade readers to accept an interpretation usually amounting to a change of direction in a research program. But instrumental documents are not really interested in interpretation or in persuasion; they attempt to create, for the purpose of maintaining the system, a narrow path of action that has been chosen or created in advance of the document's production by hierarchically arranged powers. And though they may draw upon the conventions of a democratic discourse that is open to information from diverse sources, the aim of instrumental documents is

never to treat deviant discourses with respect but always merely to take note of them, to record, them, and ultimately to treat them as "noise" in the system, which needs to be ignored or expunged. (166)

Further they assert that

the likelihood of an outsider influencing an agency action is slight. While the system constructed, maintained, and reproduced by the EIS process has little or not effect upon the lifeworld of the agency experts and primary decision makers, those whose worlds are most deeply affected are systematically excluded from participation in the process, even while their rights to be heard are ostensibly maintained. (170)

The procedure NEPA stipulates to ensure public participation, gathering individual comments, precludes public discourse itself. Rather than promoting a dialogue among interested parties, NEPA's procedures work against such a dialogue, separating "experts" from those most affected by the decision. For example, Sybil Mowrer, spokesperson for the Newport Citizens against Incineration noted that at the EIS scoping meeting, citizens had to go into a room separate from where the meeting was being held (away from agency officials and other citizens) to submit their comments on record.

Asking for a vote is different than asking for an opinion. NEPA requires that the agency considering an action potentially affecting the environment ask citizens for their comments and opinions but does not guarantee that those comments will affect the ultimate decision or, in the case of Newport, that the comments will even affect the EIS. In this light, while the NEPA regulation assumes a partial participation to public involvement in environmental decisions, the Army's interpretation of the regulation contributes to the type of pseudoparticipation discussed in chapter 2 where citizens are placated into believing that they have a voice in the decision because they are allowed to speak. Yet, in Newport anyway, the preparers of the EIS were not necessarily listening.

Other rhetoric and technical communication scholars, however, disagree with the assumption that all EISs prohibit democratic decision making. For example, David Dayton (2002) in his examination of the EIS as a genre of public decision-making discourse, argues that an EIS "can fulfill Habermas's validity norms of communicative action if the rhetorical situation creates a genuinely persuasive purpose for the agency producing the report" (356). Drawing from John Foster's adaptation of Habermas' analysis of communication practices, Dayton evaluates two EISs based on the action norms of comprehensibility, truth, sincerity, and appropriateness (367). He argues that an EIS that hopes to achieve Habermas' communicative action—and, according to Habermas and Dayton, at least—democratic decision making— must "shift from a rhetoric of advocacy" where decisions have already been made and must be defended, to a "rhetoric of inquiry" where rhetoric tries to "make sense out of the uncertain" (401–402). (A rhetoric of inquiry does seem to me a useful goal to have in matters of policy debates—an approach suggesting that multiple perspectives consider together the issues surrounding a decision.) (See Rude [1995] for a full discussion on the appropriateness and usefulness of a rhetoric of inquiry for decision making.) While the perspectives on the effectiveness of the EIS differ, I believe that we may not be able to rely on the EIS as the primary indicator of public participation in an environmental decision. Rather, we must also look to the spaces between, the more mundane, day to day practices of institutions to consider the justness of the decision-making process.

MARGINALIZING CITIZEN POWER IN THE DECISION-MAKING PROCESS

While NEPA mandates that an environmental assessment must be done in order to make an informed decision about a proposed action, and further stipulates the procedure of that assessment, it is the Army, under the direction of the Department of Defense, that is responsible for destroying the VX agent and that oversaw most of the decision making about how the VX should be destroyed. A number of agencies and programs directly involved in the chemical disposal project at Newport Chemical Depot are part of the Department of Defense (DOD): the Army, the Chemical Stockpile Disposal Program, the Program Manager for Chemical Demilitarization, the Alternative Technology Program, the Citizen Advisory Council, and the Assembly of Chemical Weapons Assessment. (In an attempt to avoid government speak in my discussion of these institutions, I spell out the name of the more unfamiliar institutions rather than incorporate an acronym on their second and subsequent use). Discussing their views on public participation together illustrates an interesting range of possible approaches to public involvement in environmental issues. Perhaps most important, it makes visible that significant public participation in decisions about environmental policy *is* possible. Sybil Mowrer, spokesperson for the Newport Citizens against Incineration, noted that the greatest obstacle to public involvement and the greatest help to public involvement were both part of the DOD (personal interview, May 7, 2000). By examining what specific practices of institutions and programs within a particular situation worked to encourage and inhibit public participation, we can gain insight into specific ways the public can be encouraged to contribute significantly to decisions about environmental policy.

Preventing Citizen Involvement

While NEPA regulations control decisions about environmental policy, the Army's involvement in this case is a result of the issue at hand—disposing of VX nerve agent. All stockpiles of chemical weapons are stored at Army installations. Moreover, as a result of Public Law 99–145, mandating that all chemical weapons be destroyed by April 2007, the Army is responsible for overseeing the safe disposal of the weapons. This mandate prompted the Army to establish two programs: the Chemical Stockpile Disposal Program, to develop a plan for the safe and efficient disposal of chemical warfare material, and the Chemical Stockpile Emergency Preparedness Program, a joint program with the Federal Emergency Management Agency (FEMA) and the Army to ensure the health and safety of the area in the event of an accident involving VX at the Newport Chemical Depot. The Army's expectation of public participation in its Chemical Stockpile Disposal Program and Program Manager for Chemical Demilitarization is one of an audience to be informed and managed. (The Program Manager for Chemical Demilitarization—along with the Soldier Biological and Chemical Command— have since been folded into a single agency: the Army's Chemical Materials Agency.) The Army's approach to public meetings is to gain approval for decisions already made. Its outreach efforts to educate the public into seeing the "correct" view of risk illustrates its assumptions that risk is not socially constructed but determined by experts. In general, for the VX disposal decision, the Army believed that it had a good plan for dealing with the situation, and the public should not ruin that plan.

Maintaining Power in the Decision-Making Process

In 1982, without public input and little publicity, the Army officials in the Chemical Stockpile Disposal Program decided that incineration would be their preferred baseline technology for chemical disposal at all Army chemical weapon stockpile sites (http://www.cwwg.org/; personal interview with Adrian Thompson; personal interview with Sybil Mowrer). At this time the Army visited each stockpile site to "announce" to the local residents its decision to destroy the chemical weapons by incineration. According to both Adrian Thompson, public affairs officer for the Newport Chemical Depot, and Sybil Mowrer, spokesperson for the Newport-based citizen group against incineration, many residents around Newport were shocked to find out that VX had been produced and was stored on site. Many, each said, were opposed to the idea of incinerating the VX. A number of industry-owned incinerators are located in and around Newport, and area residents blame the high rate of respiratory problems and the highest cancer rate in the state on these incinerators. Most residents did not complain about the industry incinerators because those plants provided jobs for the area. Many in the Newport community had mixed feelings about resisting the plan to incinerate VX at Newport because the Chemical Depot had provided so many well-paying jobs for the community since the 1960s.

While most of the community was concerned about the issue, there were fewer than ten members of the Newport Citizens against Incineration who remained active in working for an alternative disposal method (Mowrer, personal interview). This situation is not particularly unique to Newport, as often potentially hazardous waste sites are located in more rural areas where a community's economy is dependent upon the jobs provided by the sites. This often explains the apparent lack of resistance in communities where a long-time industry is discovered to be polluting the area (Bullard, 1994; Cable, 1995).

Several members were spouses of longtime Depot employees. The citizen group was not opposed to the local Army people at the Newport Chemical Depot; in fact, Mowrer claimed that the Army commanders and officials at the plant were good to them (she mentioned Adrian Thompson by name), often giving them a space at meetings to display incineration opposition posters, but she said the citizen group was opposed to the Army's assumption that it could simply announce what decision about VX disposal had been made without regard for the people who would be affected by the decision (personal interview, May 7, 2000).

Both Thompson and Mowrer noted that while Army officials only planned one information meeting where they explained their decision to incinerate VX, the public, both citizens of Newport and individuals from other areas concerned about incineration, "demanded" additional meetings. According to Thompson and Mowrer, the relationship between the citizens and the Army officials at the meeting was often hostile, with Army members appearing in suits, often standing physically above the citizens on an auditorium stage, defending their decision by arguing with the citizens.

When the Army refused to consider another approach to VX disposal, Thompson noted that the citizens began running ads in local and regional papers "inciting" large crowds at the public meetings. It was at this point, Thompson noted, that the number of citizens attending the meetings reached nearly three thousand, requiring one public meeting to be moved at the last minute to a large high school auditorium. The problem, according to Thompson, was that the citizens were basing their protest, in the ads and in the public meetings, on "misinformation" (personal interview, April, 27, 2000). At this point, Thompson asserted, the Army, deciding it was time to "start an education program" to inform the citizens about the actual risks of incineration at the Newport Chemical Depot, created the Program Manager for Chemical Demilitarization (personal interview, April 27, 2000). By casting the public as "misinformed," the Army was able to disregard their protests, maintaining all the power in the decision-making process. Further asserting its power, the Army attempted to "coerce" citizens into accepting its view of incineration by "educating" them to think like the Army did.

The Program Manager for Chemical Demilitarization was created as, and continues to be, a full-blown PR campaign for chemical weapons disposal at Army installations. Under Army leadership, the Program Manager for Chemical Demilitarization established the Newport Chemical Public Outreach and Information Office on the premise that with enough "correct" information, the public would view the decision to incinerate the VX as the "technical experts" did. Through the Newport Chemical Public Outreach and Information Office, the Program Manager for Chemical Demilitarization created and distributed a plethora of "fact sheets" describing every aspect of chemical disposal, including the sheets "Characteristics of Nerve Agent VX" and "Bulk Agent Storage." These "fact sheets" along with brochures on the history of the Newport Chemical Depot and other agencies involved in the disposal process are contained in a slick folder available at the outreach office in Newport and passed around at public meetings.

While giving the public access to information about the depot once available only to government officials with the highest level clearance is certainly a step in the right direction, the motives behind the move may be questionable. The information contained in the "fact sheets" appears accurate, but the obvious spin on the perspective is frightening. For example, the brochure "Questions and Answers about Newport Chemical Depot" describes VX agent simply as

> a member of the organo-phosphate family, similar to present day pesticides. A common misconception is that VX is a gas. VX actually is a liquid that is slightly heavier than water and evaporates more than 2,000 times more slowly than water. Under normal conditions, it is clear- to straw-colored. VX is a rapid-acting nerve agent that affects the nervous system by interfering with the signals sent from the brain to the vital organs and other parts of the body.

This quote includes the entire description of VX found in the brochure. There is no mention of VX being the deadliest substance known, no mention that when absorbed through the skin it causes the body to go into convulsions, no mention that the amount that would fit on a pin head is enough to kill a person (see appendix F).

According to Thompson, the Program Manager for Chemical Demilitarization was a success. She noted that "citizen fear about VX incineration dropped when they saw that VX looks like Karo syrup and doesn't evaporate" (personal interview, April 27, 2000). She asserted that many citizens were under the misconception that VX was a nerve gas and were surprised to find out that it is not a nerve gas, but a liquid. (The plethora of movies depicting bad guys stealing VX and threatening the world had not yet hit the big screen). Yet, assuming that citizens are, or should be, less afraid because a deadly agent looks like a food product, even though it is still as deadly as nerve gas reveals a condescending attitude toward the public and its ability to understand complex information.

Despite Thompson's assessment of the success of the Program Manager for Chemical Demilitarization, the Outreach and Information Office often worked to further separate the citizens from the decision makers. One obvious separation is seen in the fact that questions about the Newport Chemical Depot or the proposed plans for chemical weapons disposal are directed to the outreach office rather than the Army officials who make the decisions. This approach aligns with the one-way flow of information approach to risk communication discussed in chapter 2 where citizens are allowed few interactions with the decision makers and granted little power in the decision-making process—limited to being informed about a decision. In this approach, citizens are allowed, even encouraged, to ask questions and voice their concerns, but those concerns are met with packets of brochures from the Army, not with a dialogue about how those concerns might affect the disposal decision. Indeed, with this approach, the concerns are sheltered from the decision makers by the outreach office. Again, public discourse is prevented by the procedures in place to "involve" the public in the chemical disposal process.

Another Public Outreach and Information Office activity was roundtable meetings, where citizens were invited to "vent" their concerns about the VX nerve agent disposal process to public relations folk who nod and make plans to send them information to better align their concerns with "technical reality." The comments of the citizens were never recorded, never even passed along to the actual decision makers. Again, the citizens were separated from the decision-making process. This procedure works under the assumption that the public is unable to participate in discussions of technical issues in meaningful ways and has nothing to contribute to the environmental policy—assumptions that will be questioned in chapter 4.

Adrian Thompson, in her discussions of the public involvement plan, confirmed that these meetings were held every two months in different locations around the area and were announced by ads in the paper.[6]

This approach seems to fall somewhere between the "strategic action" approach to risk communication and the "pseudoparticipation" approach, both discussed in chapter 2 where the public is allowed and encouraged to voice its concerns, but those concerns are not considered valuable contributions to the decision-making process. Rather, the "education programs" of the PMCD, the outreach office where the public can go with concerns and questions, and the roundtable meetings where the Army can come to the public to hear concerns and questions, lull members of the public, at least temporarily, into believing they are being considered in the chemical weapons disposal process.

Under the Army's leadership, the Program Manager for Chemical Demilitarization also developed a site-specific public involvement strategy that outlines the Army's "responsibilities" for including the public in the chemical weapons disposal process. According to Thompson, the plan (she noted that she did not like the word *strategy* because it sounds like an attack plan) identifies the stakeholders in the chemical weapons disposal project and the steps for involving them, such as where and when to hold public meetings. Interestingly, Thompson notes that the plan was developed solely by the Army, primarily by her (that is, with no input from the public). When I asked how the Army identifies the stakeholders, Thompson said that they talked *about* the individuals they believed to be involved, about local "citizens, elected officials, citizen groups, the Russians" (Adrian Thompson, April 27, 2000). In this case, the Army defines the stakeholders and the public. If a "public" does not fit its expectation, the public will not be targeted with ads about meetings and information about the disposal process. The likelihood that a group of citizens interested, even affected, by the decision will be left out seems quite high.[7] Beyond the marginalization of some members of the public, the fact that the decision to define the public lies solely with the Army further suggests the amount of its power and control over the decision-making process in this case.

Thompson herself decides the logistics of the public meetings, including where they will be held, what time, and what format. "This," Thompson notes, "I put time into considering." She maintains that the "some Army folk back East wanted us to hold our meetings in the [local] high school auditorium." And according to Thompson, that is where the Newport meetings were held before she was brought on as the public affairs officer for the Newport Chemical Depot. However, she asserts that she found those locations "too formal" with the Army up on stage addressing the public. Instead, she suggested finding where the area residents held their meetings and hold the public meetings there so the atmosphere would feel "familiar." She mentioned meetings held at the local fire station and the Lion's Club, which became a standard meeting place, according to Thompson, because it was next door to the Public Outreach and Information Office.

While Thompson's reasoning for choosing meeting spaces seems reasonable and well intentioned, there also seemed another side to the issue as I observed the later public meetings. Spaces are never innocent, and the space chosen for the public meetings was no exception. The meeting room in the Lion's Club was quite small, with a low ceiling and few windows. The floors were concrete, and when an individual moved in the folding metal chairs provided, the noise would all but drown out the speaker. The room was smotheringly hot during the two meetings I attended in summer months and quite cold during a meeting held in mid October. Restroom facilities could only be accessed from outside the building (like the setup in old gas stations). The room itself was not large enough to hold more than sixty people comfortably. A large public library was located across the street, still within walking distance of the Public Outreach and Information Office. While I do not wish to demonize the Army's intentions on choosing the meeting site, when Army officials make assumptions about the public—such as where they believe the public feels familiar—they decontextualize the public and the public's reasons for meeting in those spaces.

The assertion of power by the Army during the public meetings them-selves was even more problematic than the meeting spaces. Mowrer asserted that the Army officials used their authority as the agency in charge of the meetings, and of the decision to dispose of the VX, to preclude significant participation through meeting procedures and intimidation. As examples she noted two meetings: one with the National Research Council (NRC), a group of members from the National Academy of Sciences, the National Academy of Engineering, and the Institute of Medicine, given the task of evaluating incineration as a method of VX agent disposal; and a special meeting between officials from the Army and the Newport Citizens against Incineration.

In the first meeting, the chair of the NRC informed the public about their on-going research and current approval of incineration as a disposal method for the VX stockpile at the Newport Chemical Depot and allowed the public to ask questions or make comments. Mowrer stated that a lawyer with the Chemical Weapons Working Group, a Kentucky-based national citizen group against incineration at all Army installations, attended to sup-port the Newport-based citizen group against incineration. During the time allotted for questions and comments, the lawyer began asking specific ques-tions about the incinerator process and asserting that it was not a safe nor appropriate technology for VX disposal.

According to Mowrer, after five minutes, an Army lieutenant colonel asked the lawyer who he was and told him that speakers were allowed five minutes each for their comments and questions. He was not allowed to make further comments even after the others wishing to speak had been heard. Further, Mowrer states that after the public comments had been heard, the lieutenant colonel said that he wanted to ask the citizens questions and did not want the same person answering every time. Mowrer indicated (to me) that she did not understand why the Army could have a spokesperson, but the citizens could not—as long as any other citizen could also speak if he or she wished.

While it seems reasonable that the Army would want different citizens to state their comments on incineration during the question segment of the meeting in order to encourage a wide representation of the different publics' concerns, forcing citizens present to *answer* questions seems more an intimi-dation tactic. Further she said that during her allotted time she spoke against incineration because it was not a "closed-loop" technology; that is, it allowed emissions to escape into the air. She said that after the meeting, the lieuten-ant colonel told her that she could not use that term in public discussions because it was not "scientific."

In another meeting the Army used intimidation tactics to discourage citizen participation. In this case, the Army would not allow area citizens to attend the meetings between the Army and the Citizen Advisory Commission, a group of citizens appointed by the governor to represent citizen input in the chemical weapons disposal decision. The Citizen Advisory Commission was created for states with low-volume chemical stockpiles as a result of the

National Defense Act of 1993. The Indiana Citizen Advisory Commission consists of nine members, seven from the stockpile region, and "two state officials with technical expertise" ("Indiana Citizen's Advisory Committee" fact sheet). While the Citizen Advisory Commission is a step in the right direction for ensuring citizen involvement in decisions about chemical weapons disposal, the idea that a citizen group must contain "technical experts" in order to participate in the discussions with the Army about chemical weapons disposal again suggests the Army's assumption that a risk is determined and a solution considered based on technical information. Further, while the Citizen Advisory Commission is required to meet at least twice a year with a representative from the secretary of the Army to discuss chemical weapons disposal, the CAC is not required to meet with concerned citizens in order to be aware of their concerns. As a result, the concerns voiced by the Citizen Advisory Commission are the concerns of seven residents, and not necessarily representative of the public. While the same can be said for any citizen group, the Citizen Advisory Commission is different in that its created purpose is to represent public participation in the chemical weapons disposal decision.

While the Army lieutenant colonel would not allow the area citizens to attend the meetings, Mowrer maintained that the lieutenant colonel called her and asked her to set up a meeting so that he and other Army representatives could talk with the area citizens about the same issues they were discussing with the Citizen Advisory Commission. According to Mowrer, the lieutenant colonel sat directly across from her during the meeting. She noted that as the meeting continued, the Lieutenant Colonel asked her how many more questions she planned to ask. Mowrer stated that if she had not seen similar "intimidation tactics" before in other negotiations in which she was involved, she would have backed down and stopped asking questions. She also stated that she repeatedly asked the Army if she could sit in on the NRC meetings that were researching incineration but was repeatedly denied access to the meetings on the grounds that the information being discussed was "too technical for you to understand." And that "the NRC is a group of top scientists. They don't work with nontechnical people." Here, and as illustrated in several of the cases in chapter 2, decisions about environmental issues are nearly always made by "technical experts" who separate the public from discussions of technical issues. Failing to see that those affected by the policy can contribute valuable knowledge can result in inappropriate plans and policies.

Undervaluing Citizen Knowledge

One consequence of the separation between the public and technical issues is that it undervalues the useful knowledge citizens can contribute to a decision or policy. This separation and subsequent undervaluing is illustrated in another Army program, the Chemical Stockpile Emergency Preparedness Program established in 1988. In its mission of ensuring the health and safety of the Newport community in the event of an accident involving VX agent, the CSEPP and FEMA are responsible for developing evacuation plans for the five counties surrounding the Newport Chemical Depot. Calendars, brochures, and videos are distributed to the residents in the five counties detailing the emergency alert equipment that is in place, as well as the route each area should take, in the case of an evacuation. The Chemical Stockpile Emergency Preparedness Program's position toward public involvement is a one-way model of communication. Its mission is based on ensuring that the public is informed about emergency action procedures. The Chemical Stockpile Emergency Preparedness Program views the public as an audience in need of knowledge that the Army and FEMA create. The public's involvement is only as end receivers of information. In this program, the public's approval is not sought, and the Chemical Stockpile Emergency Preparedness Program rests assured that their expertise can keep the public safe from harm.

The Army web site describes the Program's interpretation of a community-specific plan: "CSEPP recognizes that each community has its own particular needs for emergency preparedness. Differences such as climate, terrain and population are considered when planning your protection" (http://www.army.mil/). Differences among communities are not defined by the people and events within a community, but rather the climate, terrain, and population.

Because the Chemical Stockpile Emergency Preparedness Program's evacuation plans were never discussed with the local residents, many of the procedures outlined in the emergency preparedness plan were not appropriate for the community. For example, at a meeting to distribute copies of the final evacuation plan, a local resident asked how the plan would be altered in October and April. When the presiding officials noted that the plan was not seasonal, citizens asserted that annual community festivals attract thousands of visitors to the area and that the current plan would result in clogged roads and prevent residents from reaching a safe zone in a timely manner. When the officials, who now realized that they were faced with redesigning the plan to accommodate festival traffic, lamented that no one had told them about these events, the citizens responded, "you didn't ask us."

If officials had simply asked the residents to evaluate possible evacuation plans, the problem could have been averted. According to Mowrer, "people in the community know more about what makes sense for them. They know about events that technical experts wouldn't know about" (personal interview, May 7, 2000). The Army's failure to involve the citizens in discussions about how a VX spill would affect them has resulted in faulty alarm systems, inappropriate emergency procedures for the elderly, and potential harm to school children—examples that will be considered in detail in chapter 4.

Mowrer's perspective aligns with that of numerous scholars in technical communication and participatory design who argue that users of a product (in this case a policy or plan) have useful knowledge to contribute to the development of a product because they know how it will be used (Ehn, Johnson, Winner, Winograd). Robert Johnson (1998) asserts that citizens possess knowledge about how a technology is or would be used in, or would affect, a particular community. This understanding is something experts lack, but need in order to design a usable technology. As a result, citizens can contribute valuable information to the design and decision-making process (p. 64). Chapter 4 will further discuss the possibilities of adopting such a participatory design approach that values citizen contributions as necessary for the development of appropriate policies.

CREATING POTENTIAL SPACES FOR PUBLIC DISCOURSE IN TECHNICAL ISSUES

In 1992, despite a completed EIS proposing incineration as the Army's choice of chemical disposal, Congress mandated that the Army create an Alternative Technology Program, to consider alternative methods of disposal due to the public opposition to incineration at all of the Army installation sites including the Newport Chemical Depot. A year later the Indiana state legislator, prompted by public opposition to incineration, passed Indiana Law 13-7-8.5-13 stating that in order to receive a construction permit for chemical disposal, the Army must prove that the proposed technology is safe and effective by demonstrating that at a comparable facility 99.9999 percent of the processed chemical agent is destroyed. This requirement for receiving a permit all but eliminated the possibility of using incineration as the disposal method.

Under the 1996 Defense Appropriations Bill, Congress created the Assembled Chemical Weapons Assessment program to identify and demonstrate at least three nonincineration technologies for chemical disposal. The difference between this program and so many others created by Congress and the Army in regards to chemical disposal was that this program mandated a "dialogue process by which affected citizens, state regulators and Department of Defense officials cooperatively created technology selection criteria" (32 C. F. R. Part 178).

While the Alternative Technology Program and Assembled Chemical Weapons Assessment overlap in their mission, their positions toward public participation differ. The former was created by the Army as a result of public outcry, but by way of Congress. The ATP in isolation continued to base its decisions about chemical weapons disposal on expert reports. However, the Assembled Chemical Weapons Assessment's position toward public participation is that the public can and should contribute knowledge to technical decisions. Its procedures for determining criteria to make decisions place the public and the technical experts on an equal level—and it expect significant public contribution at all stages of the decision-making process, not only after a decision has been made.

By most accounts, the Assembled Chemical Weapons Assessment has been a success, determining six alternatives to incineration under the budget and under the deadline. Mowrer asserts that for the first time the Army and the Department of Defense (DOD) officials were on the same level with citizens; citizens' power to accept or reject a technology was equal to the scientists.' All criteria for accepting a technology and all decisions on whether a technology met those criteria were decided by consensus of all involved. Further, any affected citizen could be a part of the Assembled Chemical Weapons Assessment. In this case, citizens were granted power and epistemological status in the decision-making process. The success of the ACWA process suggests that citizens can possess the literacy practices to contribute significantly to a technical plan or decision if granted access to decision-making process and the power to influence that decision. It is such processes that create a space for citizens to participate in technical issues. Other scholars such as Frank Fischer (2000) have argued similarly that citizens can understand the technical issues involved in environmental decision making and can contribute valuable knowledge to a plan, policy, or decision. He argues that not only can citizens participate in finding appropriate solutions to environmental problems, but they often possess a local knowledge—that is knowledge about a local context—that "experts" require for effective policies, but are not privy to (xii). Yet, to be persuasive in their discussions with policy makers, citizens must adopt and adapt literacy practices that allow them to articulate their understanding of a complex issue and how their knowledge of that issue applies to the particular situation.

Surely, these literacy practices are not static but change with the context. However, according to several scholars, a minimum of technical and discourse skills may be required. For example, Fischer (2000) asserts that citizens must be able to understand the experts' research findings and "in some cases how the community can derive its own calculations" (151). Similarly, Jeff Grabill (2005) argues that often, in order to participate in policy decisions, citizens must (and can) "do their own science" and be able to articulate that science to the decision makers. Drawing from examples of citizens in a grassroots organization dealing with an environmental hazard in their community, Grabill illustrates how these citizens used "rhetorical invention" to conduct inquiries into the science of the environmental contamination and communicate that research to decision makers. William Kinsella (2005) provides even more specific technical and discourse competencies that citizens must possess if they hope to participate fully in environmental decision making. For example, Kinsella asserts that citizens must have a "working vocabulary of scientific terms and concepts, and an overall understanding of how technical reasoning operates" that allows them to "follow evolving policy issues" (92). Noting that citizens must have not only access to pertinent information about an environmental issue but also a "critical understanding of the rhetoric and sociology of technical discourse," he quotes Laird (1993):

It is not enough that participants simply acquire new facts. They must begin, at some level, to be able to analyze the problem at hand. At the simplest level, this means understanding the different interpretations that one can draw from the facts and trying to think about ways to choose among those interpretations. At a more so-phisticated level, it means beginning to learn how and when to challenge the validity of the asserted facts, where new data would be useful, and how the kinds of policy questions being asked influence the type of data they seek. Perhaps more important, analyzing a problem means being able to challenge the formulation of the prob-lem itself, that is, for people to decide for themselves what the most important questions are. (pp. 353–354, qtd in Kinsella 93)

Not only gaining access to the pertinent information about an environmen-tal issue but also being able to investigate and analyze multiple interpreta-tions and articulate these interpretations to decision makers is a messy and complex process. The epilogue further examines the complications of access to such information—especially in the wake of post–September 11 height-ened security, while chapter 6 discusses ways in which rhetoricians and tech-nical communicators might encourage this access and these types of investigations through their work on civic web sites.

Despite a growing inaccessibility to the kind of information citizens need to understand, analyze, interpret, and articulate findings on environ-mental issues, examples such as the Newport citizens' participation in the decision to choose an appropriate disposal technology illustrate that spaces exist for citizen discourse in technical environmental issues and that citizens can successfully participate in those technical discussions.

Still, a single institution that values citizen knowledge and creates a space for citizen discourse in technical issues is not enough in a decision such as VX disposal that involves a sea of institutions that separate decision making from public participation. For example, when the Army's Alternative Technology Program managers began organizing the Assembled Chemical Weapons Assessment meetings, they said that the meetings would not be held in Indiana, Maryland, or Hawaii, where three of the Army installations are located. Many well-placed letters to Congress from citizens in those areas convinced the Army to change its plan. Yet, while Congress agreed that up to six alternatives approved by ACWA could be tested, the Army claimed that it only had funds for three. Further, there is no mention of the As-sembled Chemical Weapons Assessment anywhere in the draft or final EIS. When the Army includes reasoning for its chosen technology, it attributes the decision to the Alternative Technology Program.

Despite Army subversion tactics, the Assembled Chemical Weapons Assessment holds promise for improved environmental issue decision mak-ing. In a letter to Secretary of State Cohen, twenty-four U.S. representatives urged for continued funding of ACWA after chemical disposal at Army installation sites has been completed because the technology developed has potential for environmental clean-up projects beyond chemical weapons disposal. More programs like the ACWA are needed. Chapter 4 will examine how the approach used in ACWA might positively affect other existing barriers to significant public participation in environmental issues.

Keeping the Public from Ruining a Perfectly Good Plan: Prohibiting Significant Public Contribution in Environmental Decisions

Unfortunately, few institutions involved in the chemical weapons disposal decision function like the Assembled Chemical Weapons Assessment. Even after the success of ACWA, agencies involved in the neutralization project at the Newport Chemical Depot continued to employ procedures that marginalized public participation. The Indiana Department of Environmental Management (IDEM) is responsible for ensuring that the neutralization facility at the Newport Chemical Depot meets all environmental protection acts during construction and operation of the facility, including the Resources Conservation and Recovery Act (RCRA), the Clean Air Act (CAA), and the Clean Water Act/ National Pollutant Discharge Elimination System (CWA/ NPDES) permit. RCRA regulates all hazardous waste creation, storage, and destruction. Owners and operators of facilities that store or dispose of hazardous waste must obtain a RCRA permit. ("Environmental Permitting" fact sheet). Similarly, the CAA requires owners and operators of facilities to apply for a permit to construct and operate a facility ("Environmental Permitting").

In this case, the Army must indicate the expected air emissions that will result from the construction and operation of the neutralization facility at the Newport Chemical Depot. The CWA/ NPDES permit is an EPA-administered permit program ("Environmental Permitting"). This act and permit ensure that the wastewater from the neutralization process will not endanger the quality of the water when discharged into the Wabash. The Department of Health and Human Services (DHHS) serves as a check that the data supplied by the operating agency is accurate and meets permit requirements.

Because these permits are similar in the type of information they require from the Army and in the public comment period they require, public meetings addressing all the permits were held together under the supervision of IDEM and the EPA. Two meetings were held for the public to ask questions about the permits, the Army's application for the permits, and to comment on either. The later meeting on October 12, 1999, was held specifically for the purpose of soliciting comments from citizens about the permits. A government recorder was on hand to transcribe the meeting and take public comment. However, due in large part to the procedure of the meetings, the recorder had little work. Six EPA and IDEM officials sat behind a table in the front of the room and read to those attending the manner in which they should submit their comments so that their concerns could be recorded. They further noted that if the EPA and IDEM deemed the comment significant, it would be responded to in writing by the agencies. Once the procedures had been read, individuals wishing to speak had to adhere to strict policy procedures to be heard. For example, individuals wishing to make a comment were required to indicate their intentions on a card prior to the meeting. Citizens were to take a 4 x 5.5 inch comment card offered at the front desk near the door, write their comment on the card, and give the card to one of the attending officials. This suggests, at the very least, that dialogue among the parties was not a goal. Following this procedure, an individual cannot respond immediately to another's comment.

The representative officiating the meeting noted that no one had turned in a comment card, but asked if anyone had a comment who did not turn in a card. An audience member raised his hand and said he had a question about the safety precautions being taken to prevent groundwater contamination. Citing the procedures for recording comments, an official refused to answer questions because they were "on record." The representative added that if there were time after all comments had been made, a representative would address his question. Someone else in the audience urged him to state his question anyway. He did, and silence followed. No one else made a comment, and the meeting was adjourned four minutes after the comment period had begun. In this case the very procedures that were stipulated by regulation to allow public participation worked to crush any participation at all. Since the institutional procedures instructed citizens to create comments instead of asking questions, the officials, following the letter of the procedures, denied the man's question in other forms. The minutes of this meeting recorded that no one had commented on the policy—deceptively suggesting that the citizens had no concerns with the environmental decision. As discussed earlier, the institutional procedures in place to ensure participation dictated the form in which citizens could participate—they could submit a comment—not ask a question, not begin a conversation. If their comment was in the form of a question, it was not included in the minutes. Clearly there is a difference between being allowed to comment and encouraging a dialogue, but in this meeting, both were inhibited. In the case of the public meeting regarding the permit, the experts had already made the decision they believed to be most technically feasible and saw public input only as a way to mar the perfectly good plan they had already worked hard to devise.

I have often thought about that meeting and wondered whether I should have taken a more active role in my observations. I have wondered whether I should have suggested to the man that he state his question in the form of a comment so that it would appear on record or suggested to the officials that his question be treated as a comment. If I am arguing that rhetoricians and technical communicators can intervene in the decision-making process to bring about a more just decision, then am I not obligated to intervene? Ellen Cushman (1998) reminds us that activist researchers must be careful not to impose our beliefs onto others. She advocates instead "intervention only through invitation" (246). She and other activist researchers have worked *with* individuals and communities to help bring about significant positive social change—but they ensure that their help is wanted and the changes are ones the individuals themselves identify. I think this advice is good to keep in mind. As researchers we can work to bring about a more ethical decision-making process by working *with* those affected by the decision. This collaboration can take on many forms—an issue I will return to later.

Other Indiana Department of Environmental Management actions also worked to prevent any public input. It is IDEM's responsibility to alert concerned and affected citizens about the meetings. One such source for meeting alerts was to be IDEM's web site. But the web site maintained by IDEM to alert interested parties about site procedures was rarely updated; in fact, the page announcing upcoming public meetings never indicated the date of the meeting called explicitly to solicit public comment about the licensing permits. The web site, which could have been a good resource for concerned citizens not targeted by the IDEM or the Army as stakeholders, possibly worked to prevent this audience from attending the meeting.[8]

The Indiana Department of Environmental Management is considered a public resource for accessing information about the licensing procedure and permits. Citizens are told they can visit IDEM to read about the progress on the permits, the applications for the permits, and other background information. Yet information about proposed plans is difficult to acquire from IDEM. I was given the wrong documents three times by IDEM officials and was told the documents I wanted did not exist even though I had copies of the IDEM numbers used to identify the documents. All the while, IDEM proclaimed that public participation was key to the permit process at the Newport Chemical Depot, noting, in a letter to citizens about an upcoming meeting, "IDEM is conducting public participation to ensure all interested parties have an opportunity to comment on the State Draft Permit" (letter, September 17, 1999). Indeed IDEM officials were conducting public participation: they were controlling it throughout the permit process. IDEM's and EPA's position toward public participation is similar to NEPA's in that IDEM's and EPA's efforts to involve the public are limited to gaining the public's acceptance for decisions already made. Further, their attitude is much like the Army's in that they do not allow the public the opportunity to ruin the good plan they have for environmental management and for meetings.

RESISTING INSTITUTIONAL POWER AND THE CONSEQUENCES
OF MULTIPLE VIEWS ON PUBLIC PARTICIPATION

In some ways the most interesting, although not surprising, aspect of the VX nerve agent disposal case was the different views on public participation held by the diverse groups of citizens invested in the policy decision. Because the citizen groups envisioned different roles for the public in environmental decisions, both from one another and from the federal and state public participation procedures, their attempts at participation sometimes meshed, but often conflicted. Both Sybil Mowrer, spokesperson for the Newport-based citizen group against incineration, and Tyler Mayes, spokesperson for MEG, agreed that the regulations for public participation and institutional procedures do not allow for citizens to actively participate in decisions about environmental issues except through "subversive" measures. Yet their perspectives on the role of the public in environmental decisions differ.

Mayes asserted that Army officials only encouraged public participation because they were required to, and they made certain that the citizens were aware of that. He believed that it is only because the Army is not as sophisticated in public relations skills that citizens were able to see through the tactics used to keep them from participating, spurring citizens to seek other channels, such as Congress, to make their voices heard.

Mayes noted that MEG became involved in the events at the Newport Chemical Depot to provide technical and organizational support for the local citizens. He said that as a way to support the citizens, MEG wrote a position statement to the DOD and Indiana state representatives urging "US DOD to refrain from the incineration of nerve agent stored at Newport Chemical Depot until DOD can prove this process does not pose a threat to human health and the environment" (MEG Position Statement). He stated that many citizens and other groups followed suit by sending similar letters to DOD and their state representatives. He believed that the letters encouraged state officials to pass Indiana Law 13-7-8.5-13 stating that in order to receive a construction permit for chemical disposal, the Army must prove that the proposed technology is safe and effective by demonstrating that at a comparable facility 99.9999 percent of the processed chemical agent is destroyed (see appendix E). He noted that "the Army wouldn't listen to us, but they had to listen to the Governor, so we got the Governor to listen to us" (Tyler Mayes, personal communication, May 5, 2000). In fact, Mayes asserted that writing letters to elected officials is one of the most effective means citizens currently have for involvement in environmental issues, and the tactic most often employed by MEG.

Mowrer told a similar story, asserting that the Army's attitude throughout the disposal process has been, "We're only talking to you because Congress said we have to." She also maintained that stopping the incineration would not have been possible without the help of other citizen groups such as the Chemical Weapons Working Group (CWWG). The CWWG had representatives present at each Army installation when meetings were held about chemical weapons disposal and would contact members at other sites to let them know what had happened. They encouraged her to write letters to Congress voicing her concern about incineration and about being more involved in the decision process. For example, as a way to stall the incineration, Mowrer, along with about sixteen local residents, wrote letters, including in the letter something specific and personal about that resident's situation in regards to the Newport Chemical Depot. Those letters did indeed stall the action. On another occasion, to voice her desire to have local citizens be allowed more involvement in the decision-making process, she wrote form letters for around twenty people, had them signed, and mailed them all on the same day so that they would "flood" the Army general's office two days before he was to make a decision about the Assembled Chemical Weapons Assessment program. The decision was made in favor of the citizens.

While it is encouraging that the citizens were able to delay a decision until they could influence it, it is only because of the discourse practices the citizens were able to adopt—the alternative literacy practices of writing letters to those in power—that allowed them the agency, albeit indirectly, to affect the decision-making process. The current federal and state procedures in place actively work to prevent citizens from participating fully unless they subvert the procedures and discourse practices of public meetings and investigate alternative discourse practices to have their voices heard. Yet how do citizens develop the literacy practices they need for such situations, and how do they determine which discourse practices to adopt in which situations to gain agency to the decision-making process? This book focuses not only on creating a space for citizens to participate in the decision-making process and understanding what literacy practices are necessary to participate effectively, but also on *how* citizens develop these literacy practices. In other words, how do citizens learn to conduct their own research? How do they learn the terminology in order to talk with the experts? How do they learn what the important questions are and what research methodologies will help them address these questions? Chapter 6 suggests how we might prepare our students to address these tasks and be more active citizens capable of participating significantly in civic issues, even when those issues are complex, and the spaces are not evident.

Participation Expectations

In some instances public participation in policy comes down to the difference between what the government expects from citizens participating in the decisions about environmental policy and what citizens expect from their participation in decisions about environmental policy. In the VX disposal decision, different communities and/or institutions perceived differently the ways in which public discourse should affect how policy is written on chemical weapons disposal. Because the discourse each group used focused on its own expectations, but did not meet the expectations of other communities, the public discourse failed, and the risk communication did not work. Most government regulators and thus current regulations equate participation with getting members of the public to approve a decision or allowing them to voice their opinions on the decision. Yet that interpretation of public participation varied even within an institution, as evident in the difference between the Army's attitude toward public involvement and Assembled Chemical Weapons Assessment's procedures for public participation. Moreover, the interpretation of public participation differs even among citizen groups. For example, the spokesperson for the Newport Citizens against Incineration asserted that their group's definition of public participation includes the public helping to make the decisions while a spokesperson for MEG, the statewide activist group, maintained that its definition of public participation includes the public policing the decisions (Sybil Mowrer, May 7, 2000; Tyler Mayes, May 5, 2000).

The citizen groups' positions on public participation are interesting in that they envision different roles for the public in environmental decisions. While the Newport Citizens against Incineration believed that citizens should help make the decisions, the state-wide citizen group saw the citizens' role as more of policing decisions to ensure that the environment is not harmed. This is perhaps most evident in the Newport group's continued involvement in the events at Newport versus the state-wide group's lack of interest after incineration was no longer considered a viable means of chemical weapons disposal.

The current risk communication models used in the chemical weapons disposal case at Newport assume that the public is a unified, coherent entity with similar concerns and goals. Specifically, the officials at Newport expect the public to be local citizens and are suspicious of any "interested parties" who do not fit that description. Yet this assumption excludes a number of groups and individuals affected by the decision. According to Young, assuming a homogenous public fails to consider groups that are not culturally identified with what the institutions consider the norm. For example, the citizens from Kentucky who attended the public meetings (and who lived near the Bluegrass Chemical Depot) were seen by the Army and the Indiana Department of Environmental Management as radicals interfering with the policy decision because they did not fit the institutions' criteria for the local public. By not acknowledging a range of citizens affected by a decision, experts run the risk of marginalizing groups significantly affected by a decision. A discrepancy exists between the institutional view of "the public" and the actual heterogeneous publics that make up any community engaged in social action. Charles Willard (1996) addresses this institutional view of "the public" as "largely an idea about American democracy. It is an entry point to a way of speaking about democratic life . . . a vehicle for idealizing democratic discourse, for describing a discourse space distinct from market and state and from private and technical discourses" (11). Institutional procedures for including "the public" are often merely attempts to appear as though those institutions are proceeding democratically toward a decision. Gerald Hauser (1999) claims that references to "the public" generalize "a body of disinterested members of a society or polity and [are] no more informative to an understanding of social knowledge and social action than an undefined reference to 'they' " (32). He argues for rethinking the public as a "plurality of publics grounded on their capacity for rhetorical engagement" (14). This notion of publics—whose membership is fluid and determined by both their interest in issues that affect their lives and their ability to engage in discussions about these issues—is important for thinking about a framework for environmental decision-making because it connects the importance of considering the multiple and varied groups who are affected *and* the literacy practices necessary for those groups to participate. According to Hauser, membership requires

> rhetorical competence, or a capacity to participate in rhetorical experiences. Their members, on balance, must be receptive to alternative modes of expression, engage in active interpretation to understand what is being said and how it relates to them, and be open to change. Partners in rhetorical transactions, of necessity, must actively engage one another in attempts to understand issues, appreciate each other's views, and form their own judgments. They engage in an interpretive process in which they must consider perspectives not entirely their own. They must attend to motivations and rationales that lead to differences of opinion but that open the possibility for consensus. In short, the ability to participate in rhetorical exchanges, to have rhetorical experiences, requires a certain sort of subjectivity. (pp. 33–34)

These requirements suggest a commitment—from citizens to learn about the issue, seriously consider multiple interpretations of that issue, and articulate their understanding persuasively, and from experts to acknowledge that citizens can learn about the issue, seriously consider multiple interpretations of that issue, and articulate their understanding. A framework for democratic and ethical public involvement for environmental policy requires at the least an understanding of the public as heterogeneous—where *all* affected groups are sought out and involved and a belief that citizens can understand, consider, and contribute to technical issues.

A Notion of Multiple Publics

A notion of multiple publics is important because even seemingly similar communities, such as citizen activist groups, may hold very different agendas, concerns, and views toward a proposed technology. For example, Cable and Cable (1995) assert that there are often distinct differences between state and national environmental groups and grassroots environmental groups. Members of the state and national environmental groups are often middle- or upper-class, white individuals who see environmental activism as part of their political activities and believe the political system is "theirs to manipulate, direct, and influence" (Cable & Cable, p. 119). These members, they claim, are more likely to "seek new environmental laws" rather than challenge the system or institution itself (p. 119).

Unlike members of state and national environmental groups, Cable and Cable maintain that members of local grassroots organizations are formed in response to an environmental issue in their own community. The members of these grassroots organizations, Cable and Cable claim, "petition elites for help" when they feel "a deep sense of betrayal" and that they are "bearing the environmental cost of industry production" (p. 120). Interestingly, they add that it is the grassroots environmental conflicts that can "alter significantly the structures of [. . .] institutions" by changing local political structures (p. 121). While these descriptions seem potentially stereotypical, they also hold true for the Newport case. The state environmental group saw its role as that of a "watchdog" to ensure that a safe technology was installed. Its tactic was to call for a law against incineration in Indiana (which eventually was passed). Yet after the law was passed, MEG lost interest in the situation and pursued other issues. The Newport-based citizens against incineration, however, saw their role as affected parties with the right to participate in the decision-making process and have stayed involved even after the decision not to incinerate to work toward more participation in the decision-making process.

With so many different expectations and interpretations of public participation intersecting across so many different agencies, programs, regulations, and groups, it is little wonder that the risk communication practices failed. Yet many environmental decisions are equally complex. While a unified approach is certainly not the answer—each environmental situation is different—a heuristic to institutional approaches that focuses on the *construction* of the policy/decision, and how that policy will be used in everyday practices, rather than on the product of an accepted policy, might be a step in the right direction. Drawing on the observations in chapters 2, 3, and 4, chapter 5 will present such a heuristic and detail how it might be used to evaluate and encourage public participation in environmental policy.

As a way to further consider what literacy/discourse practices are necessary to actively participate in collaborative decision making and what practices might help integrate both expert and public knowledge in an attempt to develop more appropriate policy, chapter 4 will examine the institutional approaches discussed in this chapter in terms of models of public participation. The chapter looks for spaces where citizens could be included, and how a participatory design approach to current public participation procedures might change them to more significantly involve citizens in the decision-making process.

CHAPTER FOUR

TOWARD A PARTICIPATORY APPROACH

TO DECISION MAKING:

CREATING A SPACE FOR PUBLIC

DISCOURSE IN TECHNICAL ISSUES

The situation surrounding chemical weapons disposal at the Newport Chemical Depot, as illustrated in chapter 3, and the examples of public participation in existing risk communication cases, as illustrated in chapter 2, suggest that in many institutions related to environmental policy, there is a clear separation between technical expert decision making and public involvement. In these cases the existence of the risk, the magnitude of the risk, the potential harm of the risk, and the way in which the risk should be eliminated are all determined by a group of experts who are trained in such matters. As a result, it is easy to understand the technical experts' initial reluctance to involve the public in any significant ways in the decision-making process. Many technical experts believe that involving the public in such complex decisions will only delay and further complicate the issue because the public cannot understand the technical nature of such decisions, and as a result cannot effectively participate in decisions about such issues.

For example, the spokesperson for the Newport Citizens against Incineration at the Newport Chemical Depot repeatedly noted how she was told that the nature of the discussions in the National Research Council meetings was too technical for her to understand, too technical for her to join. She was also told that her discussions of the situation were not "scientific" and supposedly invalid or unworthy of consideration.

Frank Fischer (1992), in his discussion of public participation in risk assessment, asserts that although politicians and public interest groups have for some time now seen that decisions about risk are "too important to be left to the scientists alone," the scientific lobbies and conservative politicians have maintained the current decision-making process by arguing that, "the layman simply cannot understand and responsibly judge complex technological issues. Such participation is said to be unrealistic, if not utopic" (p. 498). As further evidence of the technical expert's attitude on public involvement, Fischer quotes the former president of the National Academy of Sciences (of which the National Research Council is a part): "Most members of the public usually don't know enough about any given complicated technical matter to make meaningful judgments. And that includes scientists and engineers who work in unrelated areas" (p. 498). Involving the public in technical decisions is also time consuming and costly. Factoring in time for planning public meetings, holding public meetings, and allowing for comment periods slows the implementation of the policy or action. In many cases, public involvement is seen as a way to mar the good plan developed by experts. With these attitudes, it is little wonder that the public participation procedures are designed in ways that limit significant public involvement in the decision-making process.

This chapter illustrates how those technical experts' attitudes manifest themselves in the public participation procedures employed by institutions involved in risk communication. Such institutional moves make one perspective on risk communication—namely, the experts'—seem the "natural" perspective. Analyzing the different approaches used by the agencies and programs in the chemical weapons disposal decision at the Newport Chemical Depot in terms of models of risk communication reveals spaces where the public might be involved and how each institution navigates those spaces. I do not analyze the approaches used by different programs in the order in which they are discussed in chapter 3—by a combination of program size and chronological order of how the situation unfolded at the Newport Chemical Depot. Rather, in this chapter, I examine the programs in terms of common models of risk communication and public participation, so I start with the most exclusionary model and work toward the approach that encourages the most public participation. In doing so, I seek a range of examples of specific risk communication practices that will illustrate ways in which citizens could more significantly participate in the decisions of environmental policy. A more critical rhetoric of public participation is needed to dissolve the separation of risk assessment from risk communication (or technical decisions from public discourse) to locate epistemology within the process that involves the public. I see participatory design as a useful approach to consider for this new approach and will examine its possibilities in this chapter.

MODELS AND APPROACHES TO PUBLIC PARTICIPATION IN ENVIRONMENTAL POLICY

Considering the numerous institutions, agencies, and programs involved in the chemical weapons disposal decision at the Newport Chemical Depot, it is not surprising that there were numerous approaches to public participation employed in different instances throughout the decision process. Nor is it surprising that the different approaches employed by these institutions reflect the most common models of risk communication articulated by social science, rhetoric, and technical communication scholars (Krimsky et al.; Waddell; Rowan; Grabill and Simmons; see also chapter 2). I borrow from Waddell (1997) the idea of illustrating through models where the public becomes involved in the decision-making process. Waddell's four models: technocratic, one-way Jeffersonian, interactive Jeffersonian, and social constructionist show an evolution of increasing public involvement. Waddell maintains that when a social constructionist model is employed, where technical information, values, and emotions are exchanged between the experts and the public, the public can effectively participate in environmental decisions. With my versions of the communication models that build on Waddell's, I hope to show two additional issues: (1) that debates often incorporate multiple models rather than single models of public involvement—complicating the notion of public participation, and (2) that the notion of public itself must be seen as complicated, diverse, and multifaceted because a homogenous notion of public fails to acknowledge the vastly different perspectives different members of the public may bring to a single debate. Viewing the public as one, unified group fails to consider groups that are not culturally identified with what the institutions consider the norm (Young, 1990) and may result in an unethical or inappropriate policy decision. The often ineffective practices that occurred in the chemical weapons disposal decisions made at the Newport Chemical Depot are closely related to these models of risk communication that inform practice. Examining each of these approaches and the way in which institutions navigated public involvement may illuminate spaces where more significant participation is possible.

SUBVERTING DEMOCRACY: TECHNOCRATIC MODELS OF PARTICIPATION

The earliest stages of decisions about chemical weapons disposal at the Newport Chemical Depot follow what Waddell (1997) calls the "technocratic model" of risk communication. This model is more of a prerisk communication model in that there is no communication at any level with the public. In the technocratic model, decisions about handling risks are left to the experts. This model works to circumvent the public by avoiding disclosure about a risk and by obscuring the steps followed in the decision-making process (see figure 4.1). The technocratic model also obscures the process from experts not included because they hold a differing view from the one adopted. This illuminates an important consideration about "experts." The notion of "expert" is nearly as problematic as "public." In issues of risk, experts are often defined in the most limited sense, excluding, as mentioned, "even scientists and engineers who work in unrelated areas" (Fischer, 2000,

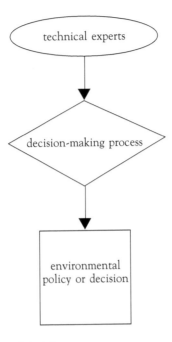

Figure 4.1: Technocratic Model

p. 498). (This, in part, explains why even arguments made by citizens with technical training and background are often dismissed by the "experts" conducting the risk assessments and the public meetings.)

Winner (1995) argues that in issues of policy debates about technology, "the lack of legitimate channels for public participation" contributes to a reliance on expert advice (p. 75). According to Winner, relying on the opinion of experts in complicated issues such as risk management is to be expected:

> Disputes about technology policy often arise in topic areas that seem to require years of training in fields of highly esoteric, science-based knowledge. [...] Because technology is regarded as an "applied science," and because the consequences of these applications involve such matters as complicated scientific measurements and the interpretation of arcane data, a common response is to turn to experts and expert research in hope of settling key policy questions. (p. 75)

Yet he asserts that consulting experts often leads to frustration because "different fields of research give very different estimates of possible hazards" and "expertise is linked to and biased by particular social interests" (p. 75). Even experts within the same field often disagree upon the appropriate mathematical model for assessing risk, resulting in significant differences in the calculated risk posed by a hazard.

Young (1990) further questions the notion of experts in decisions about environmental issues, arguing:

> Most of the insurgencies that have challenged the decision-making prerogatives of official power have also sought to demystify the ideology of expertism. Community groups challenging the decision to construct a hazardous waste treatment plant or a nuclear plant or a nuclear waste disposal site must acquire considerable technical knowledge of waste management, local geology, and law in order to conduct their campaign; in the process they discover that these matters can be understood by ordinary citizens, and that experts are rarely neutral. (p. 84)

Despite the often arbitrary distinction of "expert," the technocratic model works under the assumption that decisions about environmental risk issues are complex and technical and should therefore be restricted to individuals trained in risk assessment and risk management.

While the technocratic approach to making decisions about environmental issues is less common now than in the early days of risk management (through the early 1980s), it is still employed in cases that do not involve specific public participation regulations. Further, while many environmental decision procedures now follow other models, this model still represents the mindset of most regulatory agencies who believe that the public cannot contribute to the technical discussions about risk and that these technical and complex decisions are best left unmarred by the public.

The technocratic model represents the Army's approach to decision making in the mid-1980s when it determined, without public input, to incinerate the VX agent at the Newport Chemical Depot. This model is also reflective of Krimsky and Plough's (1985) EDB case described in chapter 2 of this study in which "all the important decisions are made in private meetings where the public is not present" (p. 27) and where the debates, and ultimately the policy, were "the responsibility of the elites" (p. 303). Not only were citizens not encouraged to participate in the decision-making process, but they were not invited to the meetings where decisions were made. This model assumes that risk policies can be determined by a defined set of principles and scientific norms—independent of citizen input. One of the most problematic aspects of this model is that the public is not allowed to participate in, or even made aware of, actions that affect their own lives. If we accept that the public should be involved in decisions that affect them and their communities, and that they, themselves, are most often the best judge of their own interests, then the technocratic approach becomes incompatible with participatory democracy.

COERCING PUBLIC PARTICIPATION:
STRATEGIC ACTION MODELS OF PARTICIPATION

Simply including the public in a model of risk communication does not guarantee the public's participation in decision making about environmental risk. Another common model of risk communication is called numerous names by different scholars,[1] but I use *strategic action* (from Habermas' theories of discourse ethics) to describe this approach to public involvement. In the strategic action model, risk communication strives to influence the public into thinking about the risk the way experts do: public perception must be brought into conformity with scientific rationality (see figure 4.2). Habermas' notion of strategic action occurs when the communicator is more interested in succeeding, or winning the argument, than in reaching an

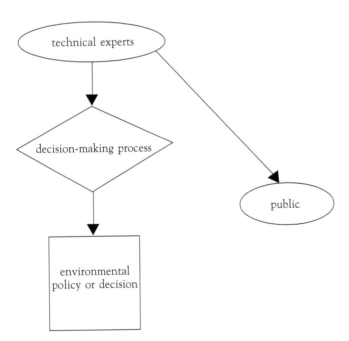

Figure 4.2: Strategic Action Model

understanding with the other parties (p. 134). This approach sees risk, issues related to risk, and ultimately the risk policy as determined by technical experts prior to communication. Effective risk communication is the result of transferring information to the public that understands and accepts it. This model reflects a one-way flow of technical information from the experts to the public where knowledge is scientifically produced prior to communication, communication is linear, and the public is seen as an audience to be managed (Grabill and Simmons, p. 422).

Both the Program Manager for Chemical Demilitarization (PMCD) and the Chemical Stockpile Emergency Preparedness Program (CSEPP) provide examples of the strategic action model of risk communication practices at the Newport Chemical Depot. The PMCD and the resulting outreach program function under the assumption that if the citizens concerned with the chemical disposal at Newport are given enough information about the issue, they will agree with the Army's decisions about chemical disposal. This is especially evident in the roundtable meetings where citizens are encouraged to voice their concerns about chemical disposal so that the Army officials can provide them with information that addresses those concerns.

The public's concerns are not even recorded or passed along to decision makers. The Army encourages the citizens to voice their concerns only so that the "misconceptions" they have can be corrected with knowledge produced by the Army. As Adrian Thompson, public affairs officer for the Newport Chemical Depot noted, the Program Manager for Chemical Demilitarization and the Newport Chemical Outreach and Information Office were established as an "education program" because the citizens were "basing their protests on misinformation" (Adrian Thompson, April 27, 2000). In this particular case, the public is present, but in very limited ways: they do not even have access to the decision makers, much less participation in the decision. If the Army is making overtures to the public to plan meetings between Army officials and the public, why could not those meetings be structured to allow genuine two-way communication between the involved parties? While there is a space for the public in this model, the space is navigated by the Army to disallow any significant public involvement. This model also falls into the strategic action quadrant discussed in chapter 2 of this study where public interaction in decision-making process and public power are both low.

Consequences of Not Involving the Public in Policy Decisions

There are at least two significant consequences of the strategic action model of risk communication and public participation for the technical experts and the involved publics. The first is that an approach that does not seek the input of publics/users on a decision risks excluding valuable situated information and thus developing a policy that is not appropriate for a particular context. For example, recall the evacuation plans that the Chemical Stockpile Emergency Preparedness Program, FEMA, and the Army developed for the five counties near the Newport Chemical Depot without soliciting the community's input on the plans. The evacuation plan failed to accommodate the large number of people who visit several of these counties during the spring and fall. The original plan would result in clogged roads, preventing residents from reaching a safe zone (VX fumes can travel quickly, leaving little time for evacuation). Mowrer noted that while the CSEPP routinely sounded the alarm system in the Newport area, it never questioned the residents about the "testing" process and did not find out for years that the alarm could not be heard by a large portion of the community. The lack of public involvement in the plans has also contributed to misinformation. She asserted that while the Chemical Stockpile Emergency Preparedness Program distributes calendars, keychains, and brochures about the evacuation plan, these promotional materials indicate that in the event of an evacuation, residents should not go to the schools to pick up their children because the teachers there have been trained to evacuate the children safely. Mowrer maintained, however, that in the nearly twenty years she has taught in the school system, she has never been told what to do with the students in the event of an evacuation during school hours.[2] These stories illustrate a significant assumption and flaw in the strategic action approach to risk communication and public participation. In this model, technical experts assume that the public has no valuable knowledge to contribute to the plan or policy, and this results in an uninformed, often problematic, plan. Yet, in the case of the evacuation plan, the area citizens possessed crucial knowledge that the Chemical Stockpile Emergency Preparedness Program officials did not.

Robert Johnson (1998) discusses a similar situation from the field of urban planning, where the city of Seattle was unable to design appropriate traffic plans until it sought public input. According to Johnson, traffic engineers in Seattle studied traffic flow using statistical techniques employed by Los Angeles traffic engineers in an effort to determine how to reroute roads, when to open and close bridges, and which bypasses to expand. Yet, after making road changes based on the data collected from studying traffic, the situation was worse (p. 65). However, a team of technical communicators from the University of Washington gathered patterns of use information from the *users* of the roads—the Seattle drivers. Using surveys, interviews, focus groups, and observations, the technical communicators found that while the drivers were not likely to alter their driving habits because of an expanded bypass, or rerouted road, they would alter their traffic route if they were given daily information about traffic patterns through town in a format/media that fit their particular needs: television, computer, telephone (p. 65). Johnson notes that rather than trying to make the users adjust to the system, the technical communicators modified the system to fit the needs of the users

(p. 65). Here it took both technical expertise and user knowledge to solve a complex and technical problem.

As in the Newport case, when decisions were based solely on the opinions of those labeled experts by the Army and did not consider the local conditions that the publics could provide, the plans were not appropriate for the particular situation. At the very least, this could cause user frustration such as congested roadways and heavy traffic, but in the case of many environmental issues, this could also result in more serious consequences, such as fatalities from inoperable evacuation plans. Rather than viewing public involvement as an opportunity to inform the public about a decision, a more effective approach would be to use the same time with the public to seek input on what conditions within a community or situation would prevent the decision/proposed plan or policy from working effectively. While ultimately this would result in a slightly longer time frame for implementing a policy, it could, in the long run, save money and time that would otherwise be needed to rework the inappropriate policy. In environmental issues such as these where the strategic action model is employed, the public remains silent, its valuable knowledge unheard.

CREATING "SIDES" AND INAPPROPRIATE POLICIES: STRATEGIC ACTION/REACTIONARY MODELS OF PARTICIPATION

In some situations where the strategic action model is employed, the publics refuse to remain silent. In this case, if the decision-making agencies do not allow a space for public input into the decision, the public will have their voices heard through other venues. Those venues may include organized appeals to Congress or protests through the media or at the institution denying input. In many instances, especially through appeals to Congress and the media, the public outcry may result in a new decision or policy (see figure 4.3). This scenario represents another consequence of the strategic action model. In the reactionary model, risk assessors consider only the technical aspects of risk during the decision-making process, not the concerns and values of each local community, resulting in public outcry against a risk or policy.

For example, both Sybil Mowrer, spokesperson for the Newport Citizens against Incineration, and Tyler Mayes, spokesperson for the Midwest Environmental Group, maintained that the revised proposal to use an alternative technology to incineration to destroy the VX stockpile at Newport Chemical Depot was due to citizen appeals to Congress. Both claimed that when it became apparent that the Army would not listen to their concerns, they believed their best recourse was to solicit help from Congress. As a result of numerous letters from individual citizens and environmental groups in both Indiana and Kentucky protesting incineration at the the Newport Chemical Depot, the Indiana State Legislature passed the law requiring the Army to prove that a proposed technology destroyed 99.9999 percent of the

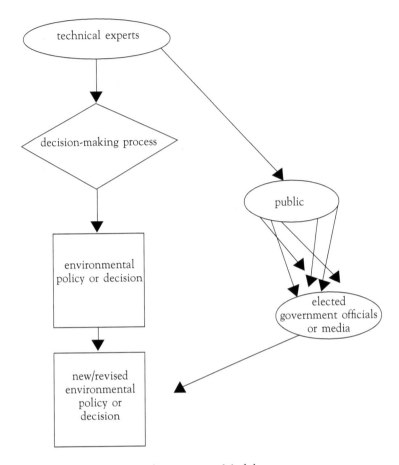

Figure 4.3: Strategic Action/Reactionary Model

processed chemical agent in order to receive a permit for chemical disposal. As a result, the Army was forced to consider an alternative to incineration for VX disposal. In this case, while the Army relegated the space for public participation to the role of passive audience, citizens, realizing that their concerns were not being heard, much less considered, found an alternative space for voicing their concerns.

McGarity (1998) asserts that this approach "reflects a high degree of distrust among the activists in the process itself. Because they strongly perceive the process to be failing, the activists seek a wider audience" (p. 3). While McGarity's essay equates activists with radicals, his perception that individuals often resent the *process* of decision-making, that is, being left out of the process, more than the actual decision has merit. Chess and Hance (1989) agree with this argument, asserting that, "communities may object as strongly to the decision-making process as to the risk itself" (as cited in Katz and Miller, p. 116). This was not entirely true in the Newport Chemical Depot VX disposal case. Sybil Mowrer, Adrian Thompson, and Tyler Mayes all commented that it was the issue of incineration that prompted the public's protest. However, Mowrer and Mayes agree that if the Army had genuinely sought citizens' input into the decision to incinerate the VX stockpile at the Newport Chemical Depot, the strategy for voicing their concerns about incineration would have been different. They both agree that it was the Army's refusal to allow public input into the decision that prompted the different public groups to take their case to Congress.

The potential problems with the strategic action/reactionary model are many. For example, when the public persuades Congress to prevent a proposed plan or enact a new one, this further fuels the hostile relations among the regulators, agencies, and publics and results in delayed implementation of the policy. McGarity (1998) notes that, "such confrontations are usually intended to be very public, they are not designed to be participatory and they are definitely not conducive to informed dialogue about risks and the measures that can be taken to reduce risks" (p. 3). While McGarity's perspective is from that of the technical expert, his point is valid. In this approach, involved parties become divided into "sides" who strive to influence a policy without the input of the other. In some cases the revised plan is not appropriate for the situation because it has been determined by Congress due to pressure from the public, without input from the technical experts. A case in point of the potential problem with this strategic action/reaction approach can be considered with the Newport Chemical Depot situation. In isolation, the Indiana Law requiring that 99.999 percent of the VX be destroyed ensures only that incineration will not be used. It does not lend itself to increasing public input into the final decision (see appendix E).

However, a few years later, due to similar citizen protests at the other eight Army installations storing chemical weapons, Congress passed the 1996 Defense Appropriations Bill, creating the Assembled Chemical Weapons Assessment (ACWA) program to identify and demonstrate at least three nonincineration technologies for chemical disposal. ACWA mandated a "dialogue process by which affected citizens, state regulators and Department of Defense officials cooperatively created technology selection criteria" (32 C.F.R., Part 178.). This outcome is perhaps a best-case scenario of the strategic action/reaction approach. In many cases, Congress directs an agency to develop another plan or policy, or simply to stop the proposed plan, but there is still no interaction among the technical experts and the public. While the public has gained power in influencing the final policy, there is little discourse between the publics and the technical experts about the decision. As mentioned in chapter 2, Iacofano and others (1990) argue that public participation in policy decisions is based on two dimensions: "the degree of political decentralization or shared power" and "the degree of desired participant interaction" (p. 197). In this strategic action/reactionary approach, the power is not "shared" by the Army, it is temporarily taken away from the Army by Congress, and the interaction among the involved parties is at a minimum. The likelihood of a final policy that is appropriate from both a technical expert/designer and publics/user point of view is slim. Rather than an adversarial model that has interested parties reacting to decisions by other interested parties, we need to strive for an approach that brings together the interested parties in discussions *before* the decision is made to consider the options and how those options will affect all involved. An approach that values the different perspectives of an environmental decision and works to balance those perspectives in a decision may work toward both a more appropriate policy and a more ethical decision-making process.

CREATING THE ILLUSION OF CITIZEN POWER: PARTIAL AND PSEUDOPARTICIPATION MODELS

Perhaps the most common risk communication/public participation model is the one stipulated by the National Environmental Policy Act (NEPA), the Resource Conservation and Recovery Act (RCRA), the Clean Water Act (CWA), and the Clean Air Act (CAA) and in the case of the Newport Chemical Depot weapons disposal decision, implemented by the Army, the EPA, and the Indiana Department of Environmental Management (IDEM). This model, which can take two approaches—partial participation and pseudoparticipation[3]—seeks public input, but in very limited ways. While the *process* of including the public is the same with the two approaches, the difference between partial and pseudoparticipation lies primarily with the institution's vision of public input. In both cases, technical experts determine a plan for addressing an environmental issue, propose that plan to the public, and establish public meetings and comment periods for collecting public concerns and opinions about the plan before it is implemented (see figure 4.4).

This model allows public feedback only at the end of the policy production process—simply to evaluate the policy, too late to actually influence the design. While this model of risk communication and public participation requires public approval before the plan is implemented, allowing only a few input points after the decision has been made does not encourage significant participation in the decision-making process. Often, at this point in the decision-making process, much time and money has been invested in the proposed plan, and technical experts are not likely to want to spend additional time significantly revising the plan to reflect public concerns. Iacofano and others (1990) similarly argue that "simply inviting citizens to comment at public meetings on environmmental planning proposals will not ensure that their concerns are readily embraced by planners and taken into account in agency decision-making" (p. 197).

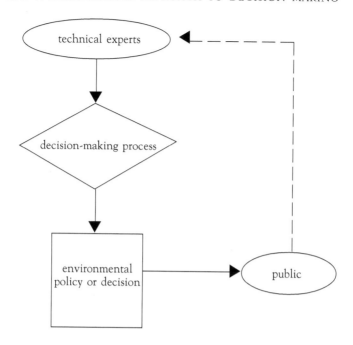

Figure 4.4: Partial Participation/Pseudoparticipation Model

This model and the two possible approaches are exemplified in the federal regulations of NEPA, RCRA, the CWA, and the CAA and their implementation through the Army, the EPA, and the IDEM. The federal regulations themselves can best be described by Iacofano's description of partial participation in the decision-making process where "two or more parties can influence each other, but the final power rests with one party only" (p. 198). This approach is often adopted in cases where citizen participation is the requirement of a federal regulation (Iacofano et al.) such as the NEPA, the RCRA, the CWA, and the CAA. Each of these regulations stipulate that a plan of action, or a permit to begin action, cannot be implemented until the public has been informed of the proposed plan or permit application and been given a set time to respond. Yet it is the responsibility of the federal agency in charge to determine how those comments will be used and whether they will impact the proposed plan or permit.

Because the final decision is ultimately that of a federal agency, the public participation activities are often staged as a strategy for fulfilling regulation requirements. This type of approach can easily "denigrate towards pseudo participation" (Iacofano et al., p. 198). Pseudoparticipation, according to Iacofano and colleagues, is often adopted for the purpose of *appearing* to actively involve citizens when a policy has already been determined by a smaller group (p. 198). Furthermore, the motivation for this approach may be to placate hostile citizen groups by making them believe that they have played a part in the development of a policy. I believe this denigration from partial participation to pseudoparticipation is what happened when the specific agencies involved in the chemical weapons disposal decision at the Newport Chemical Depot—the Army, the EPA, and IDEM—implemented the procedures for the federal regulations.

For example, while NEPA stipulates that the Army hold a "scoping" meeting to offer citizens an opportunity to express what concerns they had with the chemical weapons disposal project to help determine what issues would be included in the EIS for the Newport Chemical Depot, NEPA does not regulate that those comments actually affect what information is addressed in the EIS. Rather, it is up to the Army, as the responsible federal agency, to determine how the comment will affect the content of the EIS. In similar fashion, NEPA stipulates that the Army provide a comment period of forty-five days and hold a public meeting to solicit comments from the public once the draft EIS is published. In the case of the *Environmental Impact Statement for Pilot Testing of Neutralization/Supercritical Water Oxidation of VX Agent at Newport Chemical Depot*, the public was given an opportunity to voice concerns about the proposed plan, but because the decision on whether to incorporate those concerns into the final EIS fell to the Army, the comments amounted to no more than a listing in the appendix of the final EIS. If the federal agency responsible for preparing the EIS does not value the public comments, it can relegate the space required for public comment to a marginalized status.

The public participation requirements of the Resource Conservation and Recovery Act, the Clean Water Act, and the Clean Air Act present a similar scenario. While each of these federal regulations requires that the public be given an opportunity to comment on each permit before it is approved, the responsible agencies, in this case the EPA and IDEM, determine the format for the public meetings and whether or not the collected comments are "significant" enough to affect the permit.

The manner in which the EPA and IDEM chose to conduct the comment period and public meeting suggests that they were more concerned with placating the public than with soliciting information to help them determine whether or not to issue the permits. For example, one of the EPA officials conducting the meeting mentioned several times that this particular meeting was not required according to law but was being held as a service to the area residents. Yet, as noted in chapter 3, the EPA and IDEM officials literally prohibited a dialogue among the citizens and the officials during the public meeting to solicit comments. Individuals wishing to voice a comment were allowed to do so, but neither the officials nor the other citizens present were allowed to respond to that comment while the minutes were being recorded (observation of public meeting 8.12.99). While the meeting ad-hered to federal regulation public participation requirements, the officials were not interested in engaging in a discourse to learn about the public's input on the permits for the Newport Chemical Depot.

IDEM and the EPA's behavior regarding the permit applications for the Newport Chemical Depot aligns with the pseudoparticipation approach in which "policies may have already been made and public programs are devised so as to make participants feel that they had a useful role in creating them" (Iacofano et al., 198). This approach seems especially true in light of how the comments were all but ignored by the reviewers of the permit application as evidenced in an IDEM notice sent to interested parties. The notice, dated November 30, 1999, announced its intent to grant the hazard-ous waste operation and construction permit for the Newport Chemical Depot. It included a listing of the comments collected regarding the permit during the required forty-five-day comment period. Interestingly, the comments were divided into two categories: "responses to public comments" and "responses to facility comments." Each section contained the comment itself, IDEM's response to that comment, and what change was made in the permit appli-cation as a result of the comment. In the "response to public comments," IDEM indicated that no change occurred in the application permit as a result of public comments (even though one comment asked for clarification of how a VX leak from the containment area would affect surrounding drink-ing water wells). This issue, when voiced during a public meeting, posed great concern for several of the citizens because of the high number of residential wells in the Newport area. Further, this issue was related to the CWA, as part of the permit application, yet no clarification was made in the permit application. Yet, of the thirty-five comments made by the Army, all but four resulted in either further clarification, or a rewording. Clearly, pub-lic and facility comments were not valued equally, even when the public comment was relevant and valid.

The partial participation and pseudoparticipation models of public involvement are the most common models used in decisions of environmen-tal issues. Yet this process for including the public does not allow for input until after the policy/plan/decision has been made, making significant revi-sions as a result of public participation unlikely. Further, the way in which the process, and the federal regulations are set up, it is easy for agencies to go through the motions of collecting public comment without any intention of using the information they gather to revise the proposed plan or policy. Because public involvement comes so late in the process, even agencies interested in public input can only revise a proposed policy marginally if deadlines are imposed for reaching a policy decision (e.g., the hazardous waste incinerator in Katz and Miller [1996]). In order for citizens to contrib-ute significantly to environmental policy decisions, they must be brought into the decision-making process early enough to contribute to the *design* of the policy, and their input must be viewed as valuable knowledge capable of *constructing* risk through discourse with technical experts.

MODELS OF PUBLIC PARTICIPATION
AND THE NOTION OF PUBLIC

Though each of these models of risk communication—strategic action, reactionary, partial participation, and pseudoparticipation—is commonly employed in involving the public in decisions about environmental issues, each marginalizes the publics and the knowledge that those publics can contribute to an informed decision. A common flaw that these models share is the binary they set up between technical experts and the public. A clear hierarchy is established that preferences the technical experts above the publics. Not only does this binary set up an "us" versus "them" scenario that is often played out in current risk communication situations, but also it suggests that the public is a unified, abstract "other" with common concerns, values, opinions. This perception decontextualizes the people affected by a given risk and may therefore exclude affected groups in the construction of that risk. When the public is perceived of as the abstract other, it becomes possible to assume that public participation has been achieved through a few citizen representatives. But this assumption excludes many others affected by the decision, most often groups already oppressed or disadvantaged.

An approach to public participation that fails to account for the different communities of publics will also fail at an ethical approach to environmental decision making (Benhabib, pp. 104–105). According to Benhabib (1992), "in politics, it is less significant that 'we' discover 'the' general interest, but more significant that collective decisions be reached through procedures which are radically open and fair to all" (p. 9). Discourse and decisions are ethical only if all affected are allowed to participate (Young, 1990; Benhabib, 1992). Approaches that claim citizen participation through a few citizen representatives, that do not allow multiple publics access to decision making, or do not grant equal status to different groups, attempt to unify the public in ways that work to marginalize their contribution to the construction of a policy. In doing so, these approaches risk developing a policy that does not account for the differences of those affected and that is inappropriate for a particular situation.

As a result, throughout this study I have struggled with two questions regarding the public: (1) Who is the public? and (2) If the term *public* decontextualizes the many different communities of people involved, what is an appropriate term for the interested parties who are not a part of the federal agencies responsible for implementing an environmental policy?

Rather than try to define 'public' at this point, I look to whom the federal agencies considered the public. In order to do this—examining whom the agencies contacted about public meetings and information on the EIS and operating and construction permits. This information was sent to (1) individuals who explicitly asked to be placed on the "facility mailing list" and (2) local newspapers and radio stations including the *Danville Commercial News*, Danville, Illinois; the *Indianapolis Star*, Indiana; the *Tribune Star*, Terre Haute, Indiana; and the *Daily Clintonian*, Clinton, Indiana; WTHI, Terre Haute, Indiana; KISS, Covington, Indiana; WAXI, Rockville, Indiana; and WDNL, Danville, Illinois. Limiting notices and information to those who have asked to be placed on the mailing list and to area newspapers and radio stations suggests that the agencies involved in the Newport Chemical Depot chemical weapons disposal decision viewed the public as local residents only. This in part explains why the public affairs officer for the depot and the spokesperson for the company constructing the neutralization site were not only astonished that people from Kentucky attended several of the early public meetings, but saw their presence as an "attack" on the Army. Neither of these spokespersons mentioned that the Kentuckians might be interested in the outcome because another Army installation in Kentucky was grappling with the same chemical weapons disposal as Newport, or because they are downwind from the Newport Chemical Depot.

Even I was asked, "You aren't from here, are you?" when, during a public meeting in 1998, I explained my interest in attending the meetings concerning the Newport Chemical Depot. During each of the meetings I was viewed with downright suspicion even though I repeatedly explained that I was in favor of the neutralization project and not there to cause trouble but to observe ways in which the public was allowed to participate in decisions about environmental issues. As a further aside, it was in response to my explanation of why I attended the meetings that the spokesperson for Parsons (the company constructing the neutralization facility) noted that "public participation went against her way of thinking." Later when I interviewed the public affairs officer at the Newport Chemical Depot, I understood that some of the attention I received at the public meetings was because Parsons and the outreach office thought I must be interested in a public relations job at Parson (which three different people tried to offer me during the course of this project). When I first met the public affairs officer at the Newport Chemical Depot she said, "Oh, I know you. You came to a bunch of the meetings at the Lion's Club. We couldn't figure out who you were, so we thought you must want the public outreach job at Parsons" (personal interview, April 27, 2000). If an individual does not fit the Army, IDEM, and the EPA's narrow view of the public, his or her attendance at a public meeting is questioned.

Such a limited view of public excludes many individuals and groups affected by the issue. Individuals can be affected economically, morally, or aesthetically by an environmental decision (McGarity, p. 2), and striving to include only one group of those affected can mean developing a policy that either ignores or harms a group not invited to the decision-making table.

Rather than a model that works to include the "public" in decisions about environmental issues, an approach that works to identify "publics" affected by the issue and to include them will lead to more appropriate and just environmental policies. Here I am not suggesting that we simply replace *public* or *public participation*, the term used in federal regulations, with *publics* or *publics participation*. Working to ensure that all affected parties are heard is essential, but an examination of these common models of risk communication suggests that an ethical approach to public participation must also work to flatten the current hierarchy between technical experts and publics—to the point that each becomes seen as a multiple stakeholder. This is not to obscure the difference among the interested parties. Environmental policies cannot be constructed without technical expertise, but neither can appropriate policies be constructed without knowledge from multiple perspectives indicating how the policy could affect them. I am also not suggesting that the hierarchy can be completely flattened. Power struggles exist within all political discourse, but an approach that seeks to break down the binary of technical expert versus public by identifying multiple perspectives within those terms may lead to (1) less hostile situations among those involved in environmental issues and (2) input from all affected parties resulting in more just environmental policies.

While this approach to public participation in decisions about environmental issues might seem utopic given the most common models, one program involved in the Newport Chemical Depot weapons decision, the Assembly of Chemical Weapons Assessment, that strove to include all interested parties early in the decision-making process by all accounts (according to citizens, citizen groups, the DOD, and Congress) was successful in both involving stakeholders and making appropriate and environmental policy.

LIMITING PUBLIC PARTICIPATION: FACILITATED MODELS

The Assembly of Chemical Weapons Assessment, created by Congress to identify and demonstrate at least three nonincineration technologies for chemical disposal, established a space for all interested parties to work with representatives from the DOD to determine an appropriate disposal technology at each of the chemical weapons stockpile locations. This program mandated a "dialogue process by which affected citizens, state regulators and DOD officials cooperatively created technology selection criteria" (1996 Defense Appropriations Bill). The meetings to determine the disposal technology were held at each of the stockpile locations and opened to any interested parties. But unlike the other meetings run by representatives, these meetings were "facilitated" by an independent third party, the Keystone Institute. Keystone is an organization based in Colorado that provides facilitators for opposing environmental groups. Originally the ACWA meetings were all to be held in Arizona—significantly limiting who could attend the meetings. However, a small group of citizens presented a list of "demands" asking that the ACWA meetings be held at each installation and that an independent scientist "with full access to NRC information" be provided for the discussion as well (personal interview, May 7, 2000). The ACWA meetings function on consensus with citizens carrying an equal vote with DOD representatives. As noted in chapter 3, these meetings were the first related to the Newport Chemical Depot in which the citizens were on an equal level with scientists in a dialogue.

The ground rules for the meetings are established at the beginning by all the participants. For the ACWA meetings regarding the disposal at Newport, the citizens, independent and NRC scientists, and DOD representatives first worked together to establish criteria for choosing a disposal technology at Newport. After the criteria had been established, chemical disposal vendors (or "clean-up contractors") presented proposals for destroying the VX at the Newport Chemical Depot to the citizens, scientists, and DOD representatives. The citizens, scientists, and DOD representatives then negotiated which technology proposals they believed fit the criteria they had already established. The DOD had promised to pilot test any five technologies that passed all the established criteria. At the end of the negotiations, the group had approved six technologies that involved neutralization of the VX agent. In this approach, all involved parties worked together from the beginning, establishing criteria for a policy, then determining together by consensus whether a proposed plan fulfilled the criteria in order to decide on a proposal that all involved parties considered acceptable (see figure 4.5). Of special note is that the information presented in the vendor proposals was complex and technical. According to Mowrer, this approach was especially useful in promoting a dialogue among the participants. She notes that during negotiations, after each participant made an argument or asked a question, a facilitator would say, "I heard you say this. . . . Is that what you said?" (or "Did I understand you correctly?"). Such strategies hold promise for encouraging all the participants to listen to each comment.

This approach has also been used in a few other environmental issue decisions. McGarity (1998), calling this the mediation model, describes a dispute the Keystone Institute was asked to facilitate between a developer who wanted to construct a solid waste facility in Texas and members of the local community where the facility was to be built. According to McGarity, "at the core of the Keystone process is the idea of facilitating dialogue between the applicant and the public" (p. 5). However, according to McGarity, the reason for involving the public early in the decision-making process in this approach is to "work to reduce the potential for misinformation about local project for which risk perceptions are very high" (p. 5).

While this process for involving the public shows promise for both granting publics access to the decision-making table and for making just decisions, this model, like the partial participation model, can degrade into

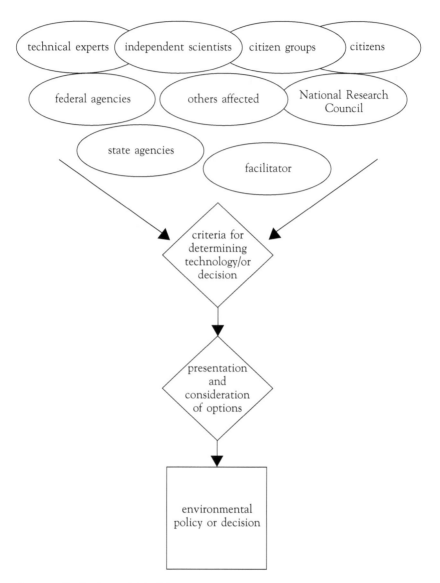

Figure 4.5: Facilitated Model

pseudoparticipation if the federal agencies, or responsible parties, are more interested in placating the publics than learning from them. In such instances the agencies may find ways to navigate the public space if they do not see the publics' input as necessary for constructing an appropriate policy. Further, while supposedly all interested parties are welcome, interested parties are not *sought out*, and notice of the meetings is not widely circulated.

There is no effort on the part of the facilitator to ensure that affected parties at least have representation. In fact, the meetings can proceed with only the Citizen Advisory Committee present to represent selected citizen viewpoints. Citizen Advisory Committees rarely represent the diverse range of perspectives a given community holds on an issue resulting in portions of the community being silenced. An approach that works as an advocate to identify and include the multiple users of a policy would better ensure an appropriate end policy. Still, I see the facilitated model as one from which we can build to create a heuristic for a more ethical approach to public participation in environmental issues.

PARTICIPATION AND POWER
AT THE NEWPORT CHEMICAL DEPOT

The many institutions and programs involved in the chemical weapons disposal decision make up a complex and conflicting picture of risk communication practices. Examining the public participation approaches used by different institutions in the chemical weapons disposal decision at the Newport Chemical Depot, we see a variety of risk communication practices and a range of public involvement within those practices. Again borrowing a framework from participatory design studies, I map the degree of power and participation each approach afforded publics as a way to reveal their often marginalized status and powerlessness in risk communication practices at the Newport Chemical Depot (see figure 4.6).

This map reveals conflicts between public participation regulations and public participation approaches used by federal agencies carrying out those regulations. For example, while the wording of the NEPA, RCRA, CWA, and CAA regulations suggests a partial participation approach to risk communication, the Army, the EPA, and the Indiana Department of Environmental Management employed a pseudoparticipation approach in the public meetings for collecting comments. Further, more than one approach may be employed by the same institution. For example, approaches used by the Army ranged from strategic action to pseudoparticipation (and to some degree full participation for their roll in the Assembled Chemical Weapons Assessment program). Perhaps most important, the map reveals that too few risk communication practices allow affected parties full participation in decisions about environmental issues. Full participation will require that affected parties be involved earlier in the decision-making process and that their input be valued, and reflected, in the resulting policy. Full participation, then, requires a redistribution of power and procedural change in current risk communication practices.

My arguments thus far assume that risk communication practices and the decision-making process of environmental issues need changing. However, if individuals are trained in the complex issues of risk assessment and

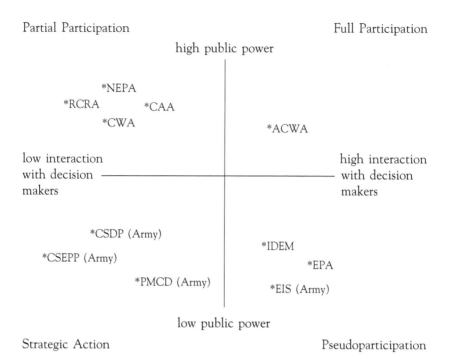

Figure 4.6: Public Participation in the Chemical Weapons Disposal Decision at the Newport Chemical Depot

risk management, why should the current decision-making process for environmental issues work toward involving the publics more significantly? Risk assessors and political scientists assert numerous reasons why the public only serves to muddle the decision-making process.

In his essay, "Informing and Educating the Public about Risk," Paul Slovic (1986) argues that including publics in decisions about environmental issues is difficult because of the "limitations of public understanding" (p. 404). Noting that "communicators must appreciate the wisdom and folly in public attitudes and perceptions," he urges risk communicators to recognize that "people's perceptions of risk are often inaccurate," that "risk information may frighten and frustrate the public," and that "naive views are easily manipulated by presentation format" (pp. 404–405). The public's role in risk decisions, according to Slovic, is to accept a decision made by technical experts, and the risk communicators' role is to provide the publics with enough information to persuade them to accept the technical expert's decision. According to *The Health Risk Communicator*, a publication of the subcommittee on risk communication and education Public Health Service

(PHS), Slovic conducts risk communication workshops for the DOD and the Army, teaching agency representatives how to involve the public in environmental risk decisions. It is little wonder then why the most common models used by the Army reflect Slovic's "inform to conform" attitude.

McGarity (1998) argues that public participation is not an "unalloyed good," noting that involving the public in technical decisions is time consuming and often results in delays to implementing policies already under tight deadlines. Further, he asserts that "allowing individuals and groups to challenge an agency's decision making forces the agency to expend resources defending itself that might otherwise be spent pursuing its statutory mission" (p. 3). He maintains that there are cases in which regulatory agencies would be justified in excluding the public from the decision-making process. McGarity argues that regulatory agencies "might legitimately attempt to limit participation to exclude irrelevant evidence and arguments" that might delay policy implementation or "exclude especially confrontational forms of participation in the interest of decorum" (p. 3). He also claims that instances where proprietary or commercially sensitive material is discussed, agencies and technological companies have the right to protect their research by excluding the public (p. 3). Conflicting with the common assumption that publics simply cannot understand the technical aspects associated with environmental risks, this argument equally marginalizes publics by assuming that their interests in risk decisions might be financial gain as competitors' spies. Clearly, there is much tension surrounding public participation. With public participation creating so many obstacles in environmental decision making, what purpose is served by working to include the public even more significantly? I argue that in the long run, risk decisions that are actively designed by both technical experts and publics are not only more ethical but also more appropriate, efficient, and economical.

Ethical environmental policies occur only when all affected parties have the ability to *actively* participate in the decision-making process (Benhabib, 1992; Foucault, 1982; Gaventa, 1980; Porter, 1997; Young, 1990). Unfortunately, ethics suits alone may not persuade federal agencies to completely overhaul their approach to public participation. Yet approaches to public participation that work to include all affected parties early in the decision-making process would, in the long run, work to the agencies' advantage. Under current models, publics, outraged because they have not been included in the decision-making process, find ways to delay or overturn environmental decisions, resulting in high costs for agencies.

For example, Belsten (1996) discusses a situation in Bloomington, Indiana, in which the EPA, Westinghouse, IDEM, Monroe county officials, and Bloomington city officials worked for ten years to determine how to remediate PCB-contaminated soil. When the agencies announced that an incinerator would be built to burn the contaminated soil, community groups lobbied elected officials to prevent the construction of the incinerator. More than fifteen years after the issue began, a policy for remediation had not been implemented (pp. 32–33). In this case, government agencies made the decision and asked the community to approve it. The community refused. The cost for the risk assessments, the public meetings to defend the decision, and court has been astronomical. And all the while the PCBs continue to pose a hazard to human health and the environment.

While there is no guarantee that another approach would have resulted in a conflict-free situation, an approach that involved the publics at the earliest stages could have at least prevented the agencies from spending ten years and large amounts of money investigating a technology that would be so adamantly rejected. And even in cases where publics do not voice objections, a policy that has been constructed without input from the users of that policy will likely experience site-specific glitches (such as the evacuation plan at Newport) resulting in the need to design another more appropriate policy. Involving affected parties at the earliest stages of decision making reduces the likelihood that a plan or policy will have to be defended for years or redesigned. Not unlike the advantages of including users in the design of computer systems, including publics in the design of policies will often increase "customer satisfaction" of the policy. In summary, working toward more ethical approaches to environmental decision making—ones that identify unequal power relations and see publics as producers of knowledge—is advantageous to agencies and publics alike.

CREATING A SPACE FOR PUBLIC DISCOURSE
IN TECHNICAL ISSUES: A PARTICIPATORY DESIGN APPROACH
TO POLICY DECISION MAKING

Changing current models of risk communication to more significantly involve the public will require getting agencies to see that citizens (1) have local knowledge that may expose problems in proposed solutions and (2) will bear the burden of the risk and risk policy and must be respected from that perspective. And while convincing agencies to change their approach is a struggle, the numerous examples of failed and inappropriate policies that resulted from lack of citizen input is slowly encouraging agencies to look for alternatives to the most common risk communication approaches (consider Assembled Chemical Weapons Assessment's use of the "new" facilitated model, for example). What is missing in the current approaches to risk communication, then, are heuristics that consider the power relations among the involved parties and strategies that work toward both creating a dialogue among those affected *and* gathering knowledge about the risk from *all* affected. In current models, public comments are often allowed but not solicited in a way in which they can often be used to point out flaws in a proposed plan. In other words, if risk assessors approached public input as a way to learn something new about the risk (for example, "Here is how we are thinking about the policy, can you think of any reason why it would not work in your community, or what would work better?") publics could take a more active role, and policies could be more appropriate and just. An approach that provides strategies for addressing those issues and gathering that knowledge is needed in risk communication and other environmental policy decisions.

Participatory design, a type of usability research often employed in the design of computer systems and urban planning, addresses these issues of power and publics knowledge and shows promise as a way to think about a more ethical approach to risk communication. An examination of how participatory design approaches address these issues of power and user participation in technical decisions may provide strategies for more significantly involving publics in the technical decisions of environmental issues.

Theorists such as Pelle Ehn (1992), Langdon Winner (1995), and Adler and Winograd (1992) have been among a recent group of technology researchers to advance arguments for involving users in product development earlier and in more substantial ways. Arguments in support of a more participatory approach point to the fact that users often have a type of expertise about how a product will be used in a particular situation that technical developers do not have. According to Ehn (1992), participatory design,[4] as a design strategy, intersects political and technical discourse by "raising questions of democracy, power, and control in the workplace" and promising "that the participation of users in the design process can contribute importantly to successful design and high-quality products" (p. 96).

Participatory design evolved out of Swedish labor union fears in the late 1960s that computers and new technologies would automate workers out of a job. As a result, participatory design approaches sought to engage workers in designing systems that would enhance rather than eliminate their jobs. For example, Pelle Ehn describes a project in the early 1980s where graphic union workers in the Swedish newspapers industry, such as typesetters, lithographers, and graphic artists, worked with management of a Stockholm newspaper and computer scientists to design a new system of computerized graphics for layout and typesetting (Ehn, pp. 112–113; Winner, pp. 78–79). Using a newly developed design approach that drew on the expertise of the designers, the management, *and* the workers, the group examined the current work practices, considered the possibilities of a new computer graphics system (and how that would affect the workers), and developed a technical document detailing the system specifications to computer suppliers (Winner, p. 79).

According to Ehn, one of the computer scientists involved in the project, participatory design assumes that "users possess the needed practical understanding but lack insight into new technical possibilities. The designer must understand the specific labor process that uses a tool" (p. 112). Ehn maintains that designing the system required mutual learning from all involved parties: "[G]raphic workers learned about the technical possibilities and constraints of computer technology, while we as designers learned about their craft or profession" (p. 112). In this project, the decisions about the design of the new computer system were made not solely by the technical experts—the computer scientists—but with the workers—the users of the computer system. Ehn maintains that a participatory approach works to create a real dialogue among affected parties in an effort to gather the different kinds knowledge about the system that different parties can offer in constructing a system that is both technically sound and usable by the workers.

At first glance participatory design appears an odd pairing with risk communication and public participation in decisions about environmental issues—in part because participatory design is about the process of *production* (of computer systems), and risk communication is about *management* (of risk, and often of citizens in that risk communication focuses its energy on persuading publics to adapt to expert views and decisions). However, this emphasis on managing creates many of the current communication problems, and risk communication would be better served to focus on the process of production. That is, rather than focusing on how to bring public perception into conformity with expert decisions, risk communication should focus on *producing* an effective, appropriate, and just risk policy. Participatory design approaches work to decentralize decision making and participation in the design process, an approach that is needed to redistribute the common imbalance of power in current risk communication practices. And unlike current risk communication models, participatory design seeks out the users/nontechnical public and sees them as able to contribute much-needed knowledge to the design of the product. Just as workers know how a computer system will affect their ability to produce graphics, publics know how a policy will affect their community (both are users of a technology) and as such can work with the technical experts to create a technology that adequately fits their needs. Specifically, Ehn asserts that participatory design is an "interactive process of production that encourages users of a product to provide feedback that informs the design of the product from its inception through its production" (p. 112). By including nontechnical users in the design or decision-making phase of technology, participatory design approaches grant users epistemological status.

It is how participatory design approaches challenge the assumption that only technical experts produce knowledge that creates a space for public participation in technical issues. According to Langdon Winner (1995),

> most thinkers in our tradition have placed technology and politics in separate categories, defining citizen roles as completely isolated from the realities of technical practice and technical change [. . .] However, participatory design created a public space for the political deliberation about the qualities of an emerging technical artifact. A diverse set of needs, viewpoints, and priorities come together to determine which material and social patterns will be designed, built, and put into operation. (pp. 78–79)

According to Ehn, even though the users did not speak the same formal languages of system analysis as the designers, the group was able to discuss complex and technical issues by addressing problems users had performing day to day tasks with the current system and working to solve those problems through usability research techniques such as mockups and scenarios (p. 112).

VALUING CIVIC DISCOURSE IN POLICY DEBATES

A look at usability research techniques may illuminate ways that technical experts and the public can work together to construct a complex and technical product—from a computer system to an environmental policy. Usability is a range of research strategies that explore how users interact with a product such as documentation, computer interfaces, or virtually any technology. By integrating information about and by the users into the design phase of the product, researchers hope to modify and improve the product to better meet the needs of actual users. In part because a number of divergent fields conduct usability studies, and contribute to the literature on usability, there exists a variety of perspectives associated with this type of research (one of which is Scandinavian participatory design). These perspectives affect both the focus of the research and how it is conducted. For example, Sullivan (1989) notes,

> psychologists and engineers in human-computer interaction typically use experiments and case studies to study the usability of interfaces and systems; sociologists and anthropologists use ethnography and field methods when they study the computing of organizations; marketers typically use interviews and surveys to study consumer preferences; document designers, educational psychologist, and writers in technical communication use various exploratory and text-based methods to study the usability of educational material. (pp. 257–258)

Because usability can refer to such a wide range of practices, some scholars have found it useful to distinguish between usability testing and usability research (Blythe, p. 3; Johnson, 1997, p. 367).

In his distinction between usability testing and research, Stuart Blythe asserts that usability testing is "a range of tests often conducted near the end of product development" (p. 3). This approach involves validating the accuracy and comprehensiveness of a near-finished product in a lab setting (Weiss, p. 175). While this type of usability can yield more effective and polished documents, it has come under criticism for its focus on the product rather than the user. Weiss asserts that "after-the-fact" usability testing is flawed because it all but eliminates the chance that the product will undergo significant design changes based on the users' responses (p. 175). For example, if users have trouble using a particular software program, rather than changing the program itself, designers frequently increase the documentation in the program's manual to prevent users from making the "errors." Instead of focusing on how actual users might utilize and modify the product in a particular context, the designers focus on making the users adapt to the product. This version of usability values the product and the designers' conception of that product over users and their needs. Further, this type of usability views users as end-of-the-line consumers without the knowledge to contribute to the design and implementation of the product (Johnson, 1998, p. 57).

Rather than end-of-the-line testing, usability research refers to an iterative process of studying how users interact with products in specific situations and of encouraging users to engage in dialogue with the designers about the design of the product from its inception through its production (Johnson, 1998; Sullivan, 1989; Blythe, 1997; Ehn, 1992). An important distinction between usability testing and usability research is the assumptions each makes about users. Unlike usability testing, usability *research* envisions meeting the needs of the users as its focus and views users as valuable and capable of contributing to the design of the product. Johnson argues that rather than seeing users merely as end-of-the-line consumers or "tool-users" those who engage in usability research see users as "producers"—those who have knowledge of how a product is used (p. 57)—and as "participatory citizens"—who have knowledge of how a product is used within a community (p. 61). He asserts that usability research values this user knowledge and grants these users the ability to participate in the decision-making process (p. 32). With this distinction, Johnson argues that a user-centered theory questions the "basic assumptions of hierarchy, power, and control" (p. 46). For example, recall Johnson's discussion of how Seattle drivers were able to help alleviate traffic problems there. Because of the drivers' knowledge of how city roads, bridges, and overpasses were used in their city, they were invited to participate in the decision-making process (p. 66). With his discussion of users as citizens, Johnson brings usability into the realm of public policy. It is here, with its research aim to determine what would improve the condition of involved users that a critical notion of usability research emerges.

Usability research methods are implemented to collect and analyze data about how users use, modify, and react to products in particular situations. There are numerous methods employed in usability research including different types of direct questioning and observations that can often be combined into one study (Sullivan, 1989, p. 259). Direct questioning methods such as surveys and interviews are useful for discovering what users anticipate happening before they use a product, their attitude about a product, and their reaction to using the product (p. 259). For example, a researcher who wants to investigate the user's reaction to a web site may use an interview to ask that user if she was able to find the information she was looking for, what problems she had using the page, if she expected something that was not there. Questioning is also useful for analyzing users' needs at the beginning of a design phase. However, Blythe notes that this approach has limitations because users may not be able to envision possible uses of products if they have no prior experience with the product (p. 6).

Observations such as protocol analysis and on-site observations provide researchers with information about how users actually use and interact with a product. In protocol analysis observations, researchers ask users to talk aloud about what they are doing, thinking about, or looking for as they use a product. This method is useful for both finding out what happens when users attempt to use a product and for tapping into the motivation for their actions (Sullivan, 1989, p. 260). On-site observations allow researchers to study users in the context of their work environment (Kukla, Clemens, Morse, and Cash, p. 45). Because on-site observation encourages users to "view the product through the needs of their work," this method allows the researcher to see the product from the user's point of view (Kukla et al., p. 45). In this less artificial setting, the users' interactions with the products may be more closely aligned with their typical use of the product, but their reasons for performing particular actions are less likely to be revealed. However, combining pre- and postobservational interviews with this approach may tap into some of the users' motivations.

Focus groups, which allow users to interact with a product and then discuss that interaction with other users and researchers, can also provide useful information about users' reactions to a product. Because users are encouraged to discuss their expectations and reactions at length with others, this method can often provide rich feedback about additional possible uses for the product. Focus groups often include moderators, sometimes the researcher, who strive to facilitate a dialogue among the users.

Similar participatory design usability techniques include scenarios, mockups, and prototyping that bring together the designers and the users in discussions of how a technology is and can be used. For example, in scenarios, designers often ask users to "tell a story about their work" that provides the designers with ideas of how the technology is used in any given circumstance (Kukla et al., p. 56). Mockups can be used to provide designers with information about how users interact with a proposed technology. According to Kukla and others, "Developers' expectations about how users will use a system are often incomplete. Users often use various tools and interfaces in completely unforeseen ways—and in many cases better ways— than those intended by the designers" (p. 48). As a result, developing a mockup of a "proposed system and a simulation strategy to allow users to interact with it allows systems engineers, human factors engineers, organizational designers, technologists, and users to work together to design useful systems" (p. 48). While mockups typically involve constructing cardboard box simulations of a proposed system, the same type of approach used in mockups—inquiring how users would interact with a proposed technology or plan—would have been useful for situations such as evacuation plans at the Newport Chemical Depot.

Another usability research technique involves prototyping a design suggested by users as a way to ensure that limitations to the design, imposed by technology, will not adversely affect its usefulness for users. Because it is possible that suggestions made by users are not technically or financially feasible, prototyping allows designers to develop a version of the proposed technology in order to examine whether the system works the way the user intended (Kukla et al., p. 49). Waiting until the system has been completely developed to test its usefulness ensures that little will be revised. This approach also provides an understanding of how the technology will affect a particular situation.

While some of these methods may be employed in isolation in the narrow conception of usability testing, it is the ongoing use of these methods in combination from the beginning of the design phase; the attempt to study the user interacting with the product in specific situations; the focus on meeting the users' needs; and the belief that actual users possess the knowledge to contribute to the design that distinguishes the methods.

Usability research is powerful because "users"—publics, stakeholders—have important knowledge often excluded from decision making, and it is this "user knowledge" that usability research methods can access. Users in all contexts are potential participants in decision making about technologies—from computer interfaces and documentation to city highways. As a result, usability research that focuses on the needs of the users from the beginning of the design process and works to allow users meaningful input throughout the entire process has the potential to bring about change. However, Ehn (1992) maintains that participation in design strategies such as these can only be successful if it makes a difference for the participants and implementation, of the results are likely. "Users," she asserts, "must have a guarantee that their design efforts are taken seriously" (p. 129).

I do not mean to suggest that publics can contribute only local or user knowledge or that they cannot understand the technical aspects of a decision about environmental issues. On the contrary, publics can (and must be able to) understand the technical aspects and contribute knowledge based upon that information, as evidenced in the Assembled Chemical Weapons Assessment meetings. My point, rather, is that regardless of technical expertise, all involved publics have knowledge about how a policy can, will, or could be used in a particular situation and that this knowledge is essential to constructing an appropriate and just policy.

Usability research, especially Scandinavian approaches that aim for democratic participation of users in designing complex technologies, shows promise as a heuristic for involving publics in decisions about complex environmental issues. Yet Scandinavian participatory design cannot be taken wholesale out of the context for which it was developed and applied to risk communication approaches. The situation surrounding union labor in Scandinavia is complexly different than the one surrounding U.S. publics concerned with environmental issues. Scandinavian approaches look at participants as workers and clients, and as such grant that these individuals have a degree of expertise because they use the complex machines. As a result there is less hierarchical baggage between their notion of expert and user (worker) and a risk assessors' notion of expert and user (citizen). Even within the context, Ehn points out limitations with the approaches, specifically the required resources and funds to allow groups of designers, workers, and union staff to work together over long periods of time.

Further, Winner (1995) mentions critics who warn that Scandinavian approaches "work at a superficial level within the technologies they confront" (p. 81). Noting that complex levels of design and operation are understood by only a few, he addresses Wengenroth's claim that technologies may be restructured only at the user-interface level as a way to placate users. While not dismissing the concern completely, Winner notes that the projects he has examined seemed "fairly deep-seeking" (p. 81). He notes that workers and designers together rejected system options that contained "entrenched forms of hierarchical work organization" that they found "anti-democratic and de-skilling" (p. 81). As illustrated in the current partial and facilitated models, using a participatory approach itself will not guarantee significant participation if the group with the ultimate say in the decision making works to subvert the public participation. While a Scandinavian participatory design approach cannot be applied to other situations without considering the differences among those situations, it does offer strategies for involving the publics that might be adapted to situations outside of computer systems.

In fact, participatory design strategies are currently used in situations quite similar to public involvement in environmental issues. Based on the belief that "communities should have a right to participate in the planning of their own future" (Sanoff, p. 6), urban planning and design studies often incorporate participatory design strategies for involving city planners, architects, and community members[5] in discussions of urban planning. According to Sanoff (1990), participatory approaches to urban planning assume,

> The designer's job is no longer to produce finished and unalterable solutions but to extract solutions from a continuous confrontation with those who still use his/her work. The designer's energy and imagination will be completely directed to raising the level of awareness of his/her partners (clients/users) in the discussion, and the solution will come out of the exchanges between the two; the designer states his/her opinions, provides technical information, and discusses the consequences of various alternatives, just as the users state their opinions and contribute their expertise. (p. 7)

Using many of the same usability research methods described above, the urban planners gather information about how specific communities would and could use a particular type of building, transportation system, roadway, or city block. Again, the situation in urban planning is somewhat different than risk communication. Risk communication often deals with decisions for remediating areas contaminated with hazardous substance, a situation that can create more conflicts than a less deadly issue. Yet, the strategies for seeking knowledge from the users of a technology seem useful despite the different situations.

According to Sanoff, what differentiates a participatory design approach to urban planning is the redistribution of power that gives citizens more say in decisions that affect them. Quoting Arnstein (1969), Sanoff argues,

> It is the redistribution of power that enables the have-not citizens, presently excluded from the political and economic process, to be deliberately included in the future.[...] Participation without redistribution of power is an empty and frustrating process for the powerless. It allows the power holders to claim that all sides were considered but makes it possible for only some of these to benefit. It maintains the status quo. (qtd in Sanoff, p. 6)

Participatory design in urban planning, according to Sanoff, does not separate the participation process from the design process. Sanoff describes a housing project in New South Wales in which citizen concerns about security, privacy, and community facilities were substantially reflected in the outcome of the project.

Integrating the participation and design process is not enough. Input must be gathered from all affected parties (Iacofano et al). In describing a project to design a "timed transfer" bus system, Iacofano and others address the need to understand how the system would affect the bus riders, bus drivers, public transportation staff, and board of commissioners for the city. They noted that while each group could provide useful information about how the system would be used, the information from each group might be gathered using different research techniques appropriate for each group. For example, bus riders were given a twenty-five-question survey and asked to participate in both a focus group and a survey (the survey was added later as a way to reach more drivers unable to attend the focus group). The staff participated in interviews, while the board of commissioners participated in two-to-one interviews about thirteen different topics of concern related to the bus system (p. 200). This illustrates an important point about participatory design. Not only are there often many different users involved but there are also different manners of gathering information. While a public meeting involving all of these affected groups together might have been useful as well, the methods used by Iacofano and colleagues worked to ensure that many voices were heard and were not drowned out by more vocal groups during a public meetings. Similar methods might be employed in risk communication situations as a way to reach citizens unable to attend public meetings often held during "business hours."

When environmental policy decision-making, then, is informed by participatory design, public knowledge of how a policy would affect a community is valued as something technical experts lack, but need to design an effective policy. Risk communication becomes an iterative process of initiating discussions and negotiations of evidence, assessments, and social concerns among involved parties who seek to construct a policy (see figure 4.7).

Notice that a participatory design approach to risk communication would look in many ways like the mediated model of risk communication used by the Assembled Chemical Weapons Assessment (see figure 4.6). There are notable differences. In most models, it is only state or federal agencies who identify issues of concern. In a participatory approach, where the public's knowledge is valued, any affected party or agency could identify an environmental concern or issue for investigation. This difference is important because it begins to dismantle the top down approach to environmental decision making and to grant citizens epistemological status. Additionally, where the mediated model employed by ACWA allowed all interested parties to participate (assuming all interested parties are able to attend the meetings), a participatory approach actively seeks participation from affected parties in the belief that they have much-needed knowledge to contribute to an effective policy. And in that belief, a participatory approach engages in research practices to gather that knowledge. (Simplistically, while an individual might simply attend a meeting based on the mediated model, in the participatory approach an individual would be asked to contribute information about how a particular technology would affect him or her in everyday life). These activities could benefit from someone who can investigate institutional procedures to consider whether all affected parties are involved and who can help initiate activities to gather information from both the technical experts and publics in a way that can lead to an informed policy. It is here that I see a role of the technical communicator. Technical communicators have long been advocates for users (Jones, Johnson-Eilola, Johnson), employing usability research techniques in situations beyond that of computer systems and documentation. Technical communicators possess the critical research skills to identify the ethical and political issues present in risk communication/ environmental policy situations and to consider approaches that grant more power to citizens. While the technical communicator/rhetorician may not fill the facilitator's role—I am not certain there is a space for us there yet—technical communicators and rhetoricians can find spaces for these investigations and activities through their community-based research work. The last chapters will investigate these roles and spaces further.

In summary, there are many models of risk communication and public participation employed in decisions about environmental issues as seen in the chemical weapons disposal decision at the Newport Chemical Depot. Yet

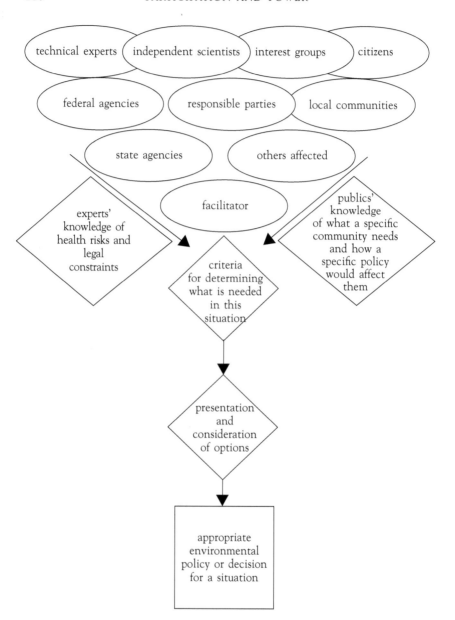

Figure 4.7: Participatory Approach

few of these approaches allow publics to be involved in significant ways. These approaches are not only unethical, in that they deny publics the right to be involved in decisions that affect their own lives, but they also lead to ineffective and inappropriate policies and plans. Strategies that seek out publics and their knowledge of how a policy would affect them may bring about more ethical and appropriate decision making. Strategies from participatory design provide useful heuristics for considering ways to gather information from the publics and more significantly involve publics in technical discourse about environmental issues. However, seeking one "model" or even approach for risk communication may not ensure that publics are allowed to actively participate in the decision-making process.

Chapter 5 looks at the institutional assumptions and procedures at work in shaping public participation and from those assumptions and procedures presents a participatory heuristic for identifying obstacles to public participation and for improving public involvement in policy decisions.

CHAPTER FIVE

PARTICIPATION AND POWER: TRANSFORMING THE POSSIBILITIES OF PUBLIC PARTICIPATION IN ENVIRONMENTAL POLICY DECISIONS

My goal for this research has been to examine ways in which the public is allowed to participate in decisions of environmental risk issues in an effort to consider ways to grant citizens more power and direct involvement in the decision-making process. Throughout this project I have argued the need for a more critical rhetoric approach to risk communication that encourages significant public participation by (1) identifying unequal power relations in the decision-making process, (2) contextualizing risk by valuing the local knowledge publics can contribute to a policy, and (3) viewing risk as socially constructed by involving the public early enough in the decision-making process to affect the resulting policy. In this chapter I want to consider the findings from my inquiry into public participation as a way to develop heuristics for evaluating whether risk communication practices encourage the kind of active participation by all affected that results in just and appropriate environmental risk policies. I draw this idea of developing heuristics from Sullivan and Porter (1998), who develop heuristics to provide criteria for judging political practices in particular settings (p. 109).

Drawing from Young (1990), I have argued that just and appropriate environmental risk policies require the active participation of all affected in the decision-making process and critiqued institutions of risk communication for preventing active participation by granting ultimate power in the decision-making process to technical experts. Because institutions regulate public participation in decisions about environmental issues, and because by critiquing institutions we can discover ways in which power is exercised (at least Foucault and others argue that we can), I frame my inquiry through the lens of critiquing the ways in which institutions constitute risk communication practices and public participation.

By examining and mapping citizen participation in existing cases of environmental public policy, we have seen the typically marginalized status of the public in environmental risk decisions. The citizens' status is marked by low interaction with the technical experts as well as little power in influencing the final policy. Risk communication practices focused on either (1) bombarding citizens with a one-way flow of information in an effort to bring their perceptions about risk into conformity with the technical experts or (2) holding public meetings and allowing public comments that attempt to placate publics but that do not influence the final policy.

Examining existing cases illustrates how the construction of risk policies is currently separated from public participation about risk. In these cases, risk assessors determined the risk and the solution and presented it to the public for approval. When these models fail to see risk as socially constructed, they fail to offer a space for significant public participation. According to the cases examined in chapter 2, publics often react, not to the technology chosen, but to not being involved in the decision-making process (Belsten, 1996; Katz and Miller, 1996). Yet institutions who involve the public in superficial ways in order to avoid hostile reactions often find that citizens are not deceived by their placating measures.

By and large, the case of chemical weapons disposal at the Newport Chemical Depot illuminates similar institutional constraints on public participation in the decision-making process. Yet the multiple perspectives that observing and interviewing allowed illuminated additional insights into the ways in which institutions inhibited active participation by publics affected by a risk decision.

INSTITUTIONS OFTEN EMPLOY RISK COMMUNICATION MODELS THAT SEPARATE POLICY CONSTRUCTION FROM PUBLIC PARTICIPATION

One of the most obvious similarities between the existing cases and the Newport case is the models of risk communication and public participation employed in both that marginalize public involvement by separating the construction of risk from public participation. While the common models range from no public participation to limited public participation, the Newport case especially illustrates how these different models have not necessarily evolved over time to include more participation, but may each still be implemented by an agency as a way to control public involvement. Remember, for example, the Army's Chemical Demilitarization Program that worked as a buffer between the concerns of the citizens and the actual decision makers. The program established the outreach office and required that public questions about the Newport Chemical Depot or the proposed plans for chemical weapons disposal be directed to the outreach office rather than to the Army officials who make the decisions. Likewise, the National Environmental Policy Act's process for public participation in EISs that allows for public input only after decisions have been made by "experts." These models resemble in many ways the Shannon and Weaver model of communication where knowledge is constructed prior to communication by the sender and any other communication by the receiver is considered "noise." According to Johnson-Eilola (1997) the task of the receiver in the Shannon and Weaver model "is to decode a preexisting code, to discover the truth—the information—of the message; the receiver, ideally, acts as the mirror image of the sender" (p. 68). He further asserts that the model has as its goals "increased technical efficiency" (p. 53). This is an understandable goal from the standpoint of technical experts who see their role as givers of knowledge and persuaders of policy decisions and view public participation as a delay in the implementation of a policy or environmental action. Yet, not only does this oppress the publics by relegating them to the role of passive receivers, with no control over decisions that affect them, but it also assumes that the technical experts alone are able to determine appropriate policies—an assumption that was challenged in the case of chemical weapons disposal at the Newport Chemical Depot. A framework that seeks to produce ethical policies will work toward dissolving the separation between policy construction and public participation by involving citizens throughout the decision making process.

TECHNICAL EXPERTISE ALONE DOES NOT CONSTRUCT AN APPROPRIATE AND JUST POLICY

While the institutions involved in the case of chemical weapons disposal at Newport Chemical Depot relied almost solely on technical experts to determine risk decisions (the Assembled Chemical Weapons Assessment program seems the only exception, and it is not acknowledged as existing in the EIS), the policies developed for the VX disposal are not necessarily technically sound or appropriate for the affected publics. Recall, for example, the evacuation plan that currently fails to accommodate the additional influx of individuals who visit the area during seasonal festivals. Local knowledge from publics could have exposed the problems in the evacuation plan before that plan was printed up on calendars and flyers and distributed through the area.

By local knowledge, I am not referring to only information from the area residents, but from all those affected by the decision. For example, citizens at another Army weapons installation may be greatly affected by the decision at Newport because that decision will likely be the one the Army proposes at other weapons installations.[1]

Further, as Young (1990) and Winner (1995) assert, expert status is often arbitrary. Given the opportunity citizens can, and often do, acquire the technical knowledge to understand the proposed risk policy (Young, p. 84). This is especially true in state and federal environmental citizen groups whose members are often experts in law, chemistry, and other fields related to environmental issues. The Assembled Chemical Weapons Assessment meetings for considering disposal technologies at Newport, which were considered a success by technical experts and Newport citizens alike, illustrates that publics and technical experts *can* participate in technical discourse about environmental issues.

As a result, institutions can benefit twofold by actively including publics in the decision-making process. First, citizens who recognize that their knowledge is being actively sought and used in constructing a policy are less likely to appeal to Congress or the state legislature to stop a decision with which they disagree. Second, technical experts can gain knowledge about how the proposed policy could be used or would affect a particular community; this knowledge is often essential in developing an appropriate policy. Yet publics' local knowledge cannot be fully realized if these publics are considered a unified, coherent group, rather than multiple groups and individuals.

CURRENT RISK COMMUNICATION PRACTICES ASSUME A UNIFIED PUBLIC

The current models used in the chemical weapons disposal case at Newport assume that the public is a unified, coherent entity with similar concerns and goals. Specifically, the officials at Newport expect the public to be local citizens and are suspicious of any "interested parties" who do not fit that description. Yet this assumption excludes a number of groups and individuals affected by the decision. According to Young, assuming a homogenous public fails to consider groups that are not culturally identified with what the institutions consider the norm. For example, the citizens from Kentucky who attended the public meetings (and who lived near the Bluegrass Chemical Depot) were seen by the Army and the Indiana Department of Environmental Management as radicals interfering with the policy decision because they did not fit the institutions' criteria for the local public. Differences exist within communities as well. Recall Ross' (1996) research illustrating how the values of the Mohawk worldview were not factored into the decision for siting a landfill because they were placed in the broad category of "public opposition" (p. 176). Communities are comprised of individuals with different perspectives, cultures, and values. When public participation models assume a unified public, or reduce public participation to a citizen advisory board, these different perspectives are lost or dismissed. And employing "representatives" does not allow affected individuals to voice their own concerns. Representative participation risks obscuring the differences among affected publics, or as Benhabib (1992) asserts, generalizes the other (p. 10). This dismissal oversimplifies the complexity of public debates and results in a decision that privileges a select few. A critical framework for ethical policy decisions *seeks out* the different perspectives of all affected. Bringing to light the multiple perspectives—just the exchange of frames—knowing how all involved parties define the problem and see themselves in relation to the problem can work toward avoiding intractable conflicts and can be a starting point for more democratic decision-making.

Further, even seemingly similar communities, such as citizen activist groups, may hold very different agendas, concerns, and views toward a proposed technology. For example, recall Cable and Cable's (1995) assertion that there are often distinct differences in the goals of state and national environmental groups and grassroots environmental groups.

Individuals and groups alike deserve a space for contributing to a decision. It may prove beneficial to have multiple means of actively seeking citizen input to accommodate the different publics and their needs. As illustrated in chapter 4, some groups may be included in focus groups—held at multiple times allowing a variety of individuals to attend—while others, unable to attend such meetings at any time, might be included with surveys or interviews. What we can learn, in part, from this experience is that as researchers in nonacademic settings we need to avoid the same assumptions of a unified community that plagued the "expert" decision makers. We need to be aware of what groups and individuals are left out of our research. And we need to consider and value the differences within a community and the different discourses of knowledges they can contribute.

INSTITUTIONAL PUBLIC PARTICIPATION PROCEDURES PROHIBIT ACTIVE INVOLVEMENT

Examining such regulations as the Comprehensive Environmental Response, Compensation, and Liability Act (CERCLA), the National Environmental Policy Act (NEPA), and the Resource Conservation and Recovery Act (RCRA) in chapters 1 and 3 illustrate how federal regulations to ensure public participation often work to prohibit it. In each of these regulations, public approval is required before the policy could be implemented, but only after the decision has been made. As illustrated in chapter 3, encouraging citizens to contribute knowledge about how a policy will affect their community at the onset of a decision-making process is quite different than allowing citizens to respond to policies already determined. Further, the regulations do not require that the citizen comments directly influence the final policy. (As illustrated in appendices B and C, they only have to be included in the appendix of an EIS). As a result, federal agencies may further marginalize public participation by holding meetings to collect public comments but not taking seriously the contributions or concerns the publics have. This was illustrated in the public meetings at Newport where a dialogue among the institutional representatives and citizens was prohibited according to "procedure," and collected public comments did not influence policy decisions. Additionally, procedures for collecting comments often created a barrier between citizens and the actual decision makers, diminishing active participation. The roundtable meetings where comments were not recorded, the outreach office that sent materials to align citizen views with expert perspectives rather than engage in a dialogue, and the plans that were determined by experts before being presented to the citizens for approval all dismissed any significant contributions and local knowledge that the citizens could offer. Allowing citizens to comment is not enough to create an ethical policy. Active involvement requires access to the decision-making process and some direct influence in the decision. Citizens must be granted epistemological status—their contributions must be valued. However, active involvement also will require that the public participation procedures in place be critiqued continually to reveal where barriers exist.

The public meetings during the chemical disposal case at the Newport Chemical Depot demonstrated that even when a partial participation model is employed, the federal agencies that oversee the meetings can easily marginalize and disregard public participation. McGarity (1998) asserts that the same marginalizing can be done with the facilitated model. This suggests that advocating a particular model for risk communication may be futile. Rather, involving citizens more significantly may require different measures such as iterative strategies that seek to ensure that participation is encouraged throughout the decision-making process and in ways that influence the final policy.

MULTIPLE INSTITUTIONS USING MULTIPLE RISK COMMUNICATION MODELS COMPLICATE PARTICIPATION

One significant difference between the reported case studies of public participation in environmental policy and the case of chemical weapons disposal at the Newport Chemical Depot was the complexity of the institutions involved and the multiplicity of the risk communication models employed in the Newport case. While most of the literature on risk communication, and indeed the existing cases on public participation in environmental issues, suggests that each case employs a single model of risk communication, the Newport case illuminated that, in many situations, multiple approaches to public participation are employed, even by the same agency, throughout the process of implementing a policy. This is due in part to the often complex web of institutions involved in the proposed environmental action. In the Newport case, because the party proposing the action was a governmental agency, the posed risk was chemical warfare, and the posed action affected air and water exposure pathways, a myriad of institutions governed the decision-making process at the Newport Chemical Depot. Yet it seems that the Newport case is not atypical in that environmental actions are often governed by multiple federal regulations and agencies.

The significance of multiple institutions is two-fold. First, different regulations and agencies are likely to employ different approaches to public participation. The chemical weapons disposal decision at Newport involved at least sixteen institutions including different federal regulations, agencies, and programs. These different institutions implemented different approaches to public participation. The Army itself implemented three different approaches to risk communication and public participation. The citizens themselves have no control over what model the institution chooses to employ.[2] This too makes it difficult to advocate for a particular model for risk communication. Second, these different models often conflict, allowing even less space for significant and sustained public involvement. It is often only in these intersections and conflicts among different procedures and communities that we see the multiple and complex literacy practices needed to participate in policy decisions. As a result, it is likely that the more institutions involved, the less opportunity there is currently for active public participation. Recall the Kimball incinerator case from chapter 2 that involved only the company hoping to build an incinerator and the citizens of the community where the company wanted to build the incinerator. In that case the company met frequently with the citizens and ultimately left the decision to build the incinerator up to the community. The company claimed it did not want to fight to build an incinerator where it was not wanted. Allowed to consider the costs and benefits of the incinerator for the community, the citizens ultimately decided in favor of the incinerator.

Other scholars have suggested that the facilitated model—where a number of lay representative are chosen to participate in technical discussions with technical experts from different areas related to risk (including risk assessors, state and federal government officials, and agency representatives)—shows the most promise (Davies 1995).[3] Yet as shown in chapter 4, this model has significant flaws. First, as just discussed, participants who are "chosen" by those in power likely do not include representatives of all affected by the decision. Further, as illustrated with the VX disposal decisions, any model of participation can be navigated by the officiating agencies to marginalize the space for public contribution. However, I believe that the frame of the model is useful. An approach that includes a facilitator may open a space for modifying models by using strategies and heuristics that aim toward actively including all affected in the decision-making process.

What most models lack is a critical theory of risk communication and public involvement that addresses issues of power and participation such as who participates, who is left out, who listens, when and how the public is involved, and how public participation affects the final policy. Yet because any model can be navigated to marginalize citizen contributions, I want to suggest instead a heuristic or strategies that seek to encourage the type of active public participation that can result in just and appropriate policies.

A HEURISTIC FOR EVALUATING PUBLIC PARTICIPATION IN ENVIRONMENTAL PUBLIC POLICY

Instead of advocating a particular model of risk communication and public participation, I draw from Sullivan and Porter (1997), Porter (1998) and Grabill (1997) to develop a critical rhetoric framework that can function as heuristics for considering decision making in environmental issues in particular situations. According to Porter (1998), rhetorical heuristics are "guidelines or strategies useful to ethical decision making in [particular] situations" (p. 18). Such rhetorical heuristics could be useful for ethical decision making in issues of environmental policy as well. Advocating heuristics instead of models seems appropriate given the complexities of environmental decision-making processes caused by (1) the variation in local sites of risk, (2) the identifications of multiple publics, and (3) the involvement of multiple government institutions. Heuristics are useful because they offer an ongoing critique of a decision-making process from the beginning of the policy development through its implementation and suggest that more than one superficial aspect of participation be fulfilled in order to "count" as active participation. As a result, a heuristic offers criteria for what might count as active participation without rigid rules that might not be applicable to the many varied and complex situations of environmental risk decisions.

The criteria that I suggest can offer guidelines for all involved (including federal agencies, citizen groups, individual citizens, facilitators, and technical communicators/rhetoricians) to consider whether a decision-making process is working to encourage a just policy. Unlike a model that can be easily manipulated—as shown in chapters 2 and 4—a decision-making process that strives to meet each criteria may result in a more ethical approach to decision-making and a more just and appropriate policy (see table 5.1).

It is important to note that achieving a particular criterion in isolation will not lead to the type of public participation that I am advocating. Rather, it is when the decision-making process aims for inclusion in all of these areas—participation, power, and process—that it is more likely to result in ethical decision-making practices and just environmental policies.

Power: Access to, and Direct Influence in, the Decision-making Process

In this framework, power indicates that citizens have access to, and direct influence in the decision-making process. Rather than following a model that goes through the motions of gathering citizen comments without any real intention of factoring them into the decision-making process, this heuristic

Table 5.1: Heuristic for Evaluating Public Participation in Environmental Policy

Criteria	Criteria for just decision-making process	Example of just decision-making process
Power: Access to the decision-making process and the ability to directly influence the decision	Takes public participation seriously and examines the following: • Who listens to publics? • Is there frequent and substantial discourse among affected parties? • How does public participation affect final policy?	Publics have direct access to and influence in actual decision-making process (which includes access to technical experts and federal representatives during the decision-making process). Further, public concerns and knowledge are valued in the decision-making process.
Participation: Seeking input from all affected parties	Actively seeks to include all affected in the decision-making process by asking the following: • Who is affected by decision? • Who participates in discussions of decision, and what is their role? • What groups or individuals are left out, and how can they be involved? (Are alternative voices being heard?)	Different communities, groups, and individuals affected by a decision are considered and each is encouraged to generate possible ways a proposed policy would affect their community.
Process: Early, iterative, and frequent participation	Sees policy construction as a process, not an end product and asks the following: • When are those affected allowed/encouraged to participate in decision? • How is public knowledge gathered?	Affected communities are brought in at the beginning of a decision-making process, and their knowledge about how a policy would affect them is sought out through focus groups, interviews, surveys, ethnographies, and histories.

approach questions how public knowledge is valued. Power in the decision-making process means that citizens can interact with the decision makers, not the public relations or outreach office that works to "inform" the public and place a barrier between them and the actual decision makers. In other words, the decision makers must be the ones who listen to the various publics. Encouraging frequent and substantial interchanges among the institutional representatives and publics is an opportunity for all affected to contribute.

Yet, unless public contributions actually influence the final policy, the interchanges become another pseudoparticipation tactic. Ehn (1992) maintains that participation in decisions is only successful if it makes a difference for the participants, and implementations are likely. If participants are not convinced that their design efforts have been taken seriously, they have not been granted power (p. 129). When the policy is socially constructed by all affected, the result is a policy that is appropriate and just for a *particular* situation.

This heuristic has implications for institutions and citizens alike. Such a heuristic would require that institutions share some of the power they possess in risk decisions but in return would provide them with a policy that both is more appropriate for a situation and less likely to be delayed by hostile citizens. More specifically, a critical rhetoric and participatory notion of power would require that institutions and "experts" acknowledge that citizens can participate in technical discussions of policy and have valuable information to contribute to the decision-making process. This critical rhetoric notion of power likewise requires that citizens be able to articulate their concerns about the technical issues of a policy in ways that are persuasive to experts. As mentioned in chapter 3, this may include adopting new and different literacy practices for participating in policy discussions such as

- having a "working vocabulary of scientific terms and concepts, and an overall understanding of how technical reasoning operates" that allows citizens to "follow evolving policy issues" (Kinsella, 92);

- "understanding the different interpretations that one can draw from the facts" and developing the ability to "think about ways to choose among those interpretations" (Laird, 353);

- learning "how and when to challenge the validity of asserted facts, where new data would be useful, and how the kinds of policy questions are being asked influence the type of data they seek" (Laird, 353); and

- knowing when to "challenge the formulation of the problem itself " and determine what are the important questions to consider (Laird, 354).

These are not easy literacies to adopt. Citizens learning to "do their own science" (Grabill) requires commitment/investment in the issue and likely the need to work with others in (and perhaps outside) their community. Some universities have established research centers to help with this very thing. For example, the University of Tennessee, Knoxville, has the Community Partnership Center, a university-based research center comprised of an interdisciplinary group of faculty members who work to initiate and support research and action partnerships with community organizations to address the needs of low-to-moderate resource communities. Partnerships between citizens and the center are often funded by external grants from places such as HUD and the Ford Foundation. The Community Partnership Center's thirteen-step model for participatory planning for sustainable community development includes activities such as determining what information is needed to understand the context, selecting methods for collecting relevant information, and analyzing mapping and other data to identify and evaluate policy alternatives. These sorts of activities can help communities persuasively discuss the technical aspects of a proposed policy with technical experts.[4]

Increasingly, academics in rhetoric and technical and scientific communication are partnering with citizens and community organizations to help them consider ways they might better participate in issues and policies that affect their lives (see Grabill, 2001; Scott). While not an easy task, if we can help citizens understand the literacy practices—the strategies they must adopt to more persuasively participate in technical discussions—we as rhetoricians and technical communicators will have helped these citizens gain more power in the decision-making process.

I am not suggesting that this changing notion of power will be easy for experts either. The powerful are rarely willing to become less so. Yet considering the growing number of stories where decisions were drawn out for more than ten years, costing thousands of dollars (see Katz and Miller), perhaps experts will become more likely to negotiate.

A critical rhetoric and participatory notion of power for ethical participation in policy decisions assumes that citizens would directly influence a decision by working with technical experts to determine a policy rather than be indirectly involved by appealing to Congress to delay a decision that blindsides them or does not go their way. This approach requires that all parties listen to one another and value the type of expertise that each brings to the table. This is perhaps easier said than done. Iris Marion Young (2000) asserts that this sort of collaboration may require viewing the decision as a shared task, adding that, "we should envision global democracy as the interaction of self-determining peoples and locals on terms of equality in which they understand obligations to listen to outsiders who claim to be affected by their decisions or actions and to resolve conflicts with them through settled procedures in a global framework of regulatory principles democratically decided on together by all the self-determining entities" (9). In other words, envisioning policy decisions as a shared and common task may enable those involved to better listen to and value the contributions of all affected and may help to dissolve the power struggle that currently plagues most policy debates.

Participation: Seeking Input from All Affected Parties

A critical rhetoric notion of participation means actively seeking out all who
are affected by an environmental policy or action. This is not an easy task,
especially for the institutions. Technical communicators may prove especially helpful. Working with involved citizens or institutions, technical communicators can help tease out who is affected, who is participating, and who
is left out. This sort of inquiry within a particular decision-making process
can help ensure that those affected have an opportunity to participate in the
decision and that alternative voices are heard. Further, this type of inquiry
examines what role the citizens are being allowed to play in the decision-
making process. This critical rhetoric framework aims for active participation, not just submitting a comment. However, such a framework might
initially meet with resistance from institutions due to the increased time
required to facilitate these sorts of meetings. The traditional public meetings
where citizens are allowed to submit comments can typically be completed
in an hour or so (especially when institutions limit each speaker to five
minutes as was the case at Newport). Yet institutions are aware that there
are flaws with their common approach to public participation. Few major
environmental policy decisions are implemented without resistance from
citizens that results in delayed action. Belsten (1996) describes talks with
several government agency officials who stated that they would try a different approach to public participation if it would bring about a less time-
consuming process. It is likely that actively involving citizens in the
decision-making process would require less time than defending lawsuits or
justifying decisions to Congress. To ensure this, it might be possible for *all*
affected parties to determine *together* at the *beginning* of a decision-making
process a set amount of time to consider the different perspectives.

Process: Early, Iterative, and Frequent Participation in the
Decision-making Process

Perhaps the biggest difference between the framework to risk communication
that I am advocating and the ones that have been advocated before is the
focus on risk communication as a process. Rather than viewing a risk policy
as a product that is developed by experts and then presented to all, a critical
rhetoric framework considers the policy an iterative process that involves all
affected in the design process from the *beginning* through the implementation
of a policy or action. In this sense, technical experts are not defending
policies they have already determined to be sound but are working with
publics to construct the policies in an effort to design a policy that is both
technically sound and appropriate for a particular situation.

    In most current policy debates, institutional procedures assume that
knowledge about a decision is produced separately by experts, *then* communicated to citizens, who are seen as end users of the policy, devoid of any

knowledge that might prove useful for producing the policy itself. According to Porter (1998), this type of communication that positions the audience members as "passive receivers" of a predetermined message, and that persuades the audience to accept a predetermined point of view, is a "rhetoric of domination" (p. 94). It is only when the audience is considered capable of participating in the dialogue, and of constructing knowledge that the communication becomes a "rhetoric of democratization" (p. 94).

When institutions (and their procedures) envision the transfer of information in terms of problems of knowledge and see knowledge as something produced separate from audiences by a select few experts, they fail to adequately conceptualize the complexity of the construction of knowledge. By denying that knowledge about a policy is socially constructed, this view positions audiences as entities to be persuaded, not as participants in the construction of policy. Further, such a view does not account for the practices of power in risk assessment and communication. In order to participate in the development of policies, the public must be seen as capable of contributing knowledge to the process and brought in early enough in the design phase to actually affect the policy.

By viewing risk communication and policy development as a process, technical experts and publics can work together to reveal what technologies are possible and how those different technologies will affect a community. This process, then, can point out problems with a proposed policy and decrease the risk that publics will be adamantly opposed to a policy that is ready to be implemented.

A critical rhetoric notion of process also means that citizen knowledge is sought out through interviews, focus groups, and other types of usability research techniques with the technical experts and facilitators, not sifted through on comment cards. Technical communicators who employ usability and participatory design strategies such as the ones described by Kukla, Clemens, Morse, and Cash (1992), Ehn (1992), and Sanoff (1990) and discussed in chapter 4 can work toward a decision-making process where multiple voices are able to contribute significant knowledge to the construction of the policy. This usability could include a wide range of research practices—a range of contextual interviewing and observation practices in particular—that necessitate researchers and technical experts to work *with* publics in the construction of knowledge (e.g., risk). Here, I am advocating the kind of participatory approaches and usability research discussed in chapter 4 that reflect an ongoing process of research that is concurrent with and continually informs the process of design (Sullivan, 1989).

CHANGING INSTITUTIONS

It is not likely that a universal solution to changing institutional practices exists; rather I believe, there are spaces and moments for different stakeholders where change is possible within a given policy decision. Because the heuristics are informed by participatory design and institutional critique, they seek to identify places where participation and change are possible. A pragmatic feature of the heuristics is that they might be adopted by any of the parties involved in the policy decisions—institutions, citizens, and technical communicators and rhetoricians—to bring about some degree of change in a given situation. Agencies may be persuaded to adopt the heuristics to avoid the costly and long-term policy delays that often occur when citizens are excluded from the decision-making process. Yet the heuristics provide citizens with strategies for active participation even if the agencies themselves have not adopted the framework. Further, rhetoricians and technical communicators involved in policy debates through their community-based research can use the participatory heuristics to help them identify oppressive power relations and look for spaces to intervene in the decision-making process.

What might prompt the agencies in power to willingly relinquish some of that power in the decision-making process? In a best-case scenario, those within the institutions of power see for themselves that changing institutional procedures and decision-making practices are necessary if they are to reach an appropriate and just decision. Yet research suggests that it is more often the case that agencies are willing to change their institutional practices only when they have reached what Roy Lewicki, Barbara Gray, and Michael Elliot (2003) define as an "intractable environmental conflict." Intractable conflicts, according to Linda Putnam and Julia Wondolleck (2003), are "conflicts that are long-standing and elude resolution" (38). Recall the VX nerve agent disposal decision, where only after years of conflict and hundreds of letters to elected officials from concerned citizens did Congress create the Assembled Chemical Weapons Assessment (ACWA) program and mandate a "dialogue process by which affected citizens, state regulators and Department of Defense officials cooperatively created technology selection criteria" (32 C. F. R. Part 178). Gray (2003) argues that these intractable conflicts often result when involved parties construct different frames (constructions and interpretations) about the nature of the conflict and how a dispute should be resolved. (Frames, in this sense, seem to function much like rhetorical stasis theory where rhetors locate and identify the issues within a conflict.) If an agency believes that it is involved in an intractable conflict, it may be willing to investigate the impasse of that conflict by looking at the different frames all involved parties have constructed about the conflict. The very admission of a conflict, then, can be a space for input from all affected. Just the exchange of frames—knowing how all involved parties define the problem—and see themselves in relation to the problem can be a starting point for more democratic decision making. The questions provided in the participatory heuristics can be used to investigate the frames that all affected see in a conflict as well as how that issue relates to them. An advantage of institutions acknowledging an intractable conflict is that in order to successfully identify the sources of the conflict—the different frames—they have to seek out all affected since different groups and individuals will likely have different frames.

The participatory heuristics can assist citizens and citizen groups as well. Because the heuristics evaluate the justness of a decision-making process, citizens may use the heuristics to identify where they are being excluded. Knowing the spaces where they should/could be included can encourage groups to work together toward claiming that space. The epilogue addresses a situation where citizens opposed the decision to transport a by-product of VX to their neighborhood for disposal. When the citizens found out that "public acceptance" was a condition of the contract between the Army and the disposal organization, they demanded that their "public refusal" be heard and used to break the contract. The heuristics can help attune citizens to the more everyday institutional practices to see that small changes can create spaces for input and that their knowledge of how a policy would affect their community is crucial in constructing an appropriate policy.

INSTITUTIONAL CRITIQUE AS AN ACTION PLAN FOR TECHNICAL COMMUNICATORS AND RHETORICIANS

Rhetoricians and technical communicators involved in policy debates through their community-based research can use the participatory heuristics to help them identify oppressive power relations and look for spaces to intervene in the decision-making process. I see analogies between the type of questions these heuristics ask and recent research by rhetoricians who have used institutional critique to identify ways to intervene in decisions about HIV/AIDS policies.

For example, Jeff Grabill's (2000) research on the ways in which HIV/AIDS services are funded by the Ryan White CARE Act argues for critical examination of institutions as a way to improve client involvement in the decision-making process and to create better procedures and policies. Federal rules mandate that at least 25 percent of the planning council for the Ryan White money must include individuals affected by the disease (in other words, clients of the services). Yet, according to Grabill, participation by this group is limited in part because these is little two-way communication between the council and clients so that clients who do participate are not made aware of what policies are made or changed because of their involvement (30). He further notes that the meeting times, locations, and procedures add barriers to client participation. In my own research, I have found that public meetings are often held during "business hours" when those affected by a decision are not available to meet. However, Grabill notes that professional writing research practices—such as questionnaires to clients to determine where and how they would feel comfortable participating in meetings—can lead to changes in decision-making procedures (42). Such changes, according to Grabill, can be as simple as including where and how meetings were conducted, and as significant as increasing the status of the committees in which the clients participate. Additionally, Grabill and those he worked with persuaded local government and the planning council that an ad hoc committee on improving client involvement needed to be a task force—a committee whose recommendations become part of the public record and require action (43). While Grabill and his colleagues did not change the policy themselves, efforts to change the decision-making procedures allowed those affected by the policy a more significant role in the policy making.

Blake Scott (2003) also draws on Foucault's notions of institutions and power to argue for more critical, responsive, and just implementation of HIV testing policies mandated by state legislatures (11). Questioning the government's assumptions that HIV testing is a "magic bullet" with intervening and empowering benefits, Scott argues that mandated testing ignores the harmful effects of positioning and "managing" certain populations considered "at risk." By examining the history and discourse surrounding HIV testing, Scott advocates more citizen involvement for more appropriate policy making through intercultural inquiry (see also Flower, Long, & Higgins, [2000]).

I include these examples not only to point to instances where technical communication researchers can intervene in institutional practices of public policy but also to show that this intervention can take many forms—often in seemingly mundane work such as researching testing practices or conducting questionnaires with clients/participants. Training in information technology, usability, and highly complex technical and scientific information can create spaces where we can become involved in changing the way public policy is constructed. It is through our research practices of involving those affected by a decision—and our ability to continually critique institutional procedures that we can work toward this change.

THE NEED FOR MORE RESEARCH OF PUBLIC DISCOURSE IN COMMUNITY-BASED SETTINGS

A growing number of scholars in rhetoric, composition, and technical communication are involved in community-based organizations through their interests and research in public policy, expertise, power, and civic discourse practices. Such projects might include observing the civic discourse involved in community planning or the development of public policy. These observations frequently show that those most affected by the policy, the local citizen, have useful knowledge to contribute to a policy, decision, or plan but are often silenced in the decision-making process. As a result of these observations, numerous scholars have begun to argue that we should be involved in community-based and public policy situations (Grabill, 2000; Johnson, 1997; Martin and Sanders, 1994; Rude, 2000, Waddell, 1996). They see rhetoricians and technical communicators as potential advocates for involving a wide range of publics in decision-making processes of public policy. This involvement seems reasonable because we possess critical and rhetorical research skills to identify ethical and political imbalances in public policy processes that deny publics active participation. Yet we must understand the various ways in which public participation is currently allowed to influence policy, and we must recognize the power structures and relations in place that work to prevent participation, as well as the literacy practices that can resist those power structures. However, we know little about the range of writing and communication practices in community contexts such as those required for participating in public policy decisions. While professional communication courses have often included public policy writing as part of their curricula, there has been little inquiry into how citizens use their professional knowledge in arguing positions in the public sphere.

Little work has been done to examine the institutional power structures of the decision-making process that encourage or inhibit public participation. By researching sites of civic discourse in community-based organizations, we can more fully understand the way policy is determined and work toward advocating a more participatory approach to the decision-making process that encourages significant contributions from all involved parties.

Sites of civic discourse, such as groups formed for community action or policy decisions, are often rich contexts of professional and technical communication. While significant professional and technical communication practices take place in these community contexts, they have remained all but invisible to professional communication research. Dale Sullivan (1990) points to a typical position when he asserts that when we limit technical communication to writing for the world of work, we "draw a boundary at the point where political [and civic] discourse picks up" (p. 377). This exclusion of political and civic discourse, he further notes, "suggests that we accept restrictions on public discourse and fail to give students power to engage in social action" (376). While I would argue that technical communication is always already situated in the realm of political and ethical, I believe that by including community-based organizations as sites of our research, we may more directly address issues of civic and political discourse that can provide insight into what literacy practices are needed to function not only in the workplaces but in everyday life as well.

My notion of civic discourse is perhaps expanded from its more traditional meanings tied to epideictic rhetoric or public democracy of a general sort, that is, speeches or sermons (as in figure 5.1). Over time our discussions of civic rhetoric have been drawn to the ways particular groups construct activist discourse, as in the ways women used civic rhetoric (see Eldred and Mortensen) or the social justice rhetoric of African American sermons, slave narratives, and African American jeremiads (see Gilyard). These discussions of civic discourse are important to our understanding of discourse practices, but civic rhetoric often neglects public policy discussions.

I see civic discourse as also the ability to participate in discussions of technical public policy decisions. A historical purpose of rhetoric has been to

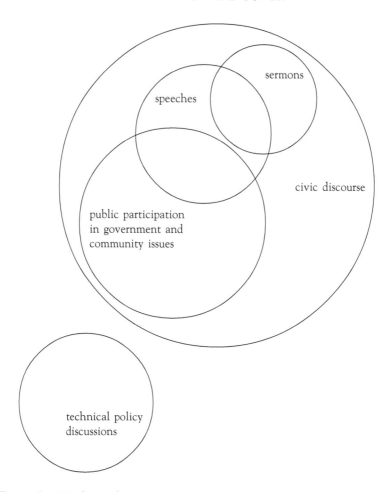

Figure 5.1: Traditional Notion of Civic Discourse

help citizens participate in public discussions necessary for democratic government. Since policies are made through discourse (Rude, 5), all policy discussions are communicative. When such discussions are highly technical and
scientific, they also fit into the realm of technical communication. Technically
complex public issues complicate the traditional notion of discourse because
technical experts claim ownership of the technical issues and close off public
debate even though these issues affect the public in very concrete ways. However, if we believe that citizens can and should participate actively in highly
technical public policy discussions, then considering such discussions as a type
of civic rhetoric may enable rhetoricians and technical communicators to
examine public policy discussions in more critical ways (see figure 5.2). Thus,

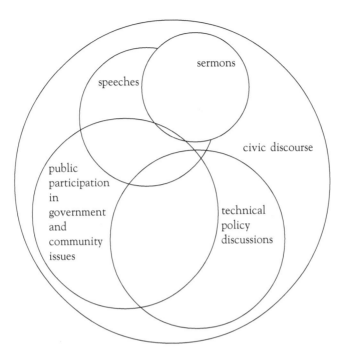

Figure 5.2: Expanded Notion of Civic Discourse

redefining rhetoric and technical communication to include studies of civic discourse, activism, as well as public policies, decisions and plans, we can glean a richer understanding of the everyday literacy practices necessary for collaborative decision making in the affected communities (Sullivan, 1990). (I take particular note of policies, decisions, and plans, because sometimes these "mundane" plans and decisions open a decision space where citizens and technical writing theory can most readily contribute.) By seeing connections between civic discourse and policy debates, one can imagine civic discourse to include the ability to participate in discussions of public policy decisions.

Understanding the literacy practices necessary to actively participate in collaborative decision making in these settings can help develop better strategies for identifying obstacles to public participation and for improving public involvement in policy decisions.

My research of the ways in which publics participate in public policy decisions in community-based contexts demonstrates some of the benefits of crossing traditional boundaries in rhetoric and technical communication. Focusing on ways in which publics have been encouraged to, or inhibited from, participating in public policy decisions, and on the actions and nonactions of institutions facilitating risk policies, we can make visible institutional assumptions about public participation in environmental policies. As rhetoricians and technical communicators we can examine such institutions and the way they exercise power, in an effort to change those practices that prevent significant public participation and provide publics with strategies for participating more fully in matters of civic discourse that affect their lives.

While decisions about environmental risk are complex and technical, they are technologies that greatly affect lives of many publics. If we accept that citizens should be able to participate in decisions that affect themselves and their communities (whether those communities be geographical, ideological, or virtual[5]), and that they, themselves, are the best judges of their own interests, then we must seek ways to include them in technical public policy discussions. A critical rhetoric approach to environmental decision making could encourage significant public participation. Adopting a critical rhetoric participatory framework for policy decision making will require changes in the discourse practices of both institutions and citizens, but it may be the first step toward a just environment.

CHAPTER SIX

TOWARD A JUST AND PARTICIPATORY ENVIRONMENT: CIVIC RESEARCH IN/FROM THE ACADEMY

"I'm not certain the average citizen, trying to find out how to dispose of household waste, is going to wade though a web site whose first page focuses on Phase II requirements—could we put all of that information in a link off the homepage?"

"I'm not sure an average citizen would follow a link with the name Phase II Requirements."

"Can we call the link something different?"

"While we are at it, do you think the citizens are going to know what half these link names mean that we were given to use?"

So began a nearly two-hour debate among graduate students in an information design class regarding how to organize and categorize information for a web site they were designing on storm water pollution prevention for a nearby county. A component of the class project required the students to gather feedback from those who would use and be affected by their communication. Gathering this feedback required students to shift their perspective from that of the EPA, which required this information to be disseminated, to that of the citizens, who would actually use the information.

The fact that the information was jargon-laden and government agency-centered was not that surprising. Nearly every other web site on storm water pollution prevention the information design students found when they were surveying and critiquing similar web sites as part of their initial research used the same jargon-laden link names and information describing something called "Phase II requirements." This very problem was what made the web site design project so appealing to me. What further interested me about the project was that it was not originally intended for the information design/ technical communication students. It was a project intended for students with subject matter expertise. But it was the technical communication students who drew on usability and information design strategies they were learning in class and who were able to construct a web site that was more usable and useful than most other storm water pollution prevention web sites. Using the participatory framework for constructing the web site, the students and I worked with the users of the web site—the local community to make it appropriate for their specific needs. In this chapter, I consider how the participatory framework informed the web site project and how it might inform other community-based projects and classroom service-learning projects to help students better understand the writing and literacy practices necessary to participate in civic discourse and their responsibility to consider the ethics of a communication situation.

I became involved in the storm water pollution prevention web site project when I was asked to be a faculty advisor for a public service project environmental science graduate students were conducting.[1] As part of its community service and education program, the Environmental Sciences program at my university divides first-year graduate students into teams to conduct environmental problem-solving research for a community partner. The team I advised worked with the Office of Environmental Quality (OEQ) in a nearby county to research storm water better management practices (BMPs) and to develop a community web site about storm water pollution prevention to increase awareness about proper waste disposal, recycling, and community events. Both the BMPs and the web site were required by the EPA to fulfill Phase II requirements.

Phase II requirements evolved from the Clean Water Act. In 1972, the Clean Water Act was passed with the hope of improving the quality of the nation's water. While water quality improved, polluted bodies of water still existed. In 1996, 40 percent of the bodies of water surveyed in the United States did not meet water quality standards (EPA fact sheet). Much of this pollution is from construction site discharges and storm water run off (EPA fact sheet). Storm water, the runoff from driveways, streets, sidewalks, and parking lots, flows into storm drains and eventually into rivers, untreated: whatever falls into a storm drain finds its way into a river or lake. In 1990, the EPA implemented a storm water program under the Clean Water Act to address this runoff. The program was divided into two phases: Phase I addresses municipal storm sewer systems serving populations of one hundred thousand or more, construction affecting five or more acres of land and some industry activity.

Phase II addresses storm sewer systems of populations fewer than one hundred thousand and construction affecting small tracts of land. Phase II's approach is to implement minimum control measures on unregulated sources of storm water discharge that have the greatest likelihood of causing environmental damage. These six "controls" include public education and out-reach, public participation and involvement, illicit discharge detection and elimination, construction site runoff control, postconstruction runoff con-trol, and pollution prevention/good housekeeping. One result of the public education and outreach requirement was a proliferation of municipality web sites that explained Phase II requirements to the community. However, most storm water public education web sites focused only on the effects of storm water and the need for Phase II requirements, not on helping citizens learn concrete, hands-on ways they could prevent storm water pollution or partici-pate in upcoming community activities. This lack of public involvement is becoming increasingly problematic for communities whose storm water pol-lution is causing erosion and polluted streams and as storm water utility bills are sent to citizens who do not understand their role in storm water pollution prevention. While the EPA states that a goal of environmental education is to "cultivate a commitment for personal action" (Ohio EPA web site), few web sites include practical information for the public or allow citizens the opportunity to provide input into what works for their own community. Further, very few sites offer the public information about upcoming public meetings and other involvement activities. Yet, if we hope to involve the general public in storm water pollution prevention, we must provide better tools for such involvement. Adopting a participatory approach to the project meant believing that the citizens themselves would help us understand what tools they needed.

Adopting a participatory framework to guide the project also required us to give special consideration to when and how often we involved the citizens; how we sought out all affected by the issue; how we incorporated their contributions into the web site; and how we ensured their needs were met along with those of the community partner and the requirements of the EPA. Working under the assumption that the citizens know best how they would use a web site aimed at pollution prevention, the Environmental Science students and I worked to identify those affected by the web site and conducted participatory observations with community residents, teachers, citizen groups, and municipal workers to determine what storm water issues were important to them and what design aspects helped them find the infor-mation they were seeking. We sought input at the beginning of the project before we committed to content or design choices. Drawing from Johndan Johnson-Eilola's (2002) distinction between usability testing and participa-tory observation and design, we asked citizens and regulators to tell us for what purpose they would use the site, then asked them try to find that information as they used the site in their own offices. Johnson-Eilola main-tains that "what users do in your usability lab or office may vary quite a bit from how they work on the job" (55). Watching users in their own work-places helped us better understand the context in which the users would interact with the web site. While we were not able to shadow the users for the long periods of time that Johnson-Eilola advocates for participatory design, allowing the community members to define their own tasks in their own contexts showed us much about the way they would use a site. As you might imagine, the local citizens often had different purposes and needs for the web site than the municipal workers. Our goal was to get feedback from as many affected as possible so that the web site was useful to the entire community, not one aspect of that community.

Participants wanted information that would help them more actively prevent storm water pollution and show them how storm water related to their day to day activities. For example, citizens indicated that they wanted a unified site for their community that would tell them not only what to recycle but also where area recycling centers for each type of recyclables are located. They also wanted to know how they could become involved in community activities through public meetings and community programs. Local contractors and developers wanted to know how they could incorporate best management practices in their construction activities. All participants wanted the web site to enable them to combine their own knowledge with the information on the web site to produce new knowledge useful for affecting their community. With this feedback, we refined the purpose of the web site to provide the public with specific strategies for incorporating better storm water practices in their communities that would still fulfill the EPA Phase II requirements.

The environmental science students researched storm water issues including best management practices and current practices of the county and then asked my information design class (with technical communication and rhetoric students) to join the project to help with the web site development.

The project encouraged the subject matter experts and the technical communicators to work together as advocates for the users of the web site to increase public participation in storm water pollution prevention. The technical communication students revised and organized the research the environmental science students provided, focusing on issues that were outside the immediate scope of the environmental science students' expertise but vital to the usefulness of the web site, such as web design, audience, usability, and accessibility. For example, they designed the web site to be compliant with the Americans with Disabilities Act and created spaces for announcing public meetings, volunteer opportunities, and other ways for the citizens to become involved in the community. This space was not included in the community partner's original vision for the web site nor was it in most of the other existing storm water pollution prevention web sites.

Drawing on audience analysis and user-centered design, the information design students critiqued the agency-centered information on existing pollution prevention web sites as well as the assumptions by the OEQ and the environmental science students about how to categorize and organize the information they had collected for this particular web site. For example, as

noted in the chapter opening, based on the feedback from the first participatory observations, the design students believed that the original site map
the OEQ provided included categories that were helpful only to subject
matter experts, not residents trying to understand how storm water pollution
prevention related to the way they disposed of materials such as oil, fertilizer,
household cleaner waste, tires, and batteries, or the manner in which they
washed their car.

To confirm that they were addressing the participants' feedback appro-
priately, the information design students conducted another round of participatory observations with members of the community several weeks into the
design phase. Organizing both the information the community believed would
help them with the information the EPA and OEQ believed should be
included in a usable design resulted in a web site that better addressed the
needs of the residents than the previously existing web sites on storm water.

The audience analysis, critiques, and usability participatory observation all served as methodologies for the students as they developed their
designs. These approaches draw from the same strategies that inform the
participatory heuristic in chapter 5: bring affected communities in at the
beginning of the process to learn about their knowledge of how a communication will affect them and how they would use the communication, seek
input from a wide range of affected individuals, and grant those affected
access to and influence in the construction of the communication. As Bickford
and Reynolds note, providing students specific methodologies and tools for
developing their community project may help them make connections to the
skills and strategies they are learning "beyond the site of their encounter"
(242). It may help the students see that the skills they are learning are useful
in their civic life as well as their work life.

The final structure, design, and categories of the web site looks very
different from the one initially envisioned by OEQ and the EPA–in part
because the experts were only a small group of the actual users of the web
site and could not anticipate how the other community members would use
the it. To address the differences, the information design students provided
rationales for their content and design decisions in an accompanying recommendation report persuading OEQ that their design better met the needs of
the citizens and was therefore more likely to encourage the citizens to become involved in pollution prevention. The site, which was adopted in
whole by OEQ, encouraged the students to see how their expertise in information design, institutional critique, usability, and participatory design created a space for public involvement. Figure 6.1 illustrates the homepage the
students created. Figure 6.2 shows a page that addresses community involvement opportunities.

One goal for the web site project was to work with community members to carve a space—in the form of a page or section—on involvement
opportunities for the citizens on each of the web sites. These opportunities

Figure 6.1: Storm Water Pollution Prevention Home Page

range from volunteer activities such as river sweeps to public meetings to reporting a spill or suspicious dumping to asking questions about water quality. A Watershed web site another technical communication class developed includes links to real time data about water quality that citizens can monitor and use in their own arguments. As discussed later in this chapter and further in the epilogue, access to this type of information—though technical and complex—is a first step toward acknowledging that citizens can and should contribute to environmental issues in significant ways and providing them with the means to do so. In a more recent web site development project—a storm water web site for another county—the citizens specifically asked us to help them develop the technical literacy they needed to participate in conversations with local experts about storm water issues by including glossaries of terms and more technical information about the issues that they learn. (Recall the spokeswoman from Newport Citizens against Incineration who was denied access to meetings because she did not know the correct technical terms.)

Through our work as technical communicators on this project, students created a space for citizen involvement where none existed before, and learned strategies for involving citizens that they can use beyond the classroom. Citi-

Stormwater Pollution Prevention

Stormwater Home
Disposal & Pollution Prevention
　Business
　Construction
　Residential
Permits & Regulations
Community Involvement
Educational Materials
Links & Resources
Contacts
OEQ Home
Site Map

Community Involvement
Visit this page frequently to learn how you can help to improve the environmental quality of Clermont County's waterways.

Computer Recycling Days
(4/15/2004)

Clean and Green Cleanup Registration Form
(4/24/2004)

Environmental Economics Conference
(4/29/2004)

Public Meetings
Participate in decisions that affect your community.

East Fork Watershed Collaborative Public Meeting
Thursday, September 9, 10 am
Perry Township Hall, U.S. Route 50 East in Fayetteville
The meeting will discuss the development of a "total maximum daily load" (TMDL) for the East Fork Little Miami River Watershed and what it means to different stakeholders. The TMDL represents the maximum amount of a particular pollutant that a surface water body can take in without showing significant signs of impairment. For more information call 513.732.7075

Volunteer Opportunities
Ohio River Sweep 2004
Volunteers are needed for the 16th annual Ohio River Sweep scheduled for Saturday, June 19, starting at 9 a.m. This year volunteers can help clean up the river banks at sites in New Richmond, Moscow, Neville, and Chilo. All supplies are provided, and all volunteers will receive a FREE River Sweep 2004 T-shirt and lunch. For more information, contact the Office of Environmental Quality at 513.732.7894.

Figure 6.2: Storm Water Pollution Prevention Community Involvement Opportunities

zens can use the created space to find information not just for educational purposes, but also for actually becoming involved in storm water issues. Such a space requires timely updates from the OEQ members, and only time will tell if that space is maintained, but for now the OEQ members as well as the area citizens know that such a space can exist and how it can function.

While the storm water pollution prevention web site project may have begun with a focus on helping the OEQ become compliant with EPA requirements, it became a way to distribute information to a wide group of citizens within a community who might not otherwise communicate. In this project, the participatory approach to designing the information resulted in a web site that attended to the needs of the citizens, provided them with tools to empower their involvement, and worked to improve the water quality of lakes and streams in the county. This tailored web site space is becoming increasingly important as a site of collaboration among citizens. According to Beth Simone Noveck (2005), "new visual and social technologies are making it possible for people to make decisions and solve complex problems collectively. These technologies are enabling groups not only to create community but also to wield power and create rules to govern their own affairs" (1). More specifically, she maintains that "technology is changing who can form a group, how the group sustains its work and what information assets the group accesses" (19). Like Laird and Young, Noveck asserts that solving complex problems most often requires working in groups. Noting the "utopic" nature of Habermasian deliberations, Noveck describes how technological tools allow groups to deliberate via shared maps and diagrams rather than the face-to-face meetings that often result in the unequal power relations that shut down or marginalize discussions (3). She argues that it is the visual screens that can encourage group interaction toward a purpose of bringing about change (7). Noveck maintains that online interfaces must enable members to see their role in relationship to the group if the group is to defy physical geography to bring about a change (11). Further, interfaces must help groups "make sense of information collectively and create it collaboratively" (14–15).

While Noveck describes examples of specific software tools that will, for instance, allow members to change the rules for participation or require a number of participants to respond to a question before the answers are posted (11)—important tools for us to examine—the ability to encourage groups to work together can also apply, I believe, to more mundane design structures in the web site. Effective civic web sites—that is, web sites designed, in part to encourage public involvement—must go beyond special software and even typical usability issues to address how useful the site is for helping citizens address the complex and messy problems they must solve to participate in environmental decisions. Understanding how citizens do engage and use the information and how the online interface both enables and disables reading, assembling, and understanding the data are issues that rhetoricians and technical communicators must address. If citizens cannot access, assemble, and analyze the information they find, they will not be able to produce the necessary knowledge to participate in decision-making processes that affect their lives and communities. While access to online technologies has shifted from few to many, the skills and literacy practices required to assemble and to produce usable knowledge from these web sites and databases are complex. Complexity is generated by the interaction between the information and the interface—between mode and media (See Kress and Van Leeuwen, 2001). Information is searched for, assembled, and analyzed differently online than in print, yet these differences are rarely acknowledged and accounted for in the interface design of civic web sites. Web sites can help establish collaboration opportunities for citizens, but a challenge to designing them is to balance helping citizens find information that is pertinent to their situation with allowing them to explore the material with multiple questions and consider multiple factors and share this information with others trying to bring about a change (Simmons & Grabill). A participatory framework for constructing civic web sites may provide us with a glimpse into understanding these necessary literacy practices.

Projects that address issues of political and civic discourse through a participatory lens can encourage our students to see the strategies they learn in composition and professional writing courses as useful for affecting social change not only in the workplace, but also their own community. For example, these strategies are useful for preparing students to be user advocates in their roles as technical communicators/rhetoricians as well as to be active citizens in their community. Preparing our students to be more active citizens capable of participating in civic issues—even when those issues are complex and the spaces are not evident—is an important skill. According to Robert Johnson (1998), "learning technical communication strategies in the service of social action instills students with the ability to act responsibly and with an awareness of the ethical dimensions of their actions" (p. 155). If we believe that individuals should participate in discussions that affect them, and that they have useful knowledge to contribute, we must help our students see how participation is possible.

At a conference presentation I gave in the spring of 2005 on increasing public participation in environmental issues, an audience member asked how we introduce our students to issues of public participation and how we encourage them to address the unequal power relations in their workplaces and community. I believe community-based projects informed by a participatory framework that aim to increase public participation, such as these web sites, are one way. While risk communication or public policy cases can offer discussions of power, policy, participation, and ethics, cases often do not provide the immediacy or real consequence that community-based projects can. Can community-based research projects provide the same tensions and unequal power relations that are often present in policy decisions? The answer depends in part upon the particular project and how we frame it. While we may not always have the opportunity to involve our students in crisis communication projects such as the VX nerve agent disposal decision, community-based projects, when carefully constructed, can offer the opportunity to explore issues of ethics, power, and participation in contexts with real consequence.

In previous chapters, I have argued that those most often affected by environmental decisions, the local community, have useful knowledge to contribute to a policy, decision, or plan but are often silenced in the decision making process. I believe that this study of citizen participation and the resulting participatory framework have implications beyond environmental decision-making. The participatory framework can inform community-based projects like the storm water pollution prevention web site in ways that prepare our students to use their expertise in discourse and information technology to identify unequal power relations and intervene in issues of civic discourse in the public sphere to bring about a more democratic environment.

Increasingly composition and technical communication instructors are incorporating service learning projects into courses with the hopes that while students work to improve a community issue and gain experience with course-related strategies, they begin to see civic engagement as part of their ongoing responsibility. The variations on service learning practices and projects are vast. Yet to be effective in preparing our students to better understand how writing and literacy functions and to become advocates for social change, the type of service learning projects we incorporate must keep these goals in mind by doing the following: ask students to write as their service to the community (Bowden and Scott, 2003); require students to consider multiple stakeholders in an issue; encourage students to see their work as change not charity (Dubinsky, 2002), address issues that are important to the participants of the research (Cushman, 1996, 1999); and include projects in multiple courses and with multiple disciplines.[1] Building on the participatory framework developed in earlier chapters, as well as existing research by scholars such as Martin and Sanders (1994), Johnson (1998), and Sullivan (1990), such service learning projects can (1) enable students to analyze the ethics of a communication situation, (2) encourage students to seek out diverse perspectives and voices on an issue as part of their social responsibility, and (3) provide students with the skills and power to build relationships with others to address and solve problems and bring about change within their communities.

If we ask students to work to bring about change, are we asking them to advocate for the organization for which they are working? Asking students to advocate for an agency—even a non-profit agency—risks asking the student to advocate for an organization that may conflict with their own ideologies. Further, it suggests that a decision has already been made, rather than an inquiry began. A participatory approach to service learning projects would ask students to advocate not for a specific organization for which they might be working, but for the individuals affected by the issue they are addressing for the organization. Being a user advocate is not a new concept for technical communicators (Johnson, 1998). Being a user advocate means getting iterative feedback from the individuals who are affected by the newsletter, proposal, brochure, web site or other communication to determine what information those affected need and want to know. This feedback requires that students consider all who are affected by the issues and seek their input, consider how the stakeholders are portrayed in the communication, and question who is excluded or not accurately portrayed. Being a user advocate means considering the ethics and power relations of any communication.

For example, in a recent undergraduate visual rhetoric course, the students designed a brochure on agricultural easements for a local land conservation agency. When the students conducted research with the targeted audience of the brochure—local farmers—they found that many of the farmers did not see themselves the way they were portrayed in the brochure. The farmers provided feedback not only on what they wanted to know about agricultural easements but also on how they believed they should be represented in the brochure. The students used this feedback to revise the brochure and discussed the changes with the land conservation agency. Encouraging students to complicate an issue by seeking out multiple stakeholders' perspectives may help them avoid essentializing a situation with a single vision of the way literacies function in the culture. It may also help them understand that envisioning a situation through a single lens does not leave space for locating conflicts among groups who have competing views of what writing/communicating should and could accomplish.

These experiences can help us point out that "alternative" voices often must be sought out, yet without these voices, the communication cannot justly represent those addressed.

Some scholars have questioned whether community-based course projects can prepare students to be user advocates outside of the classroom. I see emphasizing community advocacy in the community writing projects (and as part of their ongoing responsibility as technical communicators) as one way to discuss with our students the relationships among the classroom project, the community, and the workplace.

In participatory-informed community-based projects students focus not only on writing effective documents but also on understanding how the individuals most affected by their documents could contribute their knowledge to make these documents more reflective of the needs of the community. By including community-based projects informed by a participatory framework in the writing classroom, we can encourage students to see their ability to intervene in issues of civic discourse to involve all affected stakeholders and to work toward a more just and participatory environment.

HEIGHTENED NATIONAL SECURITY
AND PUBLIC PARTICIPATION

Nearly three years after the decision to dispose of the VX agent on-site at the Newport Chemical Depot, the Army recanted the decision and, claiming the depot was a terrorist target, dictated that the VX agent would be partially neutralized then shipped to an off-site processing plant, ignoring citizen input in both Newport and the new disposal site. This section depicts events surrounding the Army (and its contractors') decision to transport hydroly-sate—a byproduct of neutralized VX nerve agent—to an off-site location and considers ways that heightened national security prevents public participation in environmental decision making.

After the terrorist attacks of September 11, 2001, Congress ordered the Army to destroy all stockpiled chemical weapons by 2004 (AP, www.modbee. com 8.14.03). The Army decided the public would be safer if the VX agent were neutralized, but not completely disposed on-site (Ember). Modifying the original decision to use the super critical oxidation process to dispose of the VX at the Newport Chemical Depot, the Army planned a two-step process involving neutralizing the VX at Newport and then sending the hydrolysate to the Perma-Fix Environmental Services waste treatment plant in Dayton, Ohio for further treatment (Ember). The Perma-Fix facility is on the western border of Dayton, an area known as Drexel. The Army's new plan met with much resistance from the counties around Dayton. From the perspective of the residents living around the Perma-Fix facility—as well as residents living in nearby counties—sending the hydrolysate to Dayton was an issue of environmental injustice, specifically environmental racism. (See Bullard for discussion of trends in the United States to place environmental waste in low-income or minority areas.) Unlike the rural community of Newport where the residents live a little over two miles from the depot, the area of Dayton near the Perma-Fix facility has more than two thousand residents living just yards away, about 33 percent of whom live in poverty, and about 35 percent of whom are African American (Debrosse).

The citizens around the Dayton area worked with legal counsel, independent experts, and each other to oppose the Army's decision and eventually bring about a congressional hearing conducted by the House Subcommittee on National Security, Emergency Threats and International Relations to investigate Army contracting practices in the chemical weapons destruction program (McCarty). This subcommittee focuses primarily on terrorism and has oversight responsibility for the Department of Homeland Security. The environmental decision to dispose of the VX hydrolysate at the Perma-Fix facility followed the common models of decision making where citizens are informed of a plan after the decision has been made and are granted little to no power or interaction in that decision. What made this environmental decision different is two-fold. First, the quick decision to transport the VX hydrolysate to Dayton that required no revised EISs was prompted by heightened national security. Second, Perma-Fix included in its contract that it would not proceed with the disposal plan without public acceptance. Yet the definition of public acceptance became the hinge pin of the decision.

The decision to transport the VX hydrolysate to Dayton was not subject to the same process as previous environmental decisions. An EIS was not developed to consider the impact of disposing of the VX hydrolysate at the Perma-Fix location. According to testimony by Ellis Jacobs, a lawyer representing citizens who opposed the plans to transport the VX hydrolysate to Perma-Fix, neither the original EIS that was prepared to consider the environmental impact of disposing of the VX at the Army depot, nor a subsequent environmental assessment (EA) of the decision to destroy the VX in the two-step process, considered the impacts of the disposal on the area in Dayton. While the original EIS assessed the impact on the environment surrounding the Newport facility and assessed whether the action would have a "disproportionate impact on minority or low-income populations" at Newport, there was no such assessment of the area around the Perma-Fix site (Jacobs testimony[1]). This discrepancy is significant because not only is Drexel an urban, densely populated area with no sidewalks or curbs between the homes and the streets where VX hydrolysate will be transported (unlike Newport, a more rural area of 578 people who live over 2.5 miles from the depot), but the responsible crisis response team is the volunteer fire department, not a trained emergency response team like the one on-site at the Newport Chemical Depot (Congressional Hearing Testimony 10.22.03). Jacobs argues that if the Army had followed the process required by NEPA to prepare a supplemental EIS to consider the Drexel area, it would likely not have chosen to transport the VX hydrolysate to Perma-Fix at all.

Further, while an EIS certainly does not guarantee citizen input into the decision, it does offer the citizens an opportunity to learn about the proposed plan. According to testimony by an area resident before the Subcommittee on National Security, Emerging Threats and International Relations, there was little effort to inform the citizens about the decision to dispose of the VX hydrolysate at Perma-Fix. The citizen testified that Perma-Fix held a public meeting in January 2003 after the Army had already awarded Perma-Fix the contract to dispose of the VX hydrolysate. Angela Jones, a trustee of Jefferson Township where Perma-Fix is located, confirmed that the waste treatment plant did not consider informing the public until after the award had been granted. Like many environmental decisions, the public was informed only after the decision had been made, and like many public meetings, this open house was scheduled during the day, until 6:00 PM, when many individuals could not attend.

Those who were able to attend the meeting were told that VX hydrolysate was not harmful and that the project was a great thing "for us all" (Johnson testimony). Indeed, Perma-Fix maintained that "VX hydrolysate is no different than a one quart can or bottle of Drano drain cleaner" (Bristow testimony). Reminiscent of the description of VX agent as having the consistency of Kayro syrup (see chapter 3), the analogy with the drain cleaner did little to pacify the citizens' concern about VX hydrolysate. In her testimony, Mary Johnson asserted that because she and other residents received few answers at the public meeting, the residents began investigating VX and VX hydrolysate on their own. She noted that during their research they found evidence in a National Research Council publication that VX byproduct could revert to VX agent, and they subsequently researched VX and previous methods used to destroy it. They took their research to the trustees of Jefferson Township, the county commissioners, their political representatives, the Montgomery County Sanitation Department, the Army, Parsons (the contractor tasked with disposing of the VX), and Perma-Fix. The citizens obtained a copy of the contract awarding Perma-Fix the disposal job and discovered the "public acceptance" clause in the contract. According to the Parsons representative's testimony, the language used in the contract among Perma-Fix, Parsons, and the Army, required public outreach sessions to "establish a measure of public acceptance." Further, the contract states that "completion of subcontract work may be contingent upon the establishment and maintenance of public acceptance throughout the subcontract period of performance (Parsons testimony). Yet, according to the Parsons representative, public acceptance meant "the establishment of an active Public Outreach Program" and "compliance with federal, state, and local requirements" (Parsons testimony). Further, the representative claims in the testimony that "it was never Parsons intent to establish a requirement to obtain, retain, or achieve public acceptance by every citizen, but to establish a measure of community understanding that Perma-Fix could safely and effectively treat the hydrolysate generated at the Newport Chemical Depot" (Parsons testimony). The definition of public acceptance became widely contested. An area resident asserted that a more logical definition of public acceptance included public approval of the process (Johnson testimony). Ohio representative Mike Turner asked that the Army provide a definition of public acceptance before it moved forward with its plan to transport VX hydrolysate to Dayton. In response, the assistant secretary of the Army for acquisition, logistics, and technology, Claude M. Bolton Jr., asserted that "the Ohio EPA will solicit public input in connection with the approval process, and we believe that this established procedure is the most appropriate method to measure public acceptance for the Newport program" (Skaluba 5). Yet the Ohio EPA maintained that "there is no applicable public involvement process to be undertaken by this agency. Even if there were required notices or hearings, public acceptance is not one of the criteria Ohio law allows us to consider when evaluating a permit application" (Skaluba 6).

In a now familiar strategic move, the Army attempted to create a barrier between itself and the public—this time by suggesting that it was the EPA's responsibility to talk with the public to determine acceptance, not theirs. As noted in chapters 3 and 4, the "experts" often create institutional barriers between themselves and the public to separate the public from the decision-making process. When experts establish these barriers that prevent citizens from directly influencing the environmental decision, the citizens often adopt strategies for indirectly affecting the decision.

When the citizens around Dayton learned of the public acceptance clause, they collected resolutions from communities and organizations opposing the disposal decision to illustrate that there was not public acceptance. "We attended numerous meetings, sometimes as many as four in one week. We staged rallies, wrote letters to the editors and letters to public officials, made thousands of phone calls all over the United States to experts and to our elected officials, sent numerous emails and faxes, we brought in knowledgeable speakers, we produced videos, we produced a program for Dayton Access Television Station, held environmental issue forums." (Johnson testimony).

This citizen group adopted many of the literacy practices detailed in chapters 3 and 5: they educated themselves on the terminology and research about VX and VX hydrolysate; they researched different disposal technologies; and they brought in independent experts and knowledgeable speakers to help them understand the facts so that they could articulate their concerns in technical terms. Yet, because the decision-making process did not create a space for citizens to participate directly, even in well-articulated, technical discourse, the citizens were denied power to influence the decision and forced to indirectly participate through other channels, including elected officials. As we have seen, this approach to risk communication results in hostility and decisions that drag on for years because those affected by the decision are not allowed to interact directly with the experts who are making all of the decisions. Without direct access to the decision makers, the public retaliates by contacting their elected officials who intervene in the decision-making process, but only to the extent that they force the experts to develop a new plan that may not be any more appropriate for the community than the first. This process does little to progress toward a plan that is just for all affected. Rather than this indirect process that could go on for years without a resolution, a process is essential that brings together all affected at the beginning of a decision to discuss what is needed, what is wanted, and what is possible.

In the case of the VX hydrolysate disposal at Dayton, the public fulfilled its obligation for participating in a technical decision, for entering in the discourse (citizens researched and analyzed the pertinent issues at hand, but because a space did not exist for the experts and citizens to talk together for the purpose of solving the disposal issue, they did not have the power to directly influence the decision).

By some accounts, it seemed as though not only did the Army and Perma-Fix not want the public involved in the decision-making process, they did not want the public to be informed about the decision. In his testimony to the House of Representatives Committee on Government Reform: Subcommittee on National Security, Emerging Threats, and International Relations, Dennis Bristow, a coordinator in Dayton's Regional Hazardous Materials Response Team, notes that even as a part of the area's emergency first response team he was not made aware of the proposed disposal project by Perma-Fix, nor was he invited to planned meetings with fire departments, despite the fact that Perma-Fix was responsible for training all fire departments and area response teams to deal with a VX hydrolysate spill. Bristow says that when he did attend meetings (the folk at the fire department would inform him of the meetings) and questioned the experimental nature of the disposal process, he was repeatedly bombarded with the Drano analogy and realized that "Perma-Fix did not intend to share information with us" (Bristow testimony). In his testimony, Bristow maintains that Drano is not an accurate description of VX hydrolysate. Indeed, this analogy prompted much debate.

Perma-Fix, who was promised $9 million to dispose of the first 330,000 gallons of the caustic hydrolysate, conducted questionable tests to determine the safety of destroying the VX agent in its facility. Perma-Fix conducted tests with only two gallons of VX hydrolysate that did not contain the same chemical stabilizer present in the VX hydrolysate that would be shipped from Newport (AP 10.14.03). Not persuaded by Perma-Fix's own study, Montgomery County—where Drexel is located—hired a civil and environmental engineering professor as an independent expert. In his subsequent report, the independent expert argued that VX hydrolysate was not like Drano, but under the right conditions might revert back to VX nerve agent. In an interview conducted by an Indiana news station, the independent expert noted from his report that destroying VX is difficult by design because when it was produced the Army included stabilizers that "basically knit it back together and keep it from falling apart" (Hensel & Garrison). He claimed that "terrorists could form it [VX hydrolysate] back into VX by changing the PH level with household vinegar" (Hensel & Garrison). (The possibility for VX byproducts to revert back to VX agent was also acknowledged in an earlier National Research Council document cited by Mary Johnson in her testimony to the subcommittee).

On October 13, 2003, the Army contractor, Parsons, cancelled its subcontract with Perma-Fix to dispose of the VX hydrolysate. Yet the reasoning for this decision was never articulated as the lack of public acceptance. According to Parsons testimony, the decision was reached when "it became evident that constraints related to Perma-Fix's operational permit with Montgomery County would preclude the use of the Perma-Fix facility in Dayton, Ohio" (Parsons testimony). Other issues plagued the decision to transport the hydrolysate to Dayton. Adrian Thompson, spokesperson for the Newport Chemical Depot, asserted that while the Army agreed not to transport the hydrolysate off-site if the VX levels were above 20 ppb, the lowest levels they had been able to achieve were 40–80 ppb of VX (Ember).

As late as April 2005, the VX hydrolysate had not left the Newport Chemical Depot. After Dayton denied public acceptance, the Army made plans to send the VX hydrolysate to DuPont's Environmental Solutions Chamber Works facility in Deepwater, New Jersey, for biodegradation, where the treated hydrolysate would be disposed of in the Delaware River (Ember). In 2004, the town council members of Fairview Park, Indiana (12 miles south of Newport), passed a resolution opposing the transportation of VX hydrolysate through their community (Fairview Park Public Notice). The spokesperson for the Newport Citizens against Incineration, Sybil Mowrer, still involved in the disposal decision, voiced her concern for transporting the hydrolysate to a Delaware newspaper, asserting that Newport's problems should not cause trouble for someone else. In April 2005, the Centers for Disease Control and Prevention (CDC) released a report reviewing the Army's proposal for off-site treatment and disposal of VX hydrolysate from the Newport Chemical Depot. The report concluded that "more information is needed to evaluate the ecological risk of discharge of this waste in the Delaware River" (1) and that the "CDC does not recommend proceeding with treatment and disposal at Dupont until EPA's noted deficiencies in the ecological risk assessment are addressed" (2). Interestingly, while the Army's original purpose for transporting the VX hydrolysate to Dayton was to speed the destruction of the VX agent, its handling of the decision process resulted in even further delays in the disposal. The government noted this irony in a briefing memo, the "Army Contract Management: Compliance with Outreach and Public Acceptance Agreements Hearing,"

Whether or not the Army and Permafix [sic] technically had a legal requirement to "gain a measure of public acceptance" before executing the subcontract misses the point. Chemical weapon destruction is a sensitive issue that will require serious debate in any community it may affect [. . .] A project intended to accelerate the destruction of chemical weapons as a means to increase security has instead slowed the process, arguably heightening vulnerability [. . .] the Army mismanagement of the chemical weapons demilitarization program increases the American public's vulnerability to a terrorist attack by prolonging the existence of the chemical weapons stockpile. (Skaluba, 6–7, 9)

The fate of the VX is still uncertain, but it is clear that the Army's decision to bypass traditional procedures of conducting EISs and for considering how a new plan would affect a community in the name of national security forced citizens to find ways to indirectly influence a decision that they, and subsequently experts, agreed was inappropriate for their community.

On May 5, 2005, the Army began neutralizing the VX nerve agent onsite at the Newport Chemical Depot. The process has stopped three times because of spills. One spill occurred during a testing procedure when facility workers determined that a byproduct in the process was more flammable than they originally thought (Webber). However, neutralizing the VX is only the first in a two-step process for destroying it. According to a report on the Army's Chemical Materials Agency website, the second step, super critical water oxidation, was determined to be less cost effective than completing the disposal process offsite (*Cost-benefit Analysis of Off-site Versus On-site Disposal and Treatment of Newport Caustic Hydrolysate,* pp. 5–7). As of September 2006, the neutralized VX was still stored in intermodal shipping containers at Newport in the hopes of transporting the hydrolysate offsite for final treatment (p. 2).

The effects of increased national security on citizen participation reaches beyond decisions to destroy chemical weapons. Increased national security has also affected public access to information about environmental issues that affect their lives. While all environmental decisions and policies are made through discourse, all environmental decisions and policies involve technical information. As a result, citizens must develop knowledge that would be persuasive in these technical settings. An assumption of expert decision makers is that citizens do not understand the scientific knowledge, yet, more often, the fact is that citizens do not have *access* to the scientific knowledge in a format that allows them to make sense of and use the knowledge to articulate their experiences and participate in complex discussions. In order to be heard, citizens must search for the information about their issue, select the pertinent information to their issue, and make sense out of it (Fischer, 2000; Grabill, 2005; Kinsella, 2004).

Several issues concern accessibility to information required to participate in civic matters. One issue is access to the information itself. Gaining access to information necessary to make informed decisions about issues that affect citizens is becoming more and more difficult. James Porter (2005) argues that a growing number of state and federal government policies allow federal agencies to "resist" many requests by citizens for documents that normally would fall under the Freedom of Information Act. For example, he cites a U.S. Department of Justice policy that "gives federal agencies license to withhold information that might be deemed vital to 'safeguarding our national security' " (1). Such policies, which Porter asserts were neither acts of legislature nor voting procedure (2), are also calling for the removal of information previously accessible from web sites, public archives, and libraries. As a case in point, a graduate class I teach in information design recently developed an outreach and educational web site for an area water and sewer district where we were not allowed to include addresses or any references to the location of either the drinking water or the wastewater treatment plants for fear terrorists might contaminate the county's supply of drinking water. National security is not just a recent concern, of course. Growing up near Oak Ridge, Tennessee, I remember billboards around the federal facilities reminding employees that "loose lips sink ships." Porter asserts that while some of these regulations may be necessary in the wake of post-September 11 concerns, many of the newly regulated documents would not pose a threat to national security. Yet these regulations make it more difficult for citizens to access information that enables them to make informed decisions about their lives and communities. Porter draws on Foucault to question the control on discourse and discursive practices that allows certain individuals access to discourse while systematically (and institutionally) denying others (3). This control determines who can speak and how because only those with access to information will be able to speak knowledgeably (and persuasively) about civic issues that affect them (see Simmons & Grabill). Those without access to such information are rendered powerless in the decision-making process. For example, at a meeting to discuss public records access in Ohio, a member of Jefferson Township has noted that the information from public records contributed significantly to halting the decision to transport VX hydrolysate to the Perma-Fix facility in Dayton (Ohio Citizen Action web site).

Pete Shuler (*CityBeat*, July 14, 2004) argues that while government officials are supposed to serve only as the "custodians" for public records, it is rare that the requests for such documents are filled in a timely manner, if at all. Shuler investigated 491 requests made by representatives from forty-two newspapers, the Associated Press, two radio stations, and two universities all in Ohio for information that fell within the definition of public record. He found that almost half of the requests were not filled within twenty-four hours, despite the fact that Ohio law states that "all public records shall be promptly prepared and made available for inspection to any person at all reasonable times during regular business hours" (20). He also found that when the requests are filled, certain information may be blacked out. Other times government employees required requesters to provide identification and a rationale for the need of the information, "both of which are impermissible" (*CityBeat*, 20). This growing inaccessibility to information makes it more difficult for citizens to research civic issues that affect their lives in order to persuasively articulate their concerns about those issues.[2]

How does this affect rhetoricians and technical communicators? Rhetoricians and technical communicators have long considered themselves user advocates (Johnson, 1998; Sullivan, 1990). Porter provides a new facet to this role, arguing that technical communicators should be "public advocates for access" (8). In addition to our duties to always think about how the documents we produce will affect the user, this new facet requires us to "promote wide access to information" (8) in a belief that only informed citizens have the literacy practices necessary to effectively participate in environmental decisions. If citizens hope to participate in technical decisions, they must research relevant issues. Without wide access to information, citizens will not have the opportunity to educate themselves on the issues, much less articulate in a persuasive manner their concerns to decision makers. The importance of public access to information is why service-learning and community-based projects such as the civic web site projects discussed in chapter 6 are useful for rhetoricians and technical communicators. Using our expertise in information technology and usability, we can think about what information citizens need to participate in particular issues and the ways citizens can access this information. Using a participatory framework to develop civic web sites that are useful for a community is one way rhetoricians and technical communicators can work as "public advocates for access." Often these civic web sites include information that citizens can use to make informed decisions about their environment that might otherwise be difficult for citizens to obtain on their own.

Additionally, we must help our students understand their role as public advocates for access. We must help them understand that they have the ability to understand complex material and articulate their concerns about that material whether it be a piece of technology they believe is detrimental to users or the environment or a policy that they believe is detrimental to users or the environment. Our students need to know that technical communicators are more than conduits or bridges between subject matter experts and end users. Our students must leave us believing that they have the power to bring about change because they are able to articulate their understanding of a situation and the audience affected by that situation. Students need to know that as rhetoricians and technical communicators they can bring about change in different ways: by talking with designers of the technology or policy, by working with the public, or even by talking with elected officials such as senators and legislatures.

I recently attended a "lobby day" at my state capitol where I had the opportunity to talk with state senators, representatives, and state EPA officials. This particular lobby day was organized by a state-wide environmental group, the Ohio Environmental Council (OEC), to provide citizens concerned about particular environmental issues an opportunity to explain their concern to the elected officials and ask for specific actions to be taken to address those concerns. For this lobby day, the state-wide environmental group briefed the attending citizens on current environmental issues and how they corresponded to current legislation. The OEC also provided the attending citizens with a briefing book that detailed these issues and offered specific recommendations to make to the elected officials and lawmakers. (It is important to note that the speakers for this environmental group did not suggest to the attending citizens that they had to talk about one of these designated topics or lobby for the specific recommendations; rather these briefings offered specific, detailed, and useful information that the citizens could chose to use if they desired). The speakers for the environmental group also briefed the attending citizens on effective ways to lobby their elected officials and lawmakers, including providing specific details to explain why the issue is a problem, explaining how the issue affects you and the elected official's district, stating specifically what you want the elected official to do, and being polite because it is easier to catch flies with honey than with vinegar. After the briefing sessions, the attending citizens were divided into groups of three or four and given times that had been scheduled for them to visit a specified elected official. When possible, attending citizens were assigned to elected officials in their district. (Attending citizens were also provided handouts on the type of homework they need to do before they talk with the elected officials and information about each elected officials' political party and district). During the scheduled appointments, each citizen had the opportunity to talk for five to ten minutes.

I spoke with two state senators' aides (both senators were members of a committee that had been called to the floor during our scheduled appointments) and several EPA officials about the importance of public access to information. In my discussion with the senators' aides, I argued that while experts often assume that citizens cannot effectively participate in policy decisions, the fact is that citizens are often denied the information they need to effectively participate in policy decisions. I asked that citizens be given access to the debate, testimony, and discussions that occur during committee hearings and that these discussions be searchable by topic and bill number. While the proposed bill, how the bill would amend existing law, and the resulting votes are currently available online, the heart of each legislature, law, or policy, is the discourse that shaped the final decision. Having access to this discourse could help citizens better understand the multiple perspectives of the issue and how they can articulate their own concerns if they want to be valued. Since the space already exists for posting the proposed bill and the outcome, adding a transcript of the discussion is logistically a small change. Yet providing access to the committee hearing discussions reveals much about the individual officials and institutions and the way knowledge and legislature are created—knowledge that lawmakers may be hesitant to share.

When as part of a group I spoke with the state EPA officials, others and I voiced concern about a proposed bill that would slash the time the public has to comment on an environmental plan from thirty to fifteen days. I noted that if we hope for citizen concerns to be taken seriously, we must give them adequate time to not only read the plan but also to educate themselves on an issue by researching multiple perspectives regarding that issue, analyzing those different perspectives, and understanding the important questions regarding the issue. Reducing the comment time to fifteen days not only denies citizens the time to do their research but also further marginalizes public comments, making the assumption that public comments are not carefully researched or constructed.

Will my few minutes with lawmakers and state EPA officials bring about change? These discussions will probably not bring as much change as developing civic web sites with communities or conducting usability research for an environmental decision. However, while changing institutional practices requires change from within that institution, lawmakers can encourage change with new legislation. Perhaps in talking with lawmakers we can open a dialogue or spark a thought that they had not considered about the need for public access to information. And as rhetoricians and technical communicators, we must consider all available means for enacting change that empowers citizens to participate in the issues that affect their lives and communities.

APPENDIX A:

PUBLIC NOTICE SAMPLE

PUBLIC NOTICE

Notice of Public Meeting

Notice is hereby given by the Indiana Department of Environmental Management (IDEM) of a meeting to educate the interested public on the public participation process involved in the issuance of permits for the Newport Chemical Depot (NECD). The IDEM Offices of Air, Water and Solid and Hazardous Waste are working jointly to provide this opportunity for the public to ask questions and learn how to better effectively participate in the permitting process. The meeting will provide the public with information about public review of the draft permits and the associated public hearing. NECD is seeking air, water and waste permits as applicable to the operation of a facility to destroy VX nerve agent currently stored at NECD.

IDEM and the Program Manager for Chemical Demilitarization (PMCD) are inviting the public to attend this meeting on Thursday August 12, 1999 at the Newport Lions Club located at 240 South Main Street in Newport. A poster session and opportunity for one on one discussion IDEM and/or Army staff will begin at 5:00. A presentation by the regulators describing the public participation process for the various permits required for the facility will begin at 6:30. Additional time for questions and comments will be provided after the presentation.

For further information, please contact Ms. Michelle Timmermann at, IDEM at 317/232-3264.

APPENDIX B: SAMPLE OF COMMENTS

SECTION FROM DRAFT ENVIRONMENTAL

IMPACT STATEMENT

APPENDIX B

SCOPING FOR THIS ENVIRONMENTAL IMPACT STATEMENT

This appendix summarizes the environmental issues identified by the public during the scoping process for the Newport Chemical Agent Disposal Facility (NECDF) environmental impact statement (EIS). The comment period was initiated with the publication in the *Federal Register* of a Notice of Intent to prepare the NECDF EIS (62 *Fed. Regist.* 30315), which solicited written comments on the proposed project. In addition, a public scoping meeting was held in Clinton, Indiana (Vermillion County), on June 30, 1997, to provide a forum for individuals and organizations to offer oral comments on the proposed action. The oral and written comments offered by the public during the scoping period assisted in the identification of the important environmental issues and concerns deserving detailed analysis in the EIS.

B.1 BACKGROUND

In January, 1988, a public hearing was held in Vermillion County, Indiana, to discuss the Army's Final Programmatic Environmental Impact Statement concerning the disposal of agent stored at multiple sites around the country. Four years later, a public scoping meeting was held in Vermillion County concerning the preparation of a site-specific environmental impact statement on disposal of agent stored at NECD. In both meetings, large numbers of community members attended, made statements, and queried Army representatives. The dominant concern expressed at both events had to do with the safety of the disposal process and how it might affect nearby residents. Among the specific issues raised were the proximity of the proposed disposal site to neighboring towns and schools, the possible effects of natural disasters on plant operations, the training of on-site personnel, the adequacy of emergency management procedures, and the feasibility of shipping the agent off-site (Ace-Federal Reporters, Inc. 1988; Ace-Federal Reporters, Inc 1992).

In the spring and summer of 1994, staff from Battelle Pacific Northwest Laboratories conducted interviews and focus group discussions with people living in the area surrounding NECD as part of a larger effort to assess community views at all potential disposal sites. The researchers concluded that, in general, NECD was held in high regard by community members, many of whom were proud of its role in the national defense effort. Many local residents expressed trust and confidence in the Army, although others reported being shocked upon learning that VX had been manufactured at the depot decades earlier. During the late 1980s, there had been a high level of concern in the community over the Army's plans to incinerate VX on-site, but the Battelle researchers reported that community concern appeared to have waned over time. However, some community residents suggested that the lack of apparent concern could reflect the fact that the Army had taken no disposal-related actions for several years and might not indicate a genuine lack of community interest (Battelle Pacific Northwest Laboratories 1994).

Indiana, like several other states, has a Citizens' Advisory Commission (CAC) that was created by the Army to provide input on state and local concerns regarding the proposed chemical stockpile disposal program. The Indiana CAC has nine members, seven from the area surrounding NECD and two state officials. The Indiana CAC has always been very concerned with protecting the safety of Indiana residents and has expressed serious reservations concerning the proposed incineration plan. Recently, the CAC chairman voiced the Commission's support of chemical neutralization pilot testing (Indiana Citizens' Advisory Commission 1997).

B.2 PUBLIC SCOPING MEETING AND ORAL COMMENTS

Twenty-four citizens registered their attendance at the scoping meeting one June 30, 1997, and two attendees offered comments on the proposed facility. One speaker indicated that any proposed uses of the NECDF after destruction of the chemical agent should be presented to the public for consideration and discussion. The other speaker felt that the health and safety of the public and the facility workers should be the first considerations in the design, construction, and operation of the proposed facility.

B.3 WRITTEN COMMENTS

One of the speakers at the public scoping meeting also submitted a written comment. It reiterated the commentor's concern regarding potential future uses of the proposed facility and the proposed site: Any planned future uses of the facility and land should be presented to the public for comment, and comments should be solicited at not only the local level but also the regional and state levels.

B.4 RELATED SCOPING ACTIVITIES

In conjunction with the planning and evaluation stages of chemical agent demilitarization programs at Newport and other installations (e.g., Aberdeen Proving Ground in Maryland), the Army has pursued related activities that are required before the construction of the disposal facilities. These actions include preparation of the permit and permit modification applications required by the Resource Conservation and Recovery Act, the Clean Air Act, and the Clean Water Act. During these activities, the Army has noted any public concerns or comments that were expressed in those forums. Also, public comments on the Chemical Stockpile Disposal Program in general and on incineration in particular were evaluated for their applicability to this EIS. The following outline summarizes the comments received during these public involvement activities that were reviewed for their applicability to the proposed NECDF.

- Risks associated with disposal options compared with continued storage
  - quantity and condition of stockpile
  - failure of the Johnston Atoll Chemical Agent Disposal System facility to achieve a destruction efficiency of 99.9999% in the metal parts incinerator
  - transporting the stockpile as an interim safety measure
  - types and adequacy of monitoring
  - integrity of storage containers
  - types and hazards of nonstockpile chemical materiel onsite (e.g., buried chemical warfare materiel, former production facilities)
  - stockpile risks in the context of other activities and materials onsite
  - existing security measures are inadequate, making the stockpile vulnerable to sabotage or acts of terrorism
- Accidents
  - proximity of public facilities such as airports
  - need for indoor storage of stockpile
  - nearby population
- Socioeconomic impacts and community issues
  - public opposition to hazardous waste incinerators
  - public perception of the adequacy of the institutional structure to protect their safety
  - federal agency and Department of Defense attention to affected communities
  - need to institutionalize active, meaningful public involvement
  - providing assistance to citizens advisory commissions
  - involving the public in the decision making process rather than simply measuring public reaction to selected disposal option
  - employment
  - impacts on local infrastructure, public services, tourism, property values, and quality of life
  - socioeconomic differences among the counties most affected by the facility
  - importance of the installation's role in the social and economic development of the region
  - adequacy of existing emergency planning and preparedness capability in the community
  - cost of the proposed action and alternatives
  - environmental justice (locating the incinerator in an area that may not have the social, political, and financial resources to oppose it effectively)
- Emergency planning and preparedness measures
  - onsite and offsite
  - public notification systems
  - evacuation of the surrounding area would be impossible

- Ecology
  - nature, extent, and environmental impacts of existing contamination
  - transport and migration pathways for onsite contaminants (for both stockpile and nonstockpile chemicals and for both normal and nonroutine events)
  - environmental impacts of routine base operations
  - impacts on local agriculture
- Water quality
  - deposition of emissions on nearby surface water bodies (e.g., Wabash River)
  - solubility of agent and contaminants
- Noise
  - from existing operations and from construction and operation of the incinerator facility
- Air quality
  - quantity and components of emissions from incinerator
  - existing air quality (poor, would be further degraded by incinerator emissions)
  - nonattainment areas
  - "synergistic effects" of incinerator emissions and existing air pollutants, especially during inversions
- Human health
  - need for site-specific risk and exposure assessment
  - evaluation of the non-lethal health effects of incineration
  - health effects of existing onsite contamination
  - properties and effects of agents
  - regional cancer rates are high and would increase with incinerator emissions
  - health risk studies should include infants and young children
- Alternative demilitarization technologies
  - need for increased research into alternatives
  - reliability of data supporting safety of incineration
  - all alternatives need to be considered (e.g., burial/entombment)
  - more rigorous and extensive research needed on neutralization and biodegradation, possibly resulting in its selection as the preferred option for destruction of chemical agent
  - dependability and reliability of incineration
- Cost of incineration facility
  - unjustifiable cost compared with other alternatives
  - unjustifiable for "temporary" facility

REFERENCES

ACE—Federal Reporters, Inc. 1988. *Transcript of Proceedings: Public Hearing on the Final Environmental Impact Statement (FEIS) by Department of the Army, Clinton, Indiana, Tuesday, January 26, 1988.*

ACE—Federal Reporters, Inc. 1992. *Transcript of Proceedings: Public Scoping Meeting for the Proposed Newport Chemical Agent Disposal Facility, Vermillion Co., Indiana, Friday, April 3, 1992.*

APPENDIX C: SAMPLE OF COMMENTS
SECTION FROM FINAL ENVIRONMENTAL
IMPACT STATEMENT

APPENDIX H

PUBLIC COMMENTS ON THE DRAFT VERSION OF THIS ENVIRONMENTAL IMPACT STATEMENT

This appendix displays copies of letters received from agencies and the public commenting on the Draft Environmental Impact Statement (EIS). All letters received by the Army during the comment period (June 12 to July 27, 1998) are included verbatim. Two of the comments displayed in this appendix were received in writing during a public meeting held in Newport, Indiana, on July 7, 1998. Another set of remarks was provided at that meeting and is displayed in the transcript of that meeting in this appendix.

Individual comments from each agency or person were assigned numbers, as shown in boldface in the left margins of the letters displayed on the following pages. Army responses are provided on the right-hand side of the same page that displays the subject letter. In each response, the Army states either that (1) the text was revised for this Final EIS, (2) provides an explanation of why the text in the Draft EIS was adequate and did not need to be revised, or (3) answers questions that were asked by the commentor. If the response does not mention text revisions, then the corresponding text in the Draft EIS was not revised. Note that section numbers in this Final EIS are the same as those in the Draft EIS; however, page numbers referenced in letters commenting on the Draft EIS are not necessarily the same as the page numbers in this Final EIS.

7-1. The Army appreciates the comment.

7-2. Equipment specification requires the vendor of the carbon filters to meet a performance level of 99 percent removal of volatile organic compounds (VOCs) or an undetectable level (<5 ppbw), whichever is more restrictive, for emissions from the gas/liquid separators. Additional equipment specifications call for a performance level of 99.9999 percent for VX constituents for each carbon filter unit, for emissions from the Chemical Demilitarization Building. Calculations have been performed to describe the adequacy of the carbon filter to remove toxic vapors during a bounding case (release of agent). The calculation indicates that two of the six carbon filters are sufficient to remove 50 times the calculated release. These requirements are considerably more stringent than the regulatory requirement.

7-3. See response to Comment 7-2.

7-4. The Army does not plan to reactivate carbon filters.

7-5. Current plans are to transport the solid waste (salts) off-site to a permitted treatment, storage and disposal facility (TSDF). In the unlikely event of on-site disposal of the salts, the Army would be required to comply with RCRA regulations which include the avoidance of future reactivity problems.

7-6. The Army is required to comply with numerous permit requirements (see Sect. 4.9 of this EIS) specified by the Indiana Department of Environmental Management and the U.S. Environmental Protection Agency to protect human health. The monitoring requirements mentioned in the comment have yet to be determined by these agencies.

7-7. The Army will continue to keep Newport and other nearby communities, as well as the State of Indiana, informed on a regular basis if a decision is made to proceed with construction and operation of the proposed facility.

7-8. The comment is noted.

Program Manager For Chemical Demilitarization
ATTN: SFAE-CD-M
Aberdeen Proving Ground, Maryland 21010--5401

July, 26-1990

Re: Comments on the Draft Environmental Impact Statement of construction and operation of a pilot test chemical neutralization of VX followed by supercritical water oxidation at Newport Chemical Depot.

7-1 As members of C.A.I.N. we are delighted with the fact that the Army is proposing to pilot the destruction of VX by neutralization and SCWO.

We still have some concerns as follows:

7-2 1. Emission of agent into the air from possible inadequate filtering of exhaust gases.
A. that monitors provide short term information on emissions.

7-3 B. That all filtering processes be redundant.

7-4 2. How is the reactivation of contaminated carbon filters contemplated?
There should be no incineration of carbon filters.

7-5 3. Final disposition of the solid waste (salts) from the SCWO, if contemplated on-site should require the drilling and analysis of the present fill content to determine possible reactions with the new material.

7-6 4. Monitoring and disposition of the waste water after leaving the NECD plant. We hope that the disposal of all wastes would be monitored during the process.

7-7 5. That the Army keeps the entire community up to date during the construction and operation of the facility.

7-8 We appreciate the efforts of all those who have helped make sure that the concerns of the local community were and are being heard.

Mark Hudson and Rainer Zengerl on behalf
of C A I N

8-1. The Army appreciates the comment. It should be noted, however, that the baseline incinerations process (which is not an alternative considered in this EIS) does not result in the release of atmospheric emissions (i.e., vapors) harmful to human health or the environment.

8-1

The following comments were received by FAX on July 28, 1998, by Matt Hurlburt of PMCD. The commentor was Mr. Kevin Rudduck of NECD. They have been retyped for legibility.

Pilot testing of Neutralization/Supercritical Water Oxidation of VX Agent at Newport Chemical Depot, Indiana (April 1998)

11-1   Page 2-4, Table 2.2, VX Nominal Fill WT/TC should be 682 Kg/1500 lb. Remainder of metric/standard conversions in chart should be checked.

11-2   Page 2-5, para 4, Temperatures - 650%C is not 1110% F.

11-3   Page 2-9, Fig. 2.3, "Existing lagoons" do not exist.

11-4   Page 2-16, Para 2.2.3.3, adequately describes SCWO but Fig 2.5 is less clear -- into which stream is O_2 fed on entry to SCWO reactor?

11-5   Page 3-3, para 2. Chemical Plant constructed 1959 - 1961 Not 1962.

11-6   Page 3-15, para 3. This paragraph, as written, would seem to indicate that LRC water is still being degraded by past discharge practices even though LRC has not been used to discharge industrial/sanitary wastes since the early 1970's. (Is there any recovery in LRC?) Industrial/ sanitary wastes have been discharged to the Wabash River (via forced main) since 1973.

11-7   Page 3-15, para 4. Use of retention basins 30007, 30008, and 30009 should be further qualified in the narrative. It should be stated that the retention basins were not used to process industrial waste from the Chemical (VX) Plant.

11-1.   Table 2.2 has been revised to indicate the proper fill weight as indicated in the comment.

11-2.   The correct metric unit for the temperature has been inserted into this final version of the EIS.

11-3.   Figure 2.3 has been revised to delete the lagoons.

11-4.   Figure 2.5 has been revised to clarify the process stream.

11-5.   The language in this final EIS has been revised to reflect the construction dates provided in the comment.

11-6.   The language in Sect. 3.3.1.1 of this Final EIS has been revised to reflect the historical nature (i.e., prior to 1973) of these discharges.

11-7.   The language in Section 3.3.1.1 of this final EIS has been revised to clarify historical usage of the retention basins mentioned in the comment. The retention basins were not used to process industrial chemical waste from the manufacture of VX agent; only water from boiler drains and heat exchangers was pumped to these basins.

APPENDIX D: SAMPLE OF COMMENTS

SECTION FROM IDEM NOTICE

OF DECISION

RESPONSE TO COMMENTS
RCRA DRAFT PERMIT
NEWPORT CHEMICAL DEPOT
NEWPORT, INDIANA
IN1210022272

INTRODUCTION

The public comment period for the Newport Chemical Depot (NECD) Draft Permit began on September 17, 1999, with a public notice in the Tribune Star. Terre Haute. Indiana; Indianapolis Star. Indianapolis. Indiana; The Daily Clintonian. Clinton. Indiana; Danville Commercial News, Danville. Illinois and a radio announcement on radio stations WTHI AM/FM. Terre Haute. Indiana; KISS. Covington. Indiana; WAIX FM. Rockville. Indiana; WDNL, Danville. Illinois and a mass mailing to interested parties. The notice and announcement requested comments regarding the Draft RCRA Permit and also stated that a public hearing would be held on October 18. 1999, at the Newport Lion's Club in Newport. Indiana. In addition to the comments presented at the hearing, written comments were accepted during the public comment period, which ended on November 1, 1999.

This Response to Comments is issued pursuant to 329 IAC 3.1-13-13, which requires that the Indiana Department of Environmental Management (IDEM) shall:

1. briefly describe and respond to all significant comments on the Draft Permit;

2. specify which provisions, if any, of the Draft Permit have been changed, and the reasons for the change; and

3. explain the right to request an adjudicatory hearing on the permit as specified in IC 4-21.5.3.5 (see Notice of Decision).

RESPONSE TO PUBLIC COMMENTS

The following responses have been prepared by the Indiana Department of Environmental Management (IDEM) to address the concerns expressed by the public during the public comment period. The comments are described in the following sections along with the IDEM's response and any changes made as a result of the comments.

1. Comment: It was noted in my study and in my review of the *Draft Copy of the Environmental Impact Statement*, April 1998, there are forty-nine (49) pages which are thought to be in need of corrective action due to questionable and/or misleading statements. There was information which appeared to verify noncompliance when weighed with the Indiana law 13-

7-8.5-13, 1993. The "Report" provided no statistically reliable, valid, nor reproducible data to support the human safety requirements.

Response: This comment is specific to the Draft Environmental Impact Statement, April 1998 and not the Draft Permit. However, the permit application has been evaluated to insure compliance with all applicable state and federal regulations.

Change: None.

2.   Comment: If there would be a leak to the secondary containment, how would that affect the surrounding wells? If there was contamination, how would the surrounding drinking water wells be affected?

Response: The VX agent processing buildings are designed with secondary containment to protect against the release of any agent to the environment. If there was a leak to the secondary containment during the processing of agent, the waste would be contained and the appropriate responses as indicated in the permit would be implemented. No agent will have an opportunity to impact groundwater from a leak to the secondary containment.

Change: No change.

RESPONSE TO FACILITY COMMENTS

Pursuant to the issuance of the Draft IDEM RCRA Permit dated September 18, 1999, Newport Chemical Depot (NECD) and the United States Army, Program Manager for Chemical Demilitarization (PMCD) submitted the following comments in accordance with the public comment procedures. The comments are described in the following sections along with the IDEM's response and any changes made as a result of the comments.

I. STANDARD CONDITIONS

1.   Comment: Federal section of NECD current permit Page 34 of 35, Sec. VI. "Schedule of Compliance" The current permit requires that a Hazardous Waste Reduction Plan (HWRP) be completed by December 31, every other year and a Waste Reduction Implementation Report be completed by September 30, annually. The HWRP and WRIP are not addressed in the draft permit. Request confirmation if these requirements are to be discontinued.

Response: Waste minimization requirements are addressed in Permit Condition I.G.

Change: No change.

IV.   TANK STORAGE AND TREATMENT CONDITIONS

2.   Comment: Section IV.A.1. Page 30 of 58
                    Since the treatment tanks also treat streams other than the SCWO Effluent.
                    it is requested that this condition be restated as follows: "...in permitted
                    tanks and produce a total weight of 142.77 tons per day of effluent from
                    the SCWO to the evaporator/crystalizer through treatment of hazardous
                    wastes, as designated below."

      Response: IDEM concurs.

      Change: As requested.

3.   Comment: Table IV.1.a, Page 30 of 58
                    Since hazardous wastes are stored and/or treated in these tank systems. it
                    is requested that the table heading be "Hazardous Waste *Stored/*"Treated
                    in Tank Systems"

      Response: IDEM concurs.

      Change: As requested.

4.   Comment: Section IV.C, Page 31 of 58
                    Delete "which is incorporated herein by reference" since Attachment D2 is
                    part of the permit.

      Response: IDEM concurs.

      Change: As requested.

5.   Comment: Section IV.D.4, Page 32 of 58
                    Drained Agent Reactor effluent is sent to the TCC Effluent reactor for
                    further treatment prior to having treatment verified and being sent to the
                    Hydrolysate Storage Tanks. Therefore, it is requested that this condition
                    be reworded as follows: "Liquid waste shall not be discharged from the
                    neutralization reactors to the Hydrolysate Storage Tanks until the waste
                    has been treated and waste treatment is verified in accordance with
                    methods specified in Attachment C-2."

      Response: IDEM concurs.

APPENDIX E: HOUSE ENROLLED

ACT NO. 1143

Second Regular Session 107th General Assembly (1992)

PRINTING CODE. Amendments: Whenever an existing statute (or a section of the Indiana Constitution) is being amended, the text of the existing provision will appear in this style type, additions will appear in this style type, and deletions will appear in ~~this style type.~~

Additions: Whenever a new statutory provision is being enacted (or a new constitutional provision adopted), the text of the new provision will appear in this style type. Also, the word NEW will appear in that style type in the introductory clause of each SECTION that adds a new provision to the Indiana Code or the Indiana Constitution.

HOUSE ENROLLED ACT No. 1134

AN ACT to amend the Indiana Code concerning the environment.

Be it enacted by the General Assembly of the State of Indiana:

SECTION 1. IC 13-7-8.5-13 IS ADDED TO THE INDIANA CODE AS A NEW SECTION TO READ AS FOLLOWS: Sec. 13. (a) As used in this section, "chemical munition" means any of the following:

   (1) GA (Ethyl-N, N-dimethyl phosphoramidocyanidate).

   (2) GB (Isopropyl methyl phosphonoflouridate).

   (3) H, HD (Bis(2-chloroethyl) sulfide).

   (4) HT (Sixty percent (60%) HD and forty percent (40%) T (Bis[2(2-chloroethyl-thio)ethyl]ester)).

   (5) L (Dichloro(2-chlorovinyl)arsine).

   (6) VX (O-ethyl-S-(2-diisopropylaminoethyl) methyl phosphonothiolate).

  (b) In addition to any other requirements, a permit may not be issued under this chapter for the construction or operation of a hazardous waste facility to be used for the destruction or treatment of a chemical munition unless the person applying for the permit has demonstrated the following:

   (1) The destruction or treatment technology to be used at the proposed hazardous waste facility has

179

been in operation:

(A) at a facility comparable to the proposed hazardous waste facility; and

(B) for a time sufficient to demonstrate that ninety-nine and nine thousand nine hundred ninety-nine ten-thousandths percent (99.9999%) of the chemical munition processed at the comparable facility has been destroyed or treated.

(2) Monitoring data from a comparable hazardous waste facility demonstrates that there are no emissions from the comparable facility that alone or in combination with another substance present a risk of an:

(A) acute or chronic human health effect; or

(B) adverse environmental effect.

(3) A plan to:

(A) provide sufficient training, coordination, and equipment for state and local emergency response personnel needed to respond to possible releases of harmful substances from the proposed hazardous waste facility; and

(B) evacuate persons in the geographic area at risk from the worst possible release of:

(i) the chemical munition; or

(ii) a substance related to the destruction or treatment of the chemical munition;

from the proposed hazardous waste facility;

has been funded and developed.

SECTION 2. (a) Before July 1, 1993, the solid waste management board shall adopt rules under IC 4-22-2 to add GA (Ethyl-N, N-dimethyl phosphoramidocyanidate), GB (Isopropyl methyl phosphonoflouridate), H and HD (Bis(2-chloroethyl) sulfide), HT (Sixty percent (60%) HD and forty percent (40%) T (Bis[2(2-chloroethyl-thio)ethyl]ester)), L (Dichloro(2-chlorovinyl)arsine), and VX (O-ethyl-S-(2-diisopropylaminoethyl) methyl phosphonothiolate) to the list of hazardous wastes compiled and maintained under IC 13-7-8.5-3(b).

(b) This SECTION expires July 1, 1993.

SECTION 3. This act takes effect as follows:

SECTION 1 .... July 1, 1993
SECTION 2 .... July 1, 1992

Questions & Answers

Newport Chemical Depot

Newport, Indiana

production of chemical weapons and a reduction in the stockpiles of both nations. As a storage site for a portion of the U.S. chemical weapons stockpile, the Russian Federation inspected Newport Chemical Depot in late 1994.

The multilateral Chemical Weapons Convention, or CWC, went into force April 29, 1997, when the U.S. and 87 other nations had ratified the treaty. The CWC states that the U.S. and other participating nations will destroy all of their chemical weapons stockpile within 10 years after entry into force, or April 2007. To minimize the risk to the community, the Army is committed to destroying the Newport stockpile as soon as possible.

Newport Chemical Depot is subject to future inspections under the Chemical Weapons Convention.

Q. *What is the Chemical Stockpile Disposal Program?*
Public Law 99-145 mandates the disposal of the chemical weapons stockpile in the United States.

Public law also directs development of a plan, called the Chemical Stockpile Disposal Plan, or CSDP, to define the safest and most effective way to dispose of the stockpile.

The baseline technology for destruction of the Army's stockpile is on-site incineration. In response to local public concern over incineration, the Army has been authorized to proceed with the necessary activities to pilot test an alternative technology at NECD. The proposed VX destruction pilot plant will test a low-temperature, low pressure neutralization process, followed by a post-treatment mineralization process.

The Indiana Governor has appointed a board of local community members to the Indiana Chemical Demilitarization Citizens' Advisory Commission, which relays citizen and state concerns to the Army.

Q. *What is CSEPP?*
The Chemical Stockpile Emergency Preparedness Program, or CSEPP, is a joint effort by the Federal Emergency Management Agency and the Army to protect the community in the unlikely event of an accident involving Chemical Agent VX.

The Newport Chemical Depot CSEP Plan involves two states and six counties: Vermillion, Parke, Fountain and Vigo Counties in Indiana; and Vermilion and Edgar Counties in Illinois.

Each local agency is funded, staffed and trained to respond to a chemical emergency at Newport Chemical Depot.

For More Information:

Newport Chemical Depot
Offices of
Public Affairs and
Public Outreach
Newport Chemical Depot
PO Box 121
Newport, IN 47966-0121
(317)245-4597/4475

181

Q. What is Newport Chemical Depot?

Newport Chemical Depot (NECD) is a government-owned, contractor-operated military installation under the U.S. Army Chemical and Biological Defense Command.

Located in Vermillion County, two miles south of the town of Newport and 32 miles north of Terre Haute, Ind., the installation covers an area of about 7,000 acres.

Mason & Hanger Corp., the operating contractor at NECD, is the third largest employer in Vermillion County, with a work force of more than 200.

Q. What does the Army store at Newport Chemical Depot?

One of eight U.S. chemical weapons storage sites, NECD stores only Chemical Agent VX. The depot does not store munitions or other explosive material.

Though the Army produced VX at NECD in the 1960s, the plant was not intended to be a long-term storage facility. When production of the agent stopped in 1968 and the Army declared a moratorium on the shipment of VX and other chemical agents, the depot's mission became the safe and secure storage of the remaining stockpile.

Q. What is Chemical Agent VX?

VX is a member of the organo-phosphate family, similar to present day pesticides.

A common misconception is that VX is a gas. VX actually is a liquid that is slightly heavier than water and evaporates more than 2,000 times more slowly than water. Under normal conditions, it is clear- to straw-colored. VX is a rapid-acting nerve agent that affects the nervous system by interfering with the signals sent from the brain to the vital organs and other parts of the body.

Q. How is VX stored?

The stockpile at NECD is in carbon steel containers stored in a large metal building with steel beams and a sealed concrete floor.

The cylindrical ton container (named not for its weight, but for the original French manufacturer, Tonne) is 82 inches long and 30 1/2 inches in diameter. The container's sidewalls are nearly 1/2 inch thick, with 3/4-inch thick concave ends that protect the filling and draining valves. Since VX is a non-corrosive chemical, it does not erode the carbon steel containers. The ton containers are stacked three-high and clamped securely together for added safety.

Floor drains connect to a central sump so, in the unlikely event of a leak, the chemical can be contained and decontaminated.

Q. How safe is the VX stockpile?

About one-third of the work force at Newport Chemical Depot is dedicated exclusively to VX stockpile security.

Armed guards patrol the storage area 24 hours a day. The chemical storage area has a double security fence, controlled entry for vehicles and employees, and crash barriers on the entry road. There also are security lighting, motion detection and camera surveillance systems at the storage site.

No one is allowed to enter the storage area alone, and all employees who are authorized routine access to the storage area are continually screened and monitored for reliability.

Trained surety workers perform twice-weekly visual inspections of each ton container. The building also has lightning and earthquake protection systems and an air monitoring system that can detect any leakage.

Storage Configuration

Q. What is the Chemical Weapons Treaty Compliance Program?

At the 1985 Geneva Summit, President Reagan and Soviet General Secretary Gorbachev reaffirmed support for a global ban on chemical weapons and agreed to accelerate efforts toward that goal.

The United States and former Soviet Union signed in 1989 a memorandum of understanding providing for an exchange of chemical weapons data and visits between the two nations.

In 1990 Presidents Bush and Gorbachev signed a bilateral destruction agreement calling for a halt in

NOTES

CHAPTER 1

1. Since the 1960s, there has been an increasing concern for the environment in the United States. The 1962 publication of Rachel Carson's *Silent Spring* is often credited with launching the environmental movement (Belsten, Rubin & Sachs). In *Silent Spring*, Carson details the dangers of pesticides that accumulate in water, soil, and food; as a result she generated an awareness in the public eye of environmental hazard. This awareness was heightened in 1969 when a series of environmental disasters plagued the nation, including the Santa Barbara oil spill; the seizure of eleven tons of salmon in Wisconsin and Minnesota due to excessive DDT concentrations; the Cuyahoga River fire in Cleveland; and the smog alert days in Los Angeles when health official suggested that children not play outside (Belsten, p. 30; Rubin & Sachs, p. 54). 1970 brought the first Earth Day, and a "call for new initiatives to resolve environmental problems" (Belsten, p. 30). This initiative suggested that the public was no longer content to leave the fate of human health and the environment to government and scientific experts. Communities demanded not only an explanation of what risks were present, and what was going to be done about those risks, but also a hand in the decisions made about the risks.

2. This notion of the public is problematic. The public does not neatly fit into one definition. Members of the government, industry, and scientific community often spill into the group defined as public. The term *public* also tempts the dichotomy of expert versus public that is still prevalent from the early stages of risk communication but that I wish to avoid projecting. Further, the subject position of the public as coherent, unified, and identifiable decontextualizes the people affected by a given risk and therefore important participants in the construction of that risk. However, for the purposes of this study, rather than attempt to define 'public' myself, I wish to consider how institutions might define the public by examining who institutions related to a particular case identify as public. While not solving the problematic conception of 'public,' this study hopes to advocate the necessity of identifying various publics and to take seriously the differences of a given town, neighborhood, or community. Further, while I advocate that there are many publics and communities, because of the nature of this case, I have chosen to focus on two—geographical (the local communities around Newport) and ideological—the citizens and citizen groups opposed to the burning of deadly chemical warfare. While these groups are not exclusive of one another, indeed they often overlap—for example, the local citizens teamed up with citizen groups as a way to protest incineration and often used one of the citizen groups' web sites as a point of contact and way to disseminate their experiences

in the public meetings—I did not investigate the impacts of the electronic communities. An examination of these communities would prove beneficial for further research.

3. Selected passages first appeared in an article (cowritten with Jeff Grabill), "Toward a Critical Rhetoric of Risk Communication: Producing Citizens and the Role of Technical Communicators," *Technical Communication Quarterly* 7.4 (1998): 415–441.

4. The literature that does address public participation in risk policies is discussed in chapter 2 as a way to examine how public participation is practiced by institutions involved in risk communication, and subsequently, how citizens are positioned in the decision-making process.

5. Despite the number of years since the quote, the assumptions about the public remain largely unchanged. For example, I recently attended a lecture on effective risk communication by an individual who trains scientists in risk communication at a state EPA office. During this lecture, the speaker maintained that environmental risk is constructed from two factors: 1) the technical hazard, and 2) the public outrage about the hazard. According to her, all emotional, social, and political concerns fall into public outrage. What seemed most disturbing—besides the fact that this individual's view of public participation had not progressed much since the 1980s—was her response to a question I posed at the end of her lecture. I asked if characterizing all public input as "outrage" prevented the EPA from recognizing the useful knowledge that the public could contribute. She maintained that sometimes individuals could contribute to the decision-making process, but she asserted that, "public meetings are like teaching a first-grade class—you can't move on to the next level until everyone understands what you are trying to tell them." She continued to tell me that the biggest barriers to effective communication are the public's misdirected hostility and its lack of scientific knowledge. The assumption (with the analogy to first graders) is that citizens do not understand the scientific knowledge, yet, more often, the fact is that citizens do not have access to the scientific knowledge in a format that allows them to make sense of and use it to articulate their experiences and participate in complex discussions.

6. All personal names and most group names in the Newport VX disposal case are pseudonyms. Exceptions include the Newport Chemical Depot and the names of the federal agencies regulating the decision-making process. While it is possible to determine the state-wide environmental group from the web site reference, in accordance with Human Subjects Research procedures, the names have been changed. A university internal review board for the Use of Human Subjects in Research approved this study. Testimonies from the epilogue include real names because that information was retrieved from documents made available on line and in print at the hearing, not from personal interviews.

CHAPTER 3

1. The Army has owned and operated the land on which the Newport facility stands since 1941. As support for the Manhattan Project, the Army constructed a heavy-water pilot plant that employed two thousand workers who were transported into Newport from the Terre Haute area on busses and trains. In 1952 a larger heavy-water plant was constructed to support the war in Korea. The plant was shut down between 1947 and 1962 (except for a few guards). In 1962 the chemical plant to produce VX was constructed (fact sheet "Newport Chemical Depot"). VX was produced at the plant until 1967.

2. The total U.S. stockpile of chemical agents is stored at eight Army installations in the United States (and one installation on Johnston Atoll in the Pacific Ocean). Production of chemical weapons in the U.S. stopped in 1968 and, according to the Chemical Weapons Working Group web site, the Army was disposing of the obsolete weapons by deep ocean dumping, land burial, and open-pit burning. In 1972 Congress passed the Marine Protection Act prohibiting further ocean disposal (Bradbury, Branch, Heerwagen, & Liebow, 1994).

3. All personal names and most group names connected with this case are pseudonyms. Exceptions include the Newport Chemical Depot and the names of the federal agencies regulating the decision-making process. While it is possible to determine the actual state-wide environmental group from the web site reference, in accordance with Human Subjects Research procedures, the names have been changed (even though the individual at MEG with whom I have had numerous discussions gave permission to use his name and showed concern that I would attribute another name to him). Testimonies from the epilogue include real names because that information was retrieved from documents available online and in print.

4. It should be noted that while the "no action" alternative is always included in EISs, most EISs contain several alternatives, thus further suggesting that the Army had no intention of implementing any decision other than the one proposed in this EIS.

5. Often in the preparation of EISs, the research for the risk analysis will be done by another agency, often even another government agency. While the risk calculations and modelings are done by risk assessors (primarily individuals with a background in biology, mathematics, or chemistry), parts of the research are done by technical writers or research assistants. As a technical writer in the Risk Analysis Section of the Oak Ridge National Laboratory in the early 1990s, I worked on a draft EIS that assessed the risk posed to human health and the environment by the hazardous waste stored at the Department of Energy Federal Facilities.

6. Interestingly, Mowrer was surprised to hear about the meetings. She had never been invited to one and had never gotten free pizza from the Army.

7. As a case in point, a citizen at the July 1998 meeting for public comment on the draft EIS asked if the notices about the meeting could be broadcast on a different radio station than the one being used because a number of the people present did not listen to that station. Another audience member concurred and pointed out that residents of North Vermillion County listen to the Danville, Illinois, radio station, but those living in South Vermillion County listen to a station in Rockville, Indiana. By involving the citizens in the public participation plan, this type of information could help the Army better alert the citizens to public meetings and other chemical disposal information.

8. The IDEM web site no longer has information about VX disposal at the Newport Chemical Depot nor the permits for construction and operation of the disposal facility.

CHAPTER 4

1. Craig Waddell (1996) calls this approach to risk communication the "one-way Jeffersonian" because of Thomas Jefferson's assertion, "I know of no safe depository of the ultimate powers of the society but the people themselves; and if we think them not enlightened enough to exercise their control with a wholesome

discretion, the remedy is not to take it from them, but to inform their discretion by education" (142).

2. Mowrer also criticized the Chemical Stockpile Emergency Preparedness Program's "one size fits all" evacuation plan in terms of types of residents. She asserted that the elderly who live in the Newport area would have trouble hearing the alarm sirens and following the prescribed evacuation procedures, yet no alternative procedures were developed for them. When I spoke with Mowrer early in 2006, she said the CSEPP was better addressing these issues.

3. I borrow the terms *partial participation* and *pseudoparticipation* from Iacofano, Moore, and Goltsman (1990). Their descriptions of barriers to full participation align well with my own observations.

4. Ehn refers to this approach with different names. In his earlier work, *Work-oriented Design of Computer Artifacts*, he calls the approach "work-oriented design." In his article in *Usability*, he refers to the approach in places as "Scandinavian design," and "participatory work-oriented design," and "participatory design." While all participatory design is not Scandinavian in nature, I am referring to all approaches I discuss as participatory design and try to differentiate among them within the text.

5. Participatory approaches in urban planning often incorporate community children as well as adults in planning areas such as libraries and parks.

CHAPTER 5

1. While an approach to weapons disposal would best be decided at each site, the Army often maintains a "one size fits all" mindset.

2. Although, in some cases, citizens can appeal to Congress to stop or delay a particular environmental action, implementing, then, the strategic action reactionary model.

3. Davies, a sociologist, has also studied the role of power in chemical weapons disposal decisions (her study is at the Blue Grass Army Depot and focuses on the type of power the Army had in the decision-making process and how it acquired and used that power.)

4. A number of other organizations that are not affiliated with universities also have as their mission to help communities consider how social issues or policies might affect them and how they can better participate, such as the Highlander Research and Education Center in New Market, Tennessee. Highlander is a residential education center that trains community groups to use participatory research to analyze and explore options for the issues they name as most affecting them.

5. While I advocate that there are many publics and communities, because of the nature of this case, I have chosen to focus on two—geographical (the local communities around Newport) and ideology—the citizens and citizen groups opposed to the burning of deadly chemical warfare. While these groups are not exclusive of one another, indeed they often overlap; for example, the local citizens teamed up with citizen groups as a way to protest incineration and often used one of the citizen groups' web sites as a point of contact and way to disseminate their experiences in the public meetings, I did not investigate the impacts of the electronic communities. An examination of these communities would prove beneficial for further research.

CHAPTER 6

1. I discuss this storm water pollution prevention web site project as an example of how extended community-based projects in technical communication curricula can encourage civic engagement in an article under review, "Encouraging Civic Engagement through Extended Community Writing Projects: Re-writing the Curriculum."

EPILOGUE

1. I attended the congressional hearing, Army Contract Management: Compliance with Outreach and Public Acceptance Agreements, conducted by the House Subcommittee on National Security, Emerging Threats, and International Relations at the Sinclair Community College in Dayton, Ohio, on October 22, 2003. For accuracy, I have quoted the testimony made available online and in print at the hearing.

2. Selected passages from this section on public access to information appear in an article, coauthored with Jeffrey T. Grabill, "Toward a Civic Rhetoric for Technologically and Scientifically Complex Places: Invention, Performance, and Participation," forthcoming in *College Composition and Communication*.

BIBLIOGRAPHY

42 United States Code (1994). Section 4321.

42 United States Code (1995). Section 9617.

49 United States Code (1994). Section 5101.

50 United States Code (1986). Section 1521.

Aristotle. (1991). *Aristotle, on rhetoric*. Trans. George A. Kennedy. New York: Oxford University Press.

Associated Press. (2003, August 14). Army delays destruction of nerve agent. [Online]. Available: http://www.modbee.com and http://www.ohiocitizenaction.org/campaigns/dayton_vx/postpones.htm.

Bausch, C. (1992). A simple formula for crafting better NEPA documents. *Federal Facilities Environmental Journal* 3(3), 235–244.

Belsten, L. (1996). Environmental risk communication and community collaboration. In Star Muir & Thomas Veenendall (Eds.), *Earthtalk* (pp. 27–42). Westport, Connecticut: Praeger Series in Political Communication.

Benhabib, S. (1992). *Situating the self*. New York: Routledge Press.

Bickford, D. M., and Reynolds, N. (2002). Activism and service-learning: Reframing volunteerism as acts of dissent. *Pedagogy: Critical Approaches to Teaching Literature, Language, Composition, and Culture, 2(2)*, 229–250.

Blyler, N. (1994). Habermas, empowerment, and professional discourse. *Technical Communication Quarterly 3(2)*, 125–145.

Blythe, S. (1997). Wiring the usable center: Usability research and writing center practice. In Eric Hobson (Ed.), *Wiring the center*. Logan: Utah State University Press.

Bowden, M., and Scott, J. B. (2003). *Service Leaning in Technical and Professional Communication*. New York: Addison, Wesley, Longman.

Bradbury, J. A., Branch, K. M., Heerwagen, J. H., & Liebow, E. B. (1994). *Community viewpoints of the chemical stockpile disposal program*. Washington, DC: Batelle.

Bristow, D. (2003). Testimony to the House of Representatives Committee on Government Reform; Subcommittee on National Security, Emerging Threats, and International Relations. Distributed at Hearing on October 22. 2003.

Bullard, R. D. (1994). *Dumping in Dixie: Race, class, and environmental quality*. Boulder: Westview.

Burby, R. J. (2003). Making plans that matter: Citizen involvement and government action. *American Planning Association* 69(1), 33–49.

Cable, S., & Cable, C. (1995). *Environmental problems, grassroots solutions: The politics of grassroots environmental conflict*. New York: St. Martin's.

Cantrill, J. G. (1996). Gold, Yellowstone, and the search for a rhetorical identity. In Carl Herndl & Stuart Brown (Eds.), *Green culture: Environmental rhetoric in contemporary America* (pp. 166–194). Madison: University of Wisconsin Press.

Carson, R. (1962). *Silent spring*. Boston: Houghton Mifflin.

Centofanti, L. (2003, October 13). Perma-Fix of Dayton, Inc. Testimony to the House of Representatives Committee on Government Reform; Subcommittee on National Security, Emerging Threats, and International Relations. [Online] Available: ⟨http://reform.house.gov/UploadedFiles/Centofanti%20Testimony.pdf.

Chemical Weapons Working Group web site (April 25, 2000). http://www.cwwg.org/cwwg.html.

32 Code of Federal Register, Part 178.

40 Code of Federal Register, Part 1500–1508.

49 Code of Federal Register, § 107.601–620.

Cost-benefit analysis of off-site versus on-site treatment and disposal of Newport caustic hydrolysate. (April 2006). Report for the U.S. Army Chemical Materials Agency Program Manager for the Elimination of Chemical Weapons. Prepared by the Project Manager for Alternative Technologies and Approaches. [online]. Retrieved October 1, 2006 from the U.S. Army Chemical Materials Agency web site: http://www.cma.army.mil/newport.aspx.

Coppola, N. W. & Karis, B. (2000). *Technical communication, deliberative rhetoric, and environmental discourse: Connections and directions.* Norwood, NJ: Ablex.

Covello, V., von Winterfeldt, D., Slovic, P. (1986). Risk communication: A review of the literature. *Risk Abstracts 3(4), 172–182.*

Covello, V., and Allen, F. W. (1988). *Seven cardinal rules of risk communication.* U.S. Environmental Protection Agency.

Covello, V., Sandman, P., & Slovic, P. (1988). *Risk communication, risk statistics, and risk comparison: A manual for plant managers.* Washington, DC: Chemical Manufacturers Association.

Covello, V. T. (1992). Risk communication: An emerging area of health communication research. In S. A. Deetz (Ed.), *Communication Yearbook 15* (pp. 359–373). Newbury Park CA: Sage Publications.

Cushman, E. (1996). The rhetorician as an agent of social change. CCC, 47(1), 7–27.

———. (1998). *The struggle and the tools: Oral and literate strategies in an inner city community.* Albany: State University of New York Press.

———. (1999). The public intellectual, service learning, and activist research. *College English* 61(3), 328–336.

Dautermann, J. (1996). Social and institutional power relationships in studies of workplace writing. In Peter Mortensen & Gesa Kirsh (Eds.), *Ethics and representation in qualitative studies of literacy* (pp. 241–259). Urbana, IL: NCTE.

Davies, C. G. (1995). *The dialectics of power and dissent: A study of the U.S. Army's Chemical Stockpile Disposal Program.* Unpublished doctoral dissertation. University of Tennessee, Knoxville, TN.

Dayton, D. (2002). Evaluating Environmental Impact Statements as Communicative Action. *Journal of Business and Technical Communication* 16(3), 355–405.

Debrosse, J. (2003, November 21). Officials disagree on VX OK. *The Dayton Daily News Electronic Edition.* [Online]. Available: http://daytondaily.printthis.clickability.com/pt/cpt?action=cpt&expire=&ulrID=7967571.

Depoe, S. P., Delicath, J.W., and Elsenbeer, M. A. (Eds.),(2004). *Communication and public participation in environmental decision-making.* Albany: State University of New York Press.

Dubinsky, J. (2002). Service Learning as a Path to Virtue: The Ideal Orator in Professional Communication. *Michigan Journal of Community Service Learning,* 61–74.

Ehn, P. (1988). *Work-oriented design of computer artifacts.* Stockholm: Arbetslivscentrum.

———. (1992). Scandinavian design: On participation and skill. In Adler, Paul & Terry Winograd (Eds.), *Usability: Turning technologies into tools* (pp. 96–132). Oxford: Oxford University Press.

Eldred, J. & Mortensen, P. (1998). Female civic rhetoric in early America. *College English 60,* 173–188.

Ember, L. R. (2003, August 26). Destroying chemical weapons: Army's problem-plagued program more costly than originally planned. *Chemical & Engineering News Electronic Edition.* [Online]. Available: http://www.ohiocitizenaction.org/ campaigns/dayton_vx/prob_plagued.htm.

Fairfield Park Public Notice, Indiana Town Council passes VX hydrolysate transportation resolution. (2004, April 13). [Online]. Retrieved April 10, 2005 from http://fpi.homestead.com/PublicNotice.html.

Findley, R., & Farber, D. (1993). *Environmental law: In a nutshell.* St. Paul: West.

Fine, M. (1992). Passions, politics, and power: Feminist research possibilities. In Michelle Fine (Ed.), *Disruptive voices: The possibility of feminist research* (pp. 205–231). Ann Arbor: University of Michigan Press.

Fiorino, D. (1990). Citizen participation and environmental risk: A survey of institutional mechanisms. *Science, Technology, & Human Values 15(2),* 226–243.

Fischer, F. (1992). Risk assessment and environmental crisis: Toward an integration of science and participation. In Scott Campbell & Susan Feinstien (Eds.), *Readings in planning theory,* (pp. 485–506). Blackwell.

———. (2000). *Citizens, experts, and the environment: The politics of local knowledge.* Duke University Press.

Fischhoff, B., Watson, S. R., & Hope, C. (1984). Defining risk. *Policy Sciences 17,* 123–139.

Flower, L. (1997). Partners in Inquiry: A logic for community outreach. In Linda Adler-Kassner, R. Crooks, and A. Watters (Eds.), *Writing the community: Concepts and models for service-learning in composition* (95–117). Washington, DC: American Association of Higher Education.

———. (2003). Talking across difference: Intercultural rhetoric and the search for situated knowledge. *College Composition and Communication 55(1),* 38–68.

Flower, L., Long, E., and Higgins, L. (2000). *Learning to rival: A literate practice for intercultural inquiry.* Mahwah: Erlbaum.

Foucault, M. (1972). *The archeology of knowledge and the discourse on language.* (Trans. A. M. Sheridan Smith.) New York: Harper Torchbooks.

———. (1982). The subject and power. In Hubert L. Dreyfus & Paul Rabinow (Eds.), *Michel Foucault: Beyond structuralism and hermeneutics* (pp. 208–226). Chicago: University of Chicago Press.

———. (1986). Of other spaces. *Diacritics, 16,* 22–27.

Gaventa, J. (1980). *Power and powerlessness: Quiescence and rebellion in an Appalachian valley*. Urbana: University of Illinois Press.

General Accounting Office. (2003). *Chemical weapons: Sustained leadership, along with key strategic management tools, is needed to guide DoD's destruction program.*

Gilyard, K. (1999). African American contributions to composition studies. *College Composition and Communication* 50, 626–644.

Grabill, J. T. (1997). *Situating literacies and community literacy programs: A critical rhetoric for institutional change*. Unpublished doctoral dissertation, Purdue University, West Lafayette.

———. (2000). Shaping local HIV/AIDS services policy through activist research: The problem of client involvement. *Technical Communication Quarterly* 9(1), 29–50.

———. (2001). *Community literacy programs and the politics of change*. Albany: SUNY Press.

———. (2005, March 18). We may be poor but we aren't stupid. Paper presented at the Conference on College Composition and Communication, San Francisco, CA.

Grabill, J. T. and Simmons, W. M. (1998). Toward a critical rhetoric of risk communication: Producing citizens and the role of technical communicators. *Technical Communication Quarterly* 7(4), 415–441.

Gray, B. (2003). Framing of environmental disputes. In R. Lewicki, B. Gray & Elliot, M. (Eds.), *Making sense of intractable environmental conflicts* (pp. 11–34). Washington: Island.

Griggs, K. (1994). *Audience complexities in administrative law: A historical case study of an environmental policy*. Unpublished doctoral dissertation, Purdue University, West Lafayette.

Habermas, J. (1970). *Toward a rational society: Student protest, science, and politics*. (Trans. Jeremy J. Shapiro). Boston: Beacon.

———. (1979). *Communication and the evolution of society*. (Trans. Thomas McCarthy). Boston: Beacon Press.

———. (1987). *Theory of Communicative Action*. (Trans. Thomas McCarthy). Vol. 2. Boston: Beacon.

———. (1990). *Moral consciousness and communicative action*. (Trans. Christian Lenhardt and Sherry Weber Nicholsen). Cambridge: MIT Press.

Hance, B. J., Chess, C., & Sandman, P. M. (1991). *Industry risk communication manual*. Boca Raton: Lewis.

Hauser, G. (1999). *Vernacular voices: The rhetoric of publics and public spheres*. University of South Carolina Press.

Hauser, G., & Grim, A. (2004). *Rhetorical democracy: Discursive practices of civic engagement*. Mahwah, NJ: Lea.

Heap, J. (1995). Forward. In M. Campbell & A. Manicom (Eds.), *Knowledge, experience, and ruling relations* (pp. xi–xv), Toronto: University of Toronto Press.

Heath, R., & Nathan, K. (1990–91). Public relation's role in risk communication: Information, rhetoric and power. *Public Relations Quarterly*, Winter, 15–22.

Hensel, K., & Garrison, D. (2004, May 1). Project security: Indiana's WMD—Part Three. WISH-TV, News 8. Retrieved May 1, 2004, from <http://wishtv.com/Global/story.asp?S=1831079>.

Hynds, P., & Martin, W. (1995). Artisan well #5: A case study of failure in professional communication. *IEEE Transaction on Professional Communication* 38, 139–145.

Iacofano, D., Moore, R., & Goltsman, S. (1990). Public involvement in transit planning: A case study of Pierce Transit, Tacoma, Washington, USA. In H. Sanoff (Ed.), *Participatory design: Theory & techniques* (pp. 196–205). Distributed by Henry Sanoff.

Jacobs, E. (2003, October 13). Testimony in the House Subcommittee on National Security, Emerging Threats and International Relations Hearing on Army Contract Management: Compliance with Outreach and Public Acceptance Agreements. [Online] Available: http://reform.house.gov/UploadedFiles/John%20Testimony.pdf.

Johnson, M. (2003, October 13). Testimony in the House Subcommittee on National Security, Emerging Threats and International Relations Hearing on Army Contract Management: Compliance with Outreach and Public Acceptance Agreements. [Online] Available: http://reform.house.gov/UploadedFiles/John%20Testimony.pdf.

Johnson, R. (1997). Audience involved: Toward a participatory model of writing. *Computers and Composition* 14, 361–376.

———. (1998). *User-centered technology: A rhetorical theory for computers and other mundane artifacts.* Albany: State University of New York Press.

Johnson-Eilola, J. (1996). Relocating the value of work: Technical communication in a post-industrial age. *Technical Communication Quarterly* 5(3), 245–271.

———. (1997). *Nostalgic angels: Rearticulating hypertext writing.* Norwood, NJ: Ablex.

———. (2002). *Designing effective web sites: A concise guide.* Boston, Houghton Mifflin.

Jones, A. (2003, October 13). Testimony in the House Subcommittee on National Security, Emerging Threats and International Relations Hearing on Army Contract Management: Compliance with Outreach and Public Acceptance Agreements. [Online] Available: http://reform.house.gov/UploadedFiles/Jones%20Testimony.pdf.

Jones, D. (1995). A question of identity. *Technical Communication Quarterly* 4(2), 567–569.

Jonsen, A. R., & Toulmin, S. (1988). *The abuse of casuistry: A history of moral reasoning.* Berkeley: University of California Press.

Katz, S., & Miller, C. (1996). The low-level radioactive waste siting controversy in North Carolina: Toward a rhetorical model of risk communication. In Carl Herndl & Stuart Brown (Eds.), *Green culture: Environmental rhetoric in contemporary America* (pp. 111–140). Madison: University of Wisconsin Press.

Keenan, J. F. (1996). The return of casuistry. *Theoretical Studies* 57, 123–139.

Killingsworth, J. & Steffans, D. (1989). Effectiveness in the environmental impact statement: A study in public rhetoric. *Written Communication* 6, 155–180.

Killingsworth, J. & Palmer, J. S. (1992). *Ecospeak: Rhetoric and environmental politics in America.* Carbondale: Southern Illinois University Press.

Kinsella, W. J. (2005). Public expertise: A foundation for citizen participation in energy and environmental decisions. In Stephen P. Depoe, John W. Delicath, & Marie-France Aepli Elsenbeer (Eds.), *Communication and public participation in environmental decision-making* (pp. 83–95). Albany: State University of New York Press.

Kress, G. & Van Leeuwen, T (2001). *Multimodal discourse: The modes and media of contemporary communication.* London: Arnold.

Kuhn, T. S. (1970). *The structure of scientific revolutions.* 2nd ed. Chicago: University of Chicago Press.

Kukla, C., Clemens, E. A., Morse, R. S. & Cash, D. (1992). Designing effective systems: A tool approach. In Paul S. Adler & Terry A. Winograd (Eds.), *Usability: Turning technologies into tools* (pp. 41–65). New York: Oxford University Press.

Laird, F. N. (1993). Participatory analysis, democracy, and technological decision making. *Science, Technology, & Human Values* 18(3), 341–361.

Leitch, V. B. (1992). Cultural criticism, literary theory, poststructuralism. New York: Columbia University Press.

Lester, J. P., & Bowman, A.O'M. (1983). (Eds.), *The politics of hazardous waste management*. Durham: Duke University Press.

Lewicki, R. J., Gray, B., & Elliot, M. (2003). *Making sense of intractable environmental conflicts*. Washington: Island.

Martin, W., & Sanders, S. (1994). Ethics, audience, and the writing process: Bringing public policy issues into the classroom. *Technical Communication Quarterly* 3(2) 147–163.

Mayes, T. Midwest Environmental Group, spokesperson, personal interview, May 5, 2000.

McCarty, M. (2003, November 21). Neighbors battling VX plan. *The Dayton Daily News Electronic Edition*. [Online] Available: http://daytondaily.printthis.click ability.com/pt/cpt&expire=&urlID=6966124.

McGarity, T. O. (1998). *Public participation in risk regulation*. http://www.fplc.edu/risk/vol1/spring/mcgarity.htm (October 30, 1998).

Miller, B. (2004, April 14). Nerve gas disposal a political dilemma. Retrieved June 20, 2006 from http://www.delawareonline.com/newsjournal/local/2004/04/14nervegasdisposa.html.

Miller, C., & Selzer, J. (1985). Special topics of argument in engineering reports. In Lee Odell & Dixie Goswami (Eds.), *Writing in nonacademic settings* (pp. 309–341). New York: Guilford.

Mirel, B. (1994). Debating nuclear energy: Theories of risk and purposes of communication. *Technical Communication Quarterly*, 3, 41–65.

———. *Interaction design for complex problem solving*. San Francisco: Morgan Kaufmann.

Morgan, G., Fischhoff, B., Bostrom, A., Lave, L., & Atman. C. (1992). Communicating risk to the public. *Environmental Science Technology* 26(11), 2048–2056.

Mowrer, Sybil, Newport Citizens against Incineration, spokesperson, personal interview, May 7, 2000.

National Research Council. (1983). *Risk assessment in the federal government: Managing the Process*. Washington, DC: National Academy.

———. (1989). *Improving risk communication*. Washington, DC. National Academy.

———. (2002). Risk-based decision-making guidelines. [online publication]. Retrieved May 31, 2006 from <http://www.uscg.mil/hq/gm/risk/E-Guidelines/RBDM/html/vol2/00/v2-00.htm>.

Noveck, B. S. (2005). A democracy of groups. First Monday. [online publication]. Available: <http://www.firstmonday.org/issues/issue10_11/noveck/index.html>.

Ohio Citizen Action Website. (2005, February 28). Husted wants House vote on public records access soon. Retrieved June 24, 2006 from http://www.ohiocitizen.org/campaigns/dayton_vx/dayton_vx.html.

Ohio Environmental Protection Agency Web site [online]. Available: <http://www.epa.state.oh.us/>, accessed December 5, 2005.

Park, P. (1993). What is participatory research? A theoretical and methodological perspective. In Park, P, Brydon-Miller, M, Hall, B. and Jackson, T. (Eds.) *Voices of change: Participatory research in the United States and Canada.* (pp. 1–19). Ontario: The Ontario Institute for Studies in Education.

Park, P., Brydon-Miller, M., Hall, B., & Jackson, T. (1993). *Voices of change: Participatory research in the United States and Canada.* Ontario: Ontario Institute for Studies in Education.

Plough, A., & Krimsky, S. (1988). *Environmental hazards: Communicating risks as a social process.* Dover: Auburn House.

Porter, J., Sullivan, P., Blythe, S., Grabill, J. T., & Miles, E. (2000). Institutional critique: A rhetorical methodology for change. CCC 51, 610–642.

Porter, J. E. (1992). *Audience and rhetoric: An archaeological composition of the discourse community.* Englewood Cliffs, NJ: Prentice Hall.

———. (1998). *Rhetorical ethics and internetworked writing.* Greenwich, CT: Ablex and Computers and Composition.

Porter, J. E. (2005). The chilling of digital information: Technical communicators as public advocates. In Michael Day and Carol Lipson (Eds.), *Tech/Web: Technical communications and the World Wide Web in the new millennium.* Mahwah, NJ: Erlbaum.

Program Manager for Chemical Demilitarization Fact Sheets. (1997).

Public Law 99-145, Title 14, Part B, Sect. 1412.

Public Law 102-484.

Putnam, L. L., & Wondolleck, J. M. (2003). Intractability: Definitions, dimensions, and distinctions. In R. Lewicki, B. Gray, & Elliot, M. (Eds.), *Making Sense of Intractable Environmental Conflict* (pp. 35–59). Washington: Island.

Ranney, F. (2000). Beyond Foucault: Toward a user-centered approach to sexual harassment policy. *Technical Communication Quarterly* 9(1), 9–28.

Ross, S. M. (1996). Two rivers, two vessels: Environmental problem solving in an intercultural context. In Star Muir & Thomas Veenendall (Eds.), *Earthtalk* (pp. 171–190). Westport, Connecticut: Praeger Series in Political Communication.

Rowan, K. (1991). Goals, obstacles, and strategies in risk communication: A problem-solving approach to improving communication about risks. *Journal of Applied Communication Research*, November, 300–329.

———. (1994a). The technical and democratic approaches to risk situations: Their appeal, limitations, and rhetorical alternative. *Argumentation* 8, 391–409.

———. (1994b). What risk communicators need to know: An agenda for research. In Brant Burleson (Ed.), *Communication Yearbook* 18 (pp. 300–319). International Communication Association.

Rubin, D. M., & Sachs, D. P. (Eds.). (1973). *Mass media and the environment.* New York: Praeger.

Rude, C. (1995). The report for decision making: Genre and inquiry. *Journal of Business and Technical Communication* 9, 170–205.

———. (2000). Guest Editor Column. *Technical Communication Quarterly* 9(1), 5–7.

Russell, M. (1986). Communicating risk to a concerned public. *EPA Journal* 12(9), 19–21.

Sandman, P. (1990). Getting to maybe: Some communications aspects of siting hazardous waste facilities. In Thomas Glickman & Michael Gough (Eds.), *Readings in risk* (pp. 223–231). Washington, DC: Resources for the Future.

Sanoff, H. (1990). Participatory design in focus. In Henry Sanoff (Ed.), *Participatory design: Theory & techniques* (pp. 5–20). Distributed by Henry Sanoff.

Sauer, B. (1993). Sense and sensibility in technical documentation: How feminist interpretation can save lives in the nation's mines. *Journal of Business and Technical Communication*, 7(1), 63–83.

———. (2002). *The Rhetoric of risk: Technical documentation in hazardous environments*. Mahwah, NJ: Lawrence Erlbaum.

Shuler, P. (2004). Keeping public records from the public. *City Beat* (14 July 2004). 25 Oct. 2006 <http://www.citybeat.com/2004-07-14/statehouse.shtml>.

Scott, J. B. (2003). *Risky rhetoric: AIDS and the cultural practices of HIV testing.* Carbondale: Southern Illinois University Press.

Simmons, W. M., & Grabill, J. T. (in press). Toward a civic rhetoric for technologically and scientifically complex places: Invention, performance, and participation. *College Composition and Communication.*

Skaluba, C. (2003, October 17). Briefing memo for the hearing Army Contract Management: Compliance with outreach and public acceptance agreements.

Slack, J. D., Miller, D., & Doak, J. (1993). The technical communicator as author: Meaning, power, authority. *Journal of Business and Technical Communication* 7(1), 12–36.

Slovic, P. (1986). Informing and educating the public about risk. *Risk Analysis* 6, 403–415.

Smart, G. (1993). Genre as community invention: A central bank's response to its executives' expectations as readers. In Rachel Spilka (Ed.), *Writing in the workplace: New research perspectives* (pp. 124–140). Carbondale: Southern Illinois University Press.

Smith, D. (1987). *The everyday world as problematic: A feminist sociology.* Boston: Northeastern University Press.

Soja, E. (1989). *Postmodern geographies: The reassertion of space in critical social theory.* London: Verso.

Spilka, R. (1993). (Ed.). *Writing in the workplace: New research perspectives.* Carbondale: Southern Illinois University Press.

Stratman, J. E., Boykin, C., Holmes, M. C., Laufer, M. J., & Breen, M. (1995). Risk communication, metacommunication, and rhetorical stases in the aspen-EPA superfund controversy. *Journal of Business and Technical Communication* 9, 5–41.

Sullivan, D. (1990). Political-ethical implications of defining technical communication as a practice. *Journal of Advanced Composition*, 10, 375–386.

Sullivan, P. (1989). Beyond a narrow conception of usability testing. *IEEE Transactions on Professional Communication* 32(4), 256–264.

Sullivan, P., & Porter, J. (1997). *Opening spaces: Writing technologies and critical research practices.* Greenwich: Ablex.

Thompson, Adrian, Public affairs officer, Newport Chemical Depot, U.S. Army installation, personal interview, April 27, 2000.

Tinker, T. (1997). (Ed.). *The health risk communicator.* Subcommittee on Risk Communication and Education, Public Health Service (PHS).

U.S. Army. (1998). *Pilot testing of neutralization/supercritical water oxidation of VX agent at Newport chemical depot draft environmental impact statement.* Aberdeen Proving Ground, MD.

U.S. Army. (1998). *Pilot testing of neutralization/supercritical water oxidation of VX agent at Newport Chemical Depot final environmental impact statement*. Aberdeen Proving Ground, MD.

Waddell, C. (Winter 1995). Risk communication course syllabus. Michigan Tech University, Houghton.

———. (1996). Saving the Great Lakes: Public participation in environmental policy. In Carl Herndl & Stuart Brown (Eds.), *Green culture: Environmental rhetoric in contemporary America* (pp. 141–165). Madison: University of Wisconsin Press.

———. (1997).Defining sustainable development: A case study in environmental communication. *Technical Communication Quarterly* 4, 201–216.

Wartella, E. (1994). Challenge to the profession. *Communication Education* 43, 54–62.

Webber, T. (2005, November 5). VX destruction shaky. IndyStar.com. Retrieved June 24, 2006 from http://www.indystar.com/apps/pbcs.dll/article?AID=/20051105/NEWS01/511050436&SearchID=73225935857648.

Weiss, E. (1988). Usability: Stereotypes and traps. In Edward Barrett (Ed.), *Text, context, and hypertext* (pp. 175–186). Cambridge: MIT Press.

Wells, S. (1986). Jurgen Habermas, communicative competence, and the teaching of technical discourse. In Cary Nelson (Ed), *Theory in the classroom*. Urbana: University of Illinois, 245–269.

Willard, C. (1996). *Liberalism and the problem of knowledge: A new rhetoric for modern democracy*. Chicago: University of Chicago Press.

Wills-Toker, C. (2004). Public participation or stakeholder frustration: An analysis of consensus-based participation in the Georgia Ports Authority's stakeholder evaluation group. In Stephen P. Depoe, John W. Delicath, and Marie-France Aepli Elsenbeer (Eds.), *Communication and public participation in environmental decision making* (pp. 173–200). State University of New York Press.

Winner, L. (1995). Citizen virtues in a technological order. In Andrew Feenberg & Alastair Hannay, (Eds.), *Technology and the politics of knowledge* (pp. 65–84). Bloomington: Indiana University Press.

Winograd, T. (1995). Heidegger and the design of computer systems. In Andrew Feenberg & Alastair Hannay, (Eds.), *Technology and the politics of knowledge* (pp. 108–127). Bloomington: Indiana University Press.

Winograd, T. & Flores, C. F. (1986). *Understanding computers and cognition—A new foundation for design*. Norwood, NJ: Ablex.

Winsor, D. (1989). An engineer's writing and the corporate construction of knowledge. *Written Communication* 6, 270–285.

Young, I. M. (1990). *Justice and the politics of difference*. Princeton: Princeton University Press.

———. (2002). *Democracy and inclusion*. Cambridge: Oxford University Press.

INDEX

Made in the USA
Lexington, KY
10 February 2016